~THE~

Sweet Potato Queens' Guide to Life

~ THE ~

Sweet Potato Queens' Guide to Life

THE SWEET POTATO QUEENS'
BOOK OF LOVE

&

GOD SAVE THE
SWEET POTATO QUEENS

Jill Conner Browne

The Literary Guild
GARDEN CITY, NEW YORK

Published originally by Three Rivers Press, New York, New York.
Member of the Crown Publishing Group.

Random House, Inc. New York, Toronto, London, Sydney, Auckland

THREE RIVERS PRESS is a registered trademark and the Three Rivers Press
colophon is a trademark of Random House, Inc.

Printed in the United States of America

Design by Lynne Amft

ISBN 0-7394-1808-4

~ THE ~

Sweet Potato Queens'

Book of Love

To
my daughter Bailey,
who is my very heart,
and
to the sweet memory of
Beth Griffin Jones,
who believed I could write a
really funny book

CONTENTS

CONTENTS

Meet the
Sweet Potato Queens

For anyone even remotely familiar with Jackson, Mississippi, the name "Sweet Potato Queens" instantly evokes sweet memories of beautiful, somewhat augmented female forms enveloped in green sequins, towering red hairdos, provocative dances, and the haunting refrain of "Tiny Bubbles," as only Don Ho could—or would, for that matter—deliver it. If, as they say, you ain't from around here, you need some enlightening; and your life will not be complete until you get it. Nor will it ever be the same after you do.

The Sweet Potato Queens are *us*. That would be me and eight or nine of my nearest and dearest. The Sweet Potato Queens were, however, my idea, and therefore I'm the boss of the whole enterprise. This is unquestionably the best job I ever had in my entire life.

It all began back in the early 1980s. Having passed recently through a pretty thick patch of doldrums, I was feeling a mite antsy and looking for a new direction for my life. My friend Cheri told me her dad had bought some land up the road a ways in Vardaman, Mississippi, which claims to be "The Sweet Potato Capital of the World." She said he had an old beat-up pickup truck on which he had meticulously painted ANGLIN SWEET POTATO FARMS. *Farms* may suggest to the reader an enormous spread, nothing but sweet potatoes as far as the eye can see. It was, in fact, twenty acres max—what he had was a fair-sized garden. The family thought it was pretty funny of him, and so did I. She went on to tell how Vardaman was into sweet potatoes in a big way, festival and all that. It occurred to me that they might need a Queen for that festival, and so I volunteered to be it on a continuing basis to save them the trouble and expense of selecting a new one every year. She said she'd pass along my generous offer to whoever might be interested.

Somehow that interest never materialized, but I had a passing thought that I might have stumbled on to something. The prospect of being the Queen of anything at all struck a chord deep within me. But I let it slide until I got a phone call from my buddy Viv. (I was lolling about in the bathtub—all the Queens love to loll about, in bathtubs and elsewhere; it makes us no never mind.) Anyway, I was in the tub lolling, and Viv called up to say that her husband, Malcolm, was going to put on a St. Patrick's Day parade. With literally no hesitation, I spoke the words that would forever change our worlds—I truly believe it was probably some sort of divine thing.

"I'm in it," I said emphatically.

"What are you going to be?" Viv asked, in a tone of mild disdain, as if I couldn't possibly have a plan already.

"I am the Sweet Potato Queen."

"Well, so am I," she said.

I said, "Fine." And it was done.

That first year, 1982, was a confusing one for the 350,000 residents of Jackson, Mississippi. The parade was held on the actual Day of St. Patrick, which happened to be a Thursday, I think. We paraded through downtown Jackson, right at five o'clock, so that all the folks getting off work could see us and be held up in traffic a little while longer. *Were they happy.* Prior to that very moment, St. Patrick's Day had passed virtually unnoticed in Jackson. It took us a few years to get the participation of our indigenous folk, but they are quite taken with the idea now.

So Malcolm White has his parade, officially called "Mal's St. Paddy's Day Parade," every year, now always on a Saturday in the general vicinity of the actual Day of St. Patrick—sometimes before, sometimes after, but always in March, I can promise you that. Other cities, I understand, are sticklers for March 17, but we, in our Southern way, are more concerned with the convenience afforded by a Saturday parade. I can't tell you what criteria are used to determine which Saturday. The only criterion that I'm personally aware of is that the Sweet Potato Queens will be the focal point. That has never been a problem.

The newly crowned Sweet Potato Queens were the instant darlings of that first parade. Our first outfits, however, were not nearly so grand as the ones we wear today. There were four of us, and we all wore green ball gowns from family trunks or the Goodwill thrift shop. And tiaras. God, I love a tiara. Suzanne Sugarbaker of *Designing Women* was so right when she said, "There's just nothing better in life than to ride around on the back of a convertible with a crown on your head." Words to live by. We didn't actually have a convertible; we had a pickup truck. But we did have big dresses, tiaras, and long gloves. (Our first gloves were the no-longer-quite-so-white ones we found in our mothers' forgotten wardrobes. Vivid colors would come in future years.)

And we had The Wave. That beauty queen wave, the Miss America wave—back when Miss America meant something; namely, that you were the best-looking thing in the whole country and none of this ridiculous scholarship hooey. Look at the old films of the Miss America pageant. The wave changed when they started all that scholarship crap. Scholarship, my butt. Take the crown out of the deal, and see how many contenders you got left. Name me any other *scholarship* competition in the universe that induces full-grown women to have their back teeth pulled, bottom ribs removed, noses whacked, and tits—well, brains will just never reach that level of popularity, now will they? Show me another scholarship contest that necessitates the application of Firm-Grip to one's buttocks to hold one's swimsuit in place. That's so all those brains don't pop out on the runway, no doubt.

Call the thing a beauty pageant, and be done with it. Get honest. And let the winners get back to the traditional wave, the one that says, *"I am better looking than every last one of you! But I am humble about it, and I have compassion for all you little, ugly, pathetic people. I am up here, where I belong, above the crowd, so you can all see how very beee-yooo-ti-ful I am and you can see it from all angles and so fully appreciate just how much better looking I am than you. But even in my great beauty, I am still sweet and kind, and I will wave to the likes of you to prove it. See? I am waving and smiling."*

And, with her arm nearly fully extended, she ever so gently

moves just her hand, back and forth, back and forth, scarcely disturbing the air, the movement is so gentle. That's how Sweet Potato Queens wave. And I, being the Boss of Everything, am the only one who can claim ambidextrous waving skills.

So we're in this very first St. Paddy's Day parade in downtown Jackson, sitting up in the back of a green pickup truck with hand-lettered posterboard signs duct-taped to the sides proclaiming us to be the Sweet Potato Queens, riding up through some totally puzzled office workers. We just smiled and waved like we were *gen-u-wine* beauty queens, taking the whole thing very seriously, as if they should be so excited they got to see us, in person and all. And every now and then, in the tradition of Mardi Gras, we'd throw a little something to the crowds, only our throws, in keeping with who we claimed to be, were actual sweet potatoes, which are not usually as lightweight as, say, your beads or your doubloons. A sweet potato has a little heft to it, and it is fairly dense as well. Not quite the same as chunking bricks, but then actually pretty close to chunking bricks. One of the original Queens was quite the softball player, some kind of championship softball player. She could really hum them taters, let me tell you. I guess their size and odd shapes sort of affected her aim a little, since she lobbed one and nearly broke out a second-story window in the IRS building. We had to rein her in after that.

There was some initial confusion about our name. Sweet Potato Queens. Did the name describe the type of potato that we claimed to be the Queens of? Or were we the Queens of regular potatoes—Irish potatoes, maybe—possessed of good dispositions? It doesn't really matter to us. The Queen part is the only thing we care about at all.

We all knew we had what we needed to declare ourselves Queens of whatever we chose. No pageants for us. No way would *we* ever consider groveling and posturing for a bunch of strangers, in full view of a live audience, in the pitiful hope that, for reasons of their own, they would decide to give us their paltry crown. Need I point out that not only are those crowns arbitrarily awarded, there's a very tight time constraint issued at the crowning. You get that crown for one year and one year only, sweetie, and during that year, you will step and fetch at the total whim of the folks who gave it to you. You do this for one entire year, at the end of which you are no longer Queen of Anything. You are a *former Queen*. Consider, too, the status of the other pathetic ninety-nine percent who entered the fray—losers, one and all, and no doubt scarred for life by the experience. Sweet Potato Queens, on the other hand, don't have to do jackshit that anybody says, and we are Queens for Life.

And another thing: Youth is not a prerequisite to becoming a Queen. The very young can have no sense of who they are, whereas the Sweet Potato Queens have had plenty of time to cultivate this vital self-awareness. Collectively we've had approximately four hundred years to devote to our development. And we've turned out rather well, I must say. We are a marvelously diverse lot. We have not one but two former presidents of the Junior League (we knew this about them and we still embraced them as if they were normal). We could see that they had learned painfully the folly of working one's ass off for an organization that didn't provide its leadership with even the hope of a crown.

Of course, as we know, Junior League work, grueling as it is, is free labor performed in one's spare time. The Queens all have real jobs as well. We have a former district attorney (no crown for that either), a commercial real estate agent, an interior designer, and an artist. One of us owns a gourmet kitchen store and sits on the board of about a half-dozen other businesses. One Queen designs and manufactures a line of women's silk and cashmere clothing and sells it at hotsy-totsy shops all over the country. We have an exercise and fitness consultant, and one of our number even owns a funeral home.

What I'm saying here is that the Sweet Potato Queens are real live grown-up women—self-sufficient and self-actualized. But we were crownless, one and all. Who, I ask, would be more worthy and capable of wearing a crown—the women I've just described or some eighteen-year-old surgically altered twit whose sole accomplishment is finally learning all the words to "My Way"? Who indeed. We consulted our mirrors and each other, and we could see pretty damn quick that we had It—that quality, that *je ne sais quoi*, that royal air that set us apart.

For the first few years, we were a democratic lot. Basically, anybody who had balls enough to put on a green ball gown from Goodwill and a tiara and perch on the back of a pickup truck, wave, and throw sweet potatoes was welcome to join the ranks of the Sweet Potato Queens. There were not as many takers as you might imagine. There's a whole passel of folks in this world who are content just to *spectate*, and to them we say, "God love you!" because we do so love an audience, and the bigger, the better.

But then came the Year of the Outfits. I was seized with a new inspiration—a vision, if you will—for the Sweet Potato Queens. I must confess that the source of my divination was the dance troupe for a small, historically black college in Mississippi—the Golden Girls of Alcorn State University. These incredible women perform on the field at halftime for the Alcorn Braves football games. They wear matching gold-sequined swimsuit-style outfits, and their dance routines are heart-stopping. They are my idols.

I have often said that it was merely an accident of birth that prevented my being a Golden Girl. They are all black, and I, sadly, am not. It's a bitch, but there you are. Live with it, I say. I also say that in my considered opinion white people were a mistake, on God's part, I mean. If He had it to do over, I bet he'd make everybody black, or at the very least see that the melanin got distributed a little more fairly. Face it, everybody would be better looking black. Any white girl who's ever had a tan can vouch for it. Especially if you have, shall we say, figure flaws? Brown fat just does not look as bad as white fat. Hell, you can tell that by looking at a pork chop. A strip of fat around a raw pork chop is all white and globby looking. Fry that sucker, and the fat comes out all crispy and golden brown.

Anyway, forced to accept that my own whiteness and also my age were going to preclude me from ever becoming a Golden Girl, I saw a way to make my dream happen anyway. The Sweet Potato Queens would fashion our costumes after those of the Golden Girls, only ours would be St. Patrick's Day *green* sequins instead of gold. And as long as I was designing the thing, why not throw in a little figure-enhancement? And so I went to my sister-in-law, Beth, who could tailor men's suits if she wanted to—she just doesn't want to—and explained my concept to her. She indicated that this would be "no problem at all." (She probably didn't really want to do this either, but I can be persuasive, not to mention persistent.)

We bought a basic swimsuit pattern in about a size 24, sort of one-size-fits-all, you know? She made the basic size 24 suit, stuffed the top and the butt with enough batting to make fifteen good-sized teddy bears, and then took up the waistline to fit each Queen. Weighing about forty pounds apiece, these giant sequined outfits are architectural wonders. The result was mesmerizing.

We were true crowd pleasers in these suits, proving that it *is* possible to please everyone all the time. For white males, it is impossible to have tits that are too big, and for black males, you cannot get the butt big enough. At the same time, if your tits are big enough, white guys don't care how big your butt is; and if your butt's big enough, black guys don't care what's happening around front. (We know all this because the Sweet Potato Queens are multicultural and we've compared notes.)

As far as we can tell, we are the only female drag queens in existence. Gay men love us. It's entirely possible that we are gay men trapped in straight women's bodies. Our lesbian friends adore us, too, because, hey, we are WOMEN. When we made our appearance in our new outfits on parade day, the crowd was galvanized. All the men wanted us, and all the women wanted to *be* us.

Just imagine the Sweet Potato Queens in our flowing red wigs—so vital for hair-tossing, which coupled with pelvic thrusting is the mainstay of our performance—wearing our official lipstick, Revlon's Love That Pink, and our majorette boots. God, how we love our majorette boots. Women of a certain age—I need not name that age—will empathize with this at once. When we were growing up, the Sears Roebuck Christmas catalog featured a wide array of costumes—the Bride's Dress, the Cowgirl Outfit, the Nurse's Uniform, the Princess Gown, and *the Majorette Suit*. With it were some crappy little spats that were supposed to pass for boots, but you could order separately Real Live Majorette Boots. Out of all the Queens with our diverse backgrounds, not one ever got a pair of Real Live Majorette Boots, and not one had ever gotten over that bitter disappointment.

That is so much of what being a Sweet Potato Queen represents for us: correcting karma—seizing the moment, re-creating ourselves from the soles of our majorette boots to the very tip-top of our towering red wigs. Don't waste your precious life moping over the vacancies of your childhood. Hell, you're full grown now. If you don't have Real Live Majorette Boots at this stage in your life, it's your own goddamn fault. Quit whining about it and go get some!

You may wonder why there is no mention of crowns. That's because we no longer wear them. In the beginning we needed them, we thought, to establish our Queenliness. Now, we believe, to wear a tangible symbol of our intangible yet utterly pervasive air of royalty would be redundant. We *are* the Sweet Potato Queens, and everybody knows it. Symbols are superfluous. Besides, it's really hard to keep a crown fastened to that big red wig.

I've often heard it said about us, in our presence, as if we weren't there or were perhaps deaf: "They turn into someone else when they put those outfits on." This is usually said by some Queen's boyfriend or husband. In fact, nothing could be further from the truth. We are completely ourselves when we put those costumes on. The Sweet Potato Queens are at one with the universe in those outfits.

The news media were all over us in our new regalia. "How does one get to *be* a Sweet Potato Queen?" the tiny white-girl reporter asked breathlessly. "It's like this, honey," I told her, with more than a small degree of disdain, "either you *are* a Sweet Potato Queen, or you are *not*." She looked perplexed. I added, "*You* are *not*." Whining, she persisted, "Well, how did you get to be a Sweet Potato Queen?" "First of all, missy"—even more disdain here—"I am *the* Sweet Potato Queen, by divine right, and I have handpicked my court. No woman gets on this float but by me. And let me tell you—there is plenty of sucking up involved in the process."

Ever since we first trotted out those green-sequined costumes and our amazing red wigs, I've been besieged by women from all over the country, begging, pleading, offering bribes of all sorts—all dying for the chance to put on that green suit and be Queen for a Day. But it's too late, I tell them all, too late. They had their chance back in the days of thrift shop dresses, but it's gone. Now you have to wait for someone to die or move to Australia to open up a vacancy. One current Queen had to grovel in the very dirt for three full years, even after an opening became available. It was so much fun having her follow us around year after year, in desperate supplication, we sort of hated to give it up. Like all sororities, we find that half, maybe more, of the fun is in keeping others out. So much for the sweet part.

Queens serve at my pleasure alone, and don't they know it. The sucking up doesn't stop with induction. It is a lifetime process, teamed with blind obedience. I design the outfits, I select the hair color and style, I select the music and choreograph the dances. I have ultimate power, and I like it.

Lest I give anyone the erroneous impression that the Sweet Potato Queens are an insular, independent group, let me assure you—nothing could be further from the truth. There are many happy, helpful worker bees in our little hive. Their hard work and devotion make it possible for us to reign supreme and serene. For this we are truly grateful, and we try to show our gratitude constantly. Indeed, we fraternize with all of them quite freely every day of the year, save one. Here's a rundown of Team Sweet Potato Queens.

A small but dedicated band of Sweet Potato Queen Wannabes is allowed to follow our float each year. We even let them wear our old outfits and discarded wigs. They carry signs that clearly mark them as Wannabes, engaged in their sucking-up process. Whenever our float stops for us to dance provocatively for our adoring crowds, the Wannabes run and prostrate themselves in front of the float, bowing, scraping, and generally whipping up increased crowd frenzy for us, the actual Queens. The Wannabes understand that any and all attention they might possibly receive must at all times be totally derivative. They are only Something because we are Everything.

Did I mention that the Queens adhere strictly and joyfully to the principle of equal opportunity? Indeed, one of our most devoted, talented, and hardworking Wannabes is of the boy persuasion, and we are all pissed off because George's butt is cuter than ours. Nonetheless, we've voted him Most Versatile, Miss Congeniality, and Most Likely to Become a Queen, gender notwithstanding.

The Wannabes are by no means our entire entourage. With us since the very early years has been Wilson Wong, who for parade day is transformed into another persona. What do you get when you take a six-foot two-inch Chinese guy with waist-length hair and put him in a gold lamé smoking jacket and rhinestone sunglasses? You get: Lance Romance, the Official Consort to the Queens. He's the only man who has been allowed to ride on the float in anything less than a subservient capacity. Make no mistake; he *is* a veritable slave, but he's a love slave. All I can say is his wife, Lynn, is an unusually tolerant woman.

The Queens are too busy dancing and prancing in the parade these days to be bothered throwing trinkets to the masses. So we have many unpaid but happy lackeys to do our throwing for us—mostly our children, who ride in the back of the pickup truck that pulls the float. These are the "Tater Tots." People are always asking when we are going to let the kids ride on the float with us. To this ridiculous question, the answer is always the same: "When they get old enough, they can build their own damn float. We are not doing this for our children." Any idiot knows when you perform with children or animals, you become invisible, and that is not part of our plan.

The ever-growing contingent of hopeful, helpful men in our employ is known as the "Spud Studs." To say we would be nothing without them is stretching it a bit, but we would certainly be unduly in-convenienced, which is nearly as bad. And so we really love our Spud Studs, the guys who step and fetch on our behalf each and every year before and during the parade. They not only help build the float and hook up the generator and the sound system; they are solely respon-sible for getting it to the parade—no small accomplishment since this involves maneuvering a pickup truck towing a twenty-five-foot trailer bearing a fourteen-foot sweet potato down the interstate highway at three miles per hour with 250 pissed-off truckers backed up behind them for about thirty miles. The Spud Studs labor tirelessly on our be-half, literally for nothing, since most of them aren't even married to us anymore.

We could never perform without the atmosphere of safety pro-vided by our vigilant Sweet Potato Queens Security Staff, those ded-icated men and women who walk the entire arduous route alongside our float. Armed with Nerf bats, giant loofahs, and enormous loaves of rock-hard French bread, SPQ Security makes sure that the 65,000 slobbering fans who turn out to see us each year stay respectfully be-hind the police barricade. The officers of the staff—Meg, Michelle, and Rhonda—are so fetching in their little uniforms, a great deal of their time is spent defending their own honor as well.

The parade lines up on State Street, one of Jackson's main north-south thoroughfares, which you can get on and drive forever, and it will eventually take you to Chicago. We like for our float to be in about the middle of the lineup so the crowd has time to anticipate our appearance. This also puts us in position to spend a couple of hours before the parade begins looking at ourselves in the big picture windows at Lefleur's Cadillac. We like to arrive a good while before parade time to practice dancing on the float and to get accustomed to the pitch and roll of the contrivance. The float is a single-axle trailer, and that one axle makes all the difference. The float bounces around so much that dancing on it is not unlike surfing. You've got to get your sea legs early on to keep from landing out amongst the hoi polloi.

When the parade begins to roll, usually one-ish in the afternoon, we move past the sea of screaming people on State Street and turn down Capitol Street, the city's main downtown street, toward St. An-drews' Episcopal Cathedral. This is where one of the Queen's bosoms once leaped completely out of her costume and flung themselves at our friend Jerry McBride. Every year since, he has posted himself in the exact same spot but, alas, to no avail. Directly across the street from this seamy scene is the Governor's Mansion ("second oldest executive residence in the country after the White House," they say). The entire parade stops here while we work our magic on the parade judges, aka the Bucket Heads, so called because of their inexplicable fondness for wearing actual buckets on their heads. We always perform at least two dances here—one will be the theme song for that particular year, and the other is the perennial crowd favorite, "Who Wrote the Book of Love?" (Lots of pelvic thrusting in that one.) The governor himself usually comes out on his front portico to gape, and several members of the O'Tux Society will be there to curry our favor. A marching *krewe* (that's Mardi Gras lingo for "crew") of guys wearing green derbies and tuxedos with short pants, the O'Tuxers operate the flowers-for-kisses concession along the parade route. Bad boys all, at least on St. Paddy's Day.

Postperformance, we drive slowly away, leaving them all—governor, Bucket Heads, O'Tuxers, and crowd—in a state of utter satiety, and make our way down the remaining mile or so of the parade route, ending at Hal & Mal's for the street dance. Hal & Mal's, a popular Jackson watering hole owned by parade daddy Malcolm White, his Sweet Potato Queen wife, Viv, and his brother Hal, is the headquarters for the parade and quite naturally the official bar and eatery of the Sweet Potato Queens. (Hal & Mal's also has the best rest rooms in town. The men's room, our personal favorite, is a shrine to Elvis, with tributes to Elvis from famous people written on the walls, such as Billy Graham—"I think I will see Elvis Presley in Heaven." The urinals are made up to look like the front end of motorcycles.)

The Queens will make numerous appearances onstage with each band. We love all of the bands, of course, especially Raphael Semmes's local group, These Days, with lead singer Jewel Bass, but we're not shy about performing with the national acts; and Delbert McClinton is our favorite. (The greatest radio talk show guy of all time, Don Imus, loves Delbert almost as much as we do; somebody once said that Imus thinks the sun shines out of Delbert McClinton's butt, and we certainly have no evidence to the contrary.) The bands love us, too, because we can whip the crowd into a frenzy, and musicians do love a frenzied crowd. The end of the parade always comes too soon for us. Performing onstage at the street dance provides us our much-needed additional time to revel in our Queenliness.

♡

In this rarefied atmosphere of Queendom, a philosophy, a way of life, has developed over the years. We've made many observations about life from our lofty vantage point above the masses—words to live by, axioms, and even laws that have been carved in stone. Finally we have decided to share them. *The Sweet Potato Queens' Book of Love* contains Everything You Need to Know About Life and Love. Life *is* Love. The Queens are always in love, be it with the Guy du Jour or a Hal's shrimp po-boy. It all feels good, and that is what's important.

So now, whenever the song raises the age-old question "Oh, I wonder, wonder who [ba-doo-doo], who [boom], who wrote the book of love?" you will know the answer: We did.

On the pretext of maintaining some small degree of anonymity, at least outside our own community, where we are all too well known, the Queens held a meeting and decided that we would all select stage names for use in this book. Everyone wrote down her first choice on a slip of paper and submitted it to me for approval. Well, wouldn't you just know it, everybody wanted to be "Tammy." We decided, quite rightly, I think, that it would not be fair to allow any one Queen to have the name that all wanted. And so we did the only fair thing: We will all be called "Tammy" henceforth.

That Queenly Look

MAINTAINING IT IN THIS LIFETIME AND THE NEXT

Getting and keeping that Queenly Look is no small feat, and you'd be amazed at all the details to which we must constantly attend. A good portion of our lives is, of necessity, devoted to our hair, our skin tone, our figure flaws, and our clothes. On parade day, none of this is a problem: We all wear huge matching wigs, we get tan enough (if only by the bottle or the bed) to avoid causing snow blindness in our audience, and in our fantastically enhanced matching outfits, our true body shape can't be discerned. But alas, we parade only one day a year, while we are Queens for Life, twenty-four hours a day, seven days a week. Certain considerations must be taken.

When the Wigs Come Off

The Queens are split about fifty-fifty, I'd say, in the hair department. What I mean is that half of us have some—as in lots, abundant, tons—and the rest of us have about four hairs each that we try in vain to frump and twitter into the semblance of Big Hair. Big Hair is highly desirable. You must have Big Hair to perform hair-tossing and -fluffing.

This is the main activity of women in bars, and it is done not only to attract men but to intimidate other women. Because, trust me, other women are intimidated—especially if they happen to be other women to whom the hair gods were unkind. A thin, mousy mop cowers beside a Crowning Glory.

A friend of ours, Gail Pittman—an aspiring Queen who thinks she can ascend directly to the throne, bypassing the Wannabes—is a hugely successful, self-made businesswoman. She used to be a schoolteacher and now she owns and runs a gabillion-dollar company that produces her signature line of pottery and sells it in the finest shops nationwide. She has done it—made it. And in addition, she's the sweetest thing ever to draw breath. It would take a really small person to begrudge her the smashing success she has truly earned. You cannot help but love her at first sight. But sadly there are really small people in this world, and they are just the type who can only feel bigger if they make you feel smaller.

Gail was scheduled to make an appearance on a midsize town's local television talk show, and she had gotten all dolled up for the occasion, as she is wont to do: look nice for the people. For all her success and her universally renowned sweet disposition, our Gail does have a flaw; and she had the great misfortune of being in the clutches of one of those really small people, who also happened to be the local female talk show host. As the guy backstage was counting off the seconds-to-air time for them, *"Two . . . one,"* the host leaned over to Gail and said, "I thought so—you have thin hair! *You're on!"*

To say that Gail was undone does not even begin to describe it. She could hardly speak. She couldn't even think about what the creature was asking, for worrying about her hair and how very thin it must appear with all those lights shining through it and how she wished she'd worn a big hat. It was the longest ten or fifteen minutes of her entire life, and she has never fully recovered from it. We can only assume that this was the desired effect. I mean, what positive intent could be attributed to a woman who would say to another woman, immediately before a live television broadcast, "You have thin hair"?

Women with Big Hair talk with it the way Italians use their hands. They send messages with it and use it for punctuation. Their heads swivel like owls'. Women with Not Much Hair do not whip their heads about in the violent manner espoused by women with Big Hair. When desiring to look at something on the opposite side of the room from where we are currently gazing, those of us without Big Hair make a single, simple, discreet movement, one that does not disarrange our hair nor create strong wind currents that could endanger others. A Big Haired Woman, on the other hand, making the same turn will first duck her chin, then abruptly jerk it up and around, causing her massive mane to be lifted up and out in an alarming fashion, actually standing, for a moment, straight out from her head before collapsing and swirling about her head and face. Consequences to others depend on the length of said hair and the position of the hair in relation to its surroundings. Innocent bystanders can suffer lacerated eyeballs if they are not alert. Busboys have had the entire contents of their trays swept crashing to the floor by proximity to an ill-timed hair toss. An event of this magnitude, however, wouldn't be classified as a mere toss; such a grand toss is used primarily to communicate a willingness to perform sexual acts. When property damage occurs, it is usually the result of an actual hair fling, used to indicate extreme displeasure or, in the vernacular, being "pissed-off big time."

Some of the most energetic hair-flinging occurs in weight rooms. Remember that very first fitness show on TV—*The 20-Minute Workout?* It consisted, as I recall, of nearly naked women with huge hair contorting their bodies in unlikely positions and flinging their hair for twenty minutes. I don't know a single person who ever actually tried to do any of the supposed exercises. It was, however, a wildly popular show with the male demographic. The show is long gone, but hair-flinging as exercise has remained a constant in gyms all over the world. It caught on with Big Haired Women (BHW) everywhere.

The woman with normal to nominal hair, on the other hand, will simply lie down on the exercise bench, giving no attention whatsoever to the position of her hair. For her big-haired counterpart, the hair is the most important aspect and takes up most of the time. To perform, say, a leg curl, an exercise that requires one to lie facedown on a bench, the BHW, as she is lying down, will suddenly jerk her head back and then just as abruptly jerk her chin to her chest, causing all her hair to flip forward and hang off the end of the bench. No face will be visible for this exercise. Upon completion of the set, she will arise and fling it all back again. If she's performing the normal three sets of the exercise, the hair-fling will begin each and every set. If she chooses to remain on the bench in between sets, she will find it necessary to turn her head to face the other way from time to time.

This is a very tricky maneuver for the BHW, requiring major head whippage in a horizontal position. Many cervical disks have been sacrificed in the perfection of this movement.

Big Hair can become a public menace. In locations where beauty pageants are big business, like Vicksburg, Mississippi, or the entire state of Texas, many establishments have taken precautions to protect their property and the safety of their non-BHW clientele. If you get too many women with Big Hair in one room, (a) there's not enough room for anybody else and (b) it gives the fire marshals fits because nobody can see the exit signs and somebody's sure to get trampled if a fire ever breaks out.

As a result, the Big Hair Hole was developed and patented by the owner of the F & M Patio Bar in New Orleans, Trevor Palmer. Touted as the most important Big Hair development since Aqua-Net, the Big Hair Hole is not only a safety device, it also ensures that there will be ample space inside for even the most extravagant hair events. Upon arrival, Big Haired Women are directed to insert their heads into the Big Hair Hole to determine the exact size of their hair. This way, the maître d' can control the number of women with huge hair allowed inside at one sitting and can devise strategic placement as well. This provides a safe environment for participants and nonparticipants alike. In the event of a sellout crowd, latecomers are relegated to the Big Hair Holding Area until space is available.

The Unbearable Whiteness of Our Being

Several of the Queens—although, Lord knows, I love them dearly—are among those blighted individuals for whom the phrase "white people" was originally coined. *Zero* melanin in that skin, I'm saying. Freckles do not count. I, on the other hand, have been blessed with most of the melanin doled out to the white race in this hemisphere, and I'm plenty glad of it, too.

I'm also thrilled to report that my daughter got my skin and not that of her toad-belly father. When she was just a tyke, we had taken her to the beach, and she was naturally anxious to hit the sand. I cautioned her that we must wait and "grease up Dad—you know how he is." She looked thoughtful for a second and then said, "Yeah, he'll fry like a chicken in a rowboat." She was about two, and I have no idea where she came up with that analogy, let alone that perfect tone of disdain and disgust, but I've always preferred to think it was from her maternal gene pool.

Truly White People are understandably wild with envy regarding those of us with melanin-packed skin. One of the Queens, Tammy, and I had made a quick trip to Cancún to catch up on our lying down and lolling about. You don't want to get too far behind in those categories. Tammy, like most Truly Whites, had not the foggiest idea of how to get a tan; she desperately needed my expertise and assistance.

Now, in a tropical location such as the one we happened to find ourselves in, even bronze goddesses like myself must exercise a certain degree of caution about sunning. Let me just say right now that I'm well aware of all the current hoo-ha about the sun and all. And let me further state that I don't care what they say. The sun is good—for me. I believe that staying inside in fluorescent lights and working all the time is what is causing all this melanoma. I will add that I'm not a complete idiot and have no wish to look like my favorite pair of dark brown aged leather Bernardo sandals from high school. I wear 15 SPF all the time and still tan, and I love it. I will do it until I can no longer drag myself out of doors into a patch of sunlight. My theory is: Why not? We're all going to just wrinkle up and die one day anyway. If staying completely out of the sun for the rest of my life would make me look like I'm twenty-three when I'm sixty-five—I might consider it. *Might.* Na-a-ah. First, it can't happen, and second, what good would it do me to look like I'm twenty-three when I'm sixty-five? Who would I date? I have faced it: I am never going to be young and cute again, and I am over it. Let somebody else have a turn.

So Tammy wanted a tan. I knew I had my work cut out for me. We had to start the day early to handle it all. We'd go down and stake out our beach umbrella, watch the sun come up, have our breakfast poolside, and repair to the room to grease up. Tammy was stunned at the amount of preparation involved in proper tanning. Like most white people, she would typically fry herself totally the first day out and then spend the rest of her vacation in the room, watching TV standing up. She was uneducated in the proper application of sunscreen.

I explained to her, patiently, the absolute necessity of completely covering all of your flesh with lots of sunscreen and rubbing it in real good. Left to her own devices, she would have squirted a blob of sunscreen into her hand, rubbed her hands together twice, and then haphazardly smeared it on portions of assorted body parts. Some parts would have been devoid of any hope of protection, resulting in a sort of burned-in plaid or paisley design all over her body. I specified to her that any body parts she did not want crispy would have to be liberally coated with sunscreen. She was free to pick which ones she wanted to offer up to the sun god, but me, I was going to oil up *all* of my parts and go for a gentle sauté effect, leaving the deep-frying to the novices.

Tammy was also completely unaware that you are supposed to apply sunscreen twenty minutes before you actually need it, meaning you are supposed to let it soak in before you go out into the sun. Nobody reads labels. We greased up completely, no quick task given the amount of square footage we had to cover, and sat there dutifully, naked, for a full twenty minutes before suiting up and venturing out. I kept her to a rigorous schedule:

9–10 A.M.—reading under the umbrella
10–11 A.M.—sunning, thirty minutes each side, with occasional dips in the ocean
11 A.M.–noon—reading under the umbrella
noon—lunch, poolside
1–2 P.M.—nap under the umbrella
2–3 P.M.—repeat sun cycle
3–4 P.M.—repeat umbrella cycle
4 P.M.—shower, moisturize, and nap
Get up whenever, dress, and go out for dinner.
Repeat daily.j

Thanks to my expert personal tan management, Tammy did acquire a beautiful golden tan. We both developed coughs by the end of the trip, however, and we decided it was vacation pneumonia, caused by excessive lying down. We walk a fine line, don't you know, between a "therapeutic" dose and "overmedication."

How Does All That Look in the Mirror These Days?

From time to time the Queens have to make an assessment of the body situation. (Don't we all?) Unless you are Melissa Irby, our friend who grew to a flawless size two and stopped and has never added so much as a dollop of fat to her entire body—I hate her for it, we all hate her for it—I think we can safely say that this scene would best be played by candlelight. That reminds me of the guy who was going on about how his wife would never be "actually" unfaithful to him because she had had a whole bunch of kids and would never be emotionally secure enough to allow another man to see her body. I thought to myself, Now, I don't know everything; I'm just from south Jackson, after all. But down south of Raymond Road we have a little something we like to call the *dark*. He never considered the possibility that she might, if she found herself feeling frisky, just shoot out all the lightbulbs in the joint and roll around with the man of her choice until just before sunup the next day. All that is to say that the dark is our friend, and this is precisely what it was invented for. Most of us spend most of our time in the daylight, however, so it behooves us to get to the gym.

Once at the gym, you should hire a personal trainer who is knowledgeable about the two different types of muscles that make up the female body. You have your hiking-up muscles. They do just what the name implies: They hike up stuff that needs hiking up—your tits and your butt, for example. You should not need a breast reduction in order to make your waist smaller, if you catch my drift. Exercise the right muscles, and you can hike them babies back up where they belong. Then you have your pinning-down muscles; these are the ones you apply to other people. Proper use of your pinning-down muscles will assure that your man will stay right where you want him for as long as you want him there. Some muscles have dual purposes: They both hike up and pin down.

I said once that I thought a good goal for working out would be being able to Do It with the lights on. Our friend Gail said her goal was to be able to try on swimsuits while wearing knee-highs. I don't believe there's a female body in existence, even size two Melissa's, that could stand up to that test without the aid of plastic surgeons, trick lighting, and computer enhancements. We have all struggled mightily with the exercise issue. We struggle to avoid having to do it as much as anything. We resist the idea. We wish it weren't so. If we exercise, however, we do look and feel much better in our outfits, not to mention how we look *out* of our outfits. And we've found we're happiest when we are not too fat to walk.

One of our Wannabes, JoAnne (see, you don't get to be a Tammy until you are an official Queen, and thus you enjoy none of the benefits of anonymity that are afforded the Royal Court), only recently started exercising. She has spent her entire life since shortly before puberty in the avid and relentless pursuit of nonathletic endeavors. If there was a world championship title for buttsitting, JoAnne would have been a contender. Until very recently she moved around only enough to avoid getting bedsores. The only thing that could possibly have incited JoAnne to exercise was the chance to be a Wannabe, with its attendant opportunity at being an *actual* Sweet Potato Queen, if she played her cards right.

She began exercising with a vengeance. From nothing to five and six days a week in a row. Walking, riding bikes, lifting weights, doing crunches. A maniac. Well, maniac could be a trifle strong—do maniacs whine as a general rule? If not, then JoAnne would be disqualified, but she was, as they say, gettin' it with her neck out long and whining all the way. First her neck hurt, then her back had a twinge, then she was tired, then a knee started hurting—always something. But never enough to contraindicate exercise. Then she finally found what might be her ticket back to the couch: Her belly button hurt.

"Your belly button?" I asked, in a voice filled at once with incredulity and with disdain.

Those of us of a certain age were children in the time of the smallpox vaccination. You had to go to the doctor and get stuck a bunch of times on your arm. The resulting wound was expected to fester and ooze for weeks and then form a scab. And you had to be very careful of your scab; if it got knocked off before its time, you had to start all over again. Indeed, many's the kid that had to be dragged, under great protest, back to the doctor's office because the first vaccination didn't take. During that few weeks' time of incubating your vaccination, anytime something came up that you found distasteful or unpleasant, you immediately and loudly declared that you could not do *that* because it hurt your vaccination! You were bulletproof. It was the master key to the universe.

Even if parents weren't moved to pity by your pain and terror at having to be revaccinated, they were stirred to their core by the fact that you would not be allowed to enter the first grade without the requisite vaccination scar. Your starting school—and exiting the home—was vitally important to your parents, so having a freshly minted vaccination gave you pretty much carte blanche for what you would and would *not* be doing for the next few weeks. It was a heady experience of absolute power. It did not last forever, though many determined children tried to carry it on way past its time. A year later they would still be claiming alarming sensitivity in the vicinity of their vaccination.

For those of us of that generation, it has been a joke that has endured unto this very day; we can still try to weasel out of something by claiming that it hurts our vaccinations and, at the very least, count on a laugh from another *old* person. I knew a woman who would tell her exercise instructor she couldn't perform certain particularly unpleasant exercises because her eyes were dilated. She used this successfully for many years. Since the instructor knew that whenever the dilated eyes were invoked there was no future in trying to persuade Linda to do anything, she just acted sympathetic, to the amazement and disgust of the rest of the class.

Well, JoAnne may have hit on the ultimate hedge with the belly button business. If she does not, in fact, have one of those dreadful belly button hernias, which would be a tragedy and probably nip her exercise career right in the bud, she can still use it on a regular basis. Who can discern whether another person's belly button hurts? It cannot be proved or disproved, to my knowledge. We do have some leverage with her, however. There is a bylaw in the Sweet Potato Queens' Code of Conduct that prohibits being too fat to walk. If a Queen is too fat to walk, she's unable to fulfill one of her main functions, namely that of flouncing and prancing around on the float and through the crowds. She can't starve herself to achieve the desired size because she'd be too weak to perform her duties, and there's an even stronger prohibition against being skinny. Skinniness to even the slightest degree is not looked on kindly by the court. Indeed, it is simply not tolerated. No, Missy JoAnne is going to be forced to continue exercising, and we're so glad because she shows real potential. We are definitely grooming her for royalty.

She Who Laughs Last Laughs Best

The Queens do want to maintain their queenly look to the end. Another reason to get and stay fit is to try to live longer. One of the principal reasons this is such a deal, especially in the South, is that the longer you live, the longer you avoid having a typically terrible Southern obituary written about yourself. Perhaps this is not just a Southern custom, but we have certainly distilled and refined it. The first thing I read in the paper every morning is the lead obituary, which is the only one featuring comments from the grieving survivors. For many of the deceased, one could safely assume this is the only time their names have been in the newspaper. One would expect that those closest to the deceased would try to make this especially meaningful.

Here are some actual samples from real obituaries in legitimate newspapers. Honest to God. After reading them, you might want to take a moment and jot down a few notes for whoever will most likely be calling in your obit—just to be on the safe side.

He was fond of bowling and squirrels.

He enjoyed watching videos, *Matlock*, and *Wheel of Fortune* and eating candy.

She painted in oils—out of her head. She made up scenes, and she painted a lot of horses. She could make a horse look like he could talk to you. She especially enjoyed horses because her oldest granddaughter participates in high school rodeos and was named state reserve champion in the goat-tying competition.

"John" and his wife Ada Ruth have been bedridden for years but the family has continued to care for his cows.

I can never, never say what she meant to me. She was a true Christian who believed that Christianity was something you should not play with.

She never missed *Days of Our Lives* and had lunch ready to watch the stories every time.

"Sam" and his wife enjoyed raising St. Bernards. "We raised them and sold them. We sold them in about seven states in the South. They're just like most dogs. If you want them to be inside dogs, you keep them inside. Any you want to be outside dogs, you keep them outside."

She married at age thirty-three because she had been caring for her little brother who fell out of a tree when he was small.

Or they print revealing nicknames, such as "David 'Do-Nasty' Williams." But what follows is the world *champeen* obituary of all time. I will not be able to resist some commentary during the text.

Cause of death is undetermined pending the outcome of a coroner's investigation. "Betty Jo" was a friend that "Lou Ann" said she will never forget. "We have shared so many good times and there were so many things she did that turned many of our times into pure fun times." "Lou Ann" said that the deceased enjoyed cooking so much that she would cook in large portions—regardless of how many guests she would actually have. "I looked at the stove Sunday when I was at her house and I noticed what she had cooked. I honestly thought she must have planned for the students at the high school to come over and eat with her. She enjoyed cooking and eating—she would not mind telling you that." [I inferred from this that the departed one did not do so in a size four dress.] She has always loved shoes, and she will be buried in a pair of beige leather pumps her daughter "Poochy" recently bought. I am sure that when she walks through the Golden Gates [has she gone to Heaven or San Francisco?] her shoes will be shining and she will be smiling. And since she was always particular about her hair and wore it in a banana clip a lot [I swear to God, it said that], I am going to do her hair and makeup. We decided to let her look like she is getting ready for a night out—she is going to be just beautiful. We are going to let her wear it down and pushed off her face a bit so the angels can see those pretty eyes of hers. [Are we to assume that she was buried with her eyes stretched and pinned wide open?]

The lessons in all this are many, but to recap the high points for you: Stay fit and live long and prosper, but write your own obituary now, while you can, just in case.

The horrors wrought by supposedly good friends and close family members in the writing of obituaries give us food for thought on a related subject: burial clothes. If your "best" friend is going to put your hair in a banana clip while you lie helpless in your coffin and then tell the world about it in the newspaper, for crying out loud, what do you reckon the bitch will dress you in? She'll probably go out and buy you something since you probably don't own anything ugly enough to suit her. Whatever color you looked the worst in while living—you can only imagine how much worse you will look in it dead.

One of my favorite Wannabe Wannabes, Gayle Christopher, is a really pretty woman. (The Wannabes have gotten so snotty, they won't let any new ones join, so we have a whole crop of women sucking up to them now.) If you don't mention right off your own self how pretty she is, she will shortly find a way to work it into the conversation. If her best friend, Jean Hines, and I are trying to have a conversation that happens to have nothing whatsoever to do with how beautiful Gayle is, and Gayle is present, then every few minutes either Jean or I will have to glance at Gayle and say, right in the middle of our conversation, "Your hair looks great," or "That color is great on you." If we don't do this, she'll interrupt frequently with questions regarding her hair (doesn't it look great?) or her weight (doesn't it appear to be dropping rapidly?) or her nails (good color, yes?) or her general overall cuteness (I'm cuter than y'all are, right?), and so it's just easier to interrupt ourselves and give her what she wants. This woman has even pulled up beside us at a stoplight, rolled down her window, and hollered at us how she wished we could see her standing up because she had on the best-looking outfit and it looked especially cute on her. Then she punched her husband, John, in the arm and demanded, "Tell 'em how cute I look!" And just rode off, laughing, down the road. The thing is: She really is cute, and dang if part of what's so cute about her isn't how cute she says she is—unabashedly and loquaciously.

Gayle wants to leave this world looking just as cute. She has made us promise that we'll see to it that she's buried with clean and fluffy hair, with no gray showing, and wearing a pink negligee. Whenever she prepares to go out of town, she reminds us of our solemn oath concerning her burial preparations. We threaten to slap a gray granny-looking wig on her and dress her in a beige polyester double-knit pantsuit, two sizes too small so she looks fat, and with a high neck. The woman loves to cleave, if you know what I mean.

My sister, Judy, has always said that she would like to lie in state, propped up in her coffin with her eyes blared wide open, face fixed in a big grin, and have a taped greeting for all her mourners. Something real upbeat and, well, live-sounding, like:

"He-e-e-ey! Cuteshoestellyoumamahi!"

That is the gist of most conversations in the state of Texas. In Mississippi, a lot of conversations go like this:

"He-e-e-ey! KewtshewsyewthenkOleMissgoneweeun?"

(If you were born north of the Mason-Dixon line, you probably can't imagine what's being said. I suggest that you read each line aloud several times, sounding out the syllables phonetically until the words register. This would be a good preparatory exercise if you ever plan to visit the South.)

The previously mentioned Official Consort to the Sweet Potato Queens, Lance Romance, is in everyday life Wilson Wong, devoted son of Mrs. Wong. Wilson was born on the ship en route to the States when his parents immigrated from China right before the big Commie brouhaha. Mrs. Wong does not speak English. For years the family owned the best Chinese restaurant in town, and occasionally we'd try to reach Wilson there. If she happened to be there by herself, Mrs. Wong would answer the phone, and if the caller was not Chinese, like us, it was just too bad. "Wong!" she would shout into the phone, and that was it. She had said the only word she knew that could be understood by anyone outside her village.

Mrs. Wong's health has been failing of late, and when asked how she was doing, Wilson said, "Well, she has her ups and downs, but she's already been through five sets of burial clothes, so we don't know what to think." He explained that it is customary in China for a person to select his/her own burial clothes, obviously in advance of the actual day of burial. But tradition says they can't be new clothes, so you have to wear them at least once. Well, she keeps buying burial outfits and wearing them once, only to discover that she likes the outfit and keeps on wearing it. Then it ceases to be the burial outfit—apparently it can't be old clothes either—and so she has to start over. Since she cannot and will not die without proper burial clothes, we figure, at this rate she'll live forever.

The Queens had a planning session on the subject of burial

clothes. The consensus was that no new outfits need be purchased, no funeral plans or cemetery plots arranged. We think that one fine St. Patrick's Day, right at the end of the parade, we will all just ascend, in full regalia, right off the float and directly up to Heaven. It seems the only plausible ending to us, and it is the only one we could all agree on.

The True Magic Words

GUARANTEED TO GET ANY MAN
TO DO YOUR BIDDING

Given that it's not easy, painless, or inexpensive to be a Sweet Potato Queen, that tells you right off that outside assistance will be required. We postulate that this is true whether one is a Queen or not. We feel that in any area of life, it is highly desirable to get other people—men—to do things for you whenever possible. This includes, but is certainly not restricted to, performing all manner of personal services, as in cooking, cleaning, and errand-running, and especially rubbing, fawning, worshiping in word and deed, constantly, and of course, paying for things—as in everything, including, naturally, presents of all kinds, but especially the sparkly kind. We find that we are very crowlike in our affinity for things that go sparkle.

Toward this end we have formulated the True Magic Words. Let me assure you, these words used correctly just beat the hell out of *please*. As a matter of fact, if you use these words aptly, you can forget the word *please* even exists—except that you will be hearing it spoken to *you* so much, you will come to gag on it. With these simple words you will have the instant ability to persuade any man on earth to willingly, happily, and swiftly do your bidding. This is one hundred percent guaranteed. The Sweet Potato Queens, as a group, have employed this technique for more than twelve years now, and we have an absolute no-fail rate thus far.

Here's what you do: First, decide what it is that you want or need done, handled, fetched, or purchased. Then select the man you want to perform this task. It doesn't matter which man. For the purposes being discussed, they are interchangeable. Anyway, pick a guy, any guy, and outline for him, in vivid detail, exactly what you will require of him. It is vital that you cover all the bases at this point in the discussion, because once he hears the words, he will be momentarily slack-jawed and breathless, and then his brain will irretrievably lock. He is a man with a mission, and he is going to do whatever you want so fast, your head will spin, so get out of the way.

So you've followed the steps so far. You've identified your want/need. You've selected the designated guy. You've shared with him in minute catalog your heart's desire. You are ready for the Magic Words. The words have been uttered so successfully so many times in Jackson, Mississippi, and abroad by the Sweet Potato Queens that they have become known as the Sweet Potato Queens' Promise, or simply, the Promise. And what we do is this. One or more of us will visit the designated guy and make the pitch: "And if you will do this one little ole thing for us, we promise that"—and here's what clinches the whole deal, the True Magic Words—"we, all eight of us, will give you a blow job."

And then we shut up.

A traditional moment of silence is always observed immediately following the use of the Magic Words. Men are inherently slow regarding women, and the moment of silence allows for lag time. Men's brains are migratory and are usually located in their summer home, way south. The silence of the moment is palpable, just like those few seconds before the sun slips into the ocean. The man is transported. When breathing is restored, it is almost always mouth breathing.

Do not, under any circumstances, utter another word after the True Magic Words have been spoken. Any sales manual will tell you that, once you have made your offer, the next one who speaks loses. And trust me, ladies, he will speak. Okay, maybe he won't actually speak. There may not be time. He may have just launched himself out the nearest window in his rush to comply with your wishes. But the result is the same. With these few Magic Words, you will be able to persuade any man on earth to swiftly and happily perform any and all requests you make.

And now, let me hasten to explain to you, as you will to him: *There is a vast difference between the promise of something and the receipt thereof.* What he has received is the *Promise.* But it's no trouble at all to help him see that, even with only the Promise, he is miles ahead of where he was without it. He is actually in the ballpark now. It could happen. It won't, never has, but it doesn't matter. Men just love to hear you say the words.

Talk about shooting fish in a barrel. This is so easy. If it didn't make them so happy, we'd probably feel bad about it and quit. And it works so damn well! I'm telling you, we've used this technique repeatedly throughout the civilized world, very often with the same men. Not only have we never failed to get what we want, but to date not one Promise has ever been fulfilled.

The giving of the Promise has become the Sweet Potato Queens' rite of initiation. Once a woman has been selected for a position in the court, the Boss Queen, namely me, will choose a quest and a knight for her to practice on. The entire court will accompany her on her virgin mission. It is a very moving occasion.

A few years ago, at the initiation of Tammy, which was being held during happy hour at Hal & Mal's, we spied at the bar a certain high muckety-muck from the *Clarion-Ledger,* the largest newspaper in Mississippi. And we—rather, I—decided that it would be a good thing if he would ensure that there was a large, full-color, above-the-fold, front-page photo of the Sweet Potato Queens in Sunday's paper following the parade on Saturday. And so our newest Tammy went over to him, accompanied by the full court of Queens. Now he, not living under a rock, knew full well who we were, what we wanted, and what we were about to say to him in order to get it. So did everybody else at the bar, which, of course, did make him the Man of the Hour— lucky bastard. Still, not being accustomed to receiving such attention, he was slightly flustered and flushed. Meanwhile our girl Tammy, former president of the Junior League and former Queen Regent of the Girls' Auxiliary of the First Baptist Church of the little town where she grew up, was in an equal swivet at the prospect of actually delivering the Promise to this man, in full view and earshot of a hundred or so people, all of whom were respectfully silent in keeping with the import of the occasion.

All I can say is: I now have that large, full-color, above-the-fold, front-page photo framed and hanging in my office.

On another occasion a covey of Queens drove forty miles to Vicksburg because Jason D. Williams was playing outdoors on the banks of the Mississippi River, at a club over there, and the Queens were in a dancing mood. If you're in a dancing mood, Jason D. is a good man to help you out. He is a piano-playing fiend, that's what he is. He plays like Jerry Lee Lewis's wet dream. But on that night, Jason D. began positively crooning songs like "Bringing in the Sheaves," which is highly entertaining church fare but not what we had in mind for a Saturday night out of town. We made inquiries of the sound man about how long we could expect this to go on. He indicated there was just no telling what Jason D. might do or when he might do it. This was not acceptable. The Queens were in a froth to dance.

One of the Queens, possibly me, hastily scribbled a note on a cocktail napkin and marched herself through the thicket of chairs, up the steps, and across the stage and plunked the note down on the piano, right under the nose of Jason D., who was at that time right in the middle of a touching ballad. What the note said was this: "There are six of us who came over here to dance, and we will all give you a blow job if you will crank it up *right now!*" Well, I'll have you know that Jason D. kicked his piano stool off into the river and commenced flailing on that piano in a manner most exciting to the Queens. We flocked to the front and twirled and undulated to our own delight— and that of the band as well. As a result, we didn't have to pay admission to the second show, and we drank free, too.

Whenever possible, we like to make the Promise in a group. It seems to heighten the excitement for the guy. We're all laughing fit to kill, and he knows on some level—like his conscious, rational mind— that it is never going to happen. But on some other level, usually a little farther south, hope springs eternal, and we are all for keeping hope alive, especially since it serves our purpose so well.

We are mindful, however, that a power this, well, *powerful* cannot and should not be used for our own purposes alone, no matter how worthwhile and important those purposes may be. No, we feel honor-bound on occasion to use this power for the good of others as well. Draw nigh and hear testimony of our touching concern for the health and well-being of our brother. A number of years ago, one of our dearest friends and biggest fans, Sergio Fernandez, was stricken with that weird temporary paralysis stuff, Guillain-Barré syndrome. This was not a handy disease for a keyboard-playing father of two to come down with. As it progressed, he became completely paralyzed, and he spent a good bit of time in a rehab hospital. Being universally adored, Sergio had everybody breaking his or her neck to help him out. Folks were praying for him and raising money. We felt that the Queens could do more. And so we did.

Me and one of the longest-serving Queens, Tammy, suited up in full Queen regalia and paid a hospital call. When we arrived on Sergio's floor, the nurse informed us that we would find him in the patients' lounge. We made quite an entrance, as you may well imagine. Sergio was, of course, elated to see us. He said our arrival had been duly noted from the windows of the lounge by some of his fellow patients, and no one had believed him when he wheeled over, looked out, and said nonchalantly, "I know those women." So imagine their awe and his triumph when we swept in and came immediately to his side.

We sat and chatted for a bit and inquired about his progress. He was proud to announce that bath time was a happy time and that the nurses were pretty good-natured about it. He was just so ecstatic to receive confirmation on a daily basis that *everything* was not paralyzed. We said we were happy to hear that, and that brought us to the real reason for our visit. "We have come to heal you, Sergio," we told him gravely. He seemed willing. And then we told him that if he would get well and quick, we promised that we would all give him a blow job. And so, of course, he did, and, of course, we didn't. But he has never complained.

This technique will work on any man, anywhere, anytime. There are certain words and/or gestures that are the same in any language— Mayday, visa, exit, okay, grabbing your throat to tell the world you are choking. You can no doubt think of other examples. Well, blow jobs are that way—timeless, universal, always desired and appreciated. Everybody wants a blow job all the time.

Women are not like this. As much as we love sex, there are times when we really and truly are not interested. One of those times would be, say, immediately after we have eaten an entire pizza. This is known as Whole Pizza syndrome. You know, you're stuffed to the gills, your stomach looks like you ate a basketball, whole and inflated; you're starting to get that comfy, sleepy feeling, and here he comes, pawing at you. He could not have been interested before you ate the entire pizza, when you were alert and had that flat stomach. No, he wasn't interested then because he was hungry, and he can think only about his overriding primal need at any given moment. Once he has eaten, peed, had a beer, put out the fire in his hair—satisfied whatever urgent need he happens to be having at the time—then his mind immediately reverts to the one subject it is totally consumed with 99.9 percent of his life, waking or sleeping: sex, or more precisely, blow jobs.

At any rate men could do a lot better—meaning, get what they want—if they would just pay attention. If their thoughts weren't totally focused on blow jobs all the time, they might be able to think clearly enough to formulate more successful strategies than suddenly grabbing some of our body parts and inquiring bluntly whether we wanted to give them one. How many times has this happened to you, and how many times have you responded with a resounding, "Yes, I was just thinking the whole time I was drinking that pitcher of beer and eating that thirty-six-inch fully loaded pizza, that as soon as I finish all this, I'm going to pounce on you like a duck on a June bug"?

You, at this point, having just consumed an entire pizza, would rather be set on fire than have sex with anybody, let alone anybody as stupid as he is to think that you'd be in the mood. This has happened after virtually every meal you've ever shared with him. Men are persevering little shits; you've got to give 'em that. They'll just keep right on trying. The puzzle is this: Why, when something doesn't work ever, do they keep trying the same thing? Why does it never occur to them to change strategies? Just once, why can't he figure out that everybody loves cold pizza *after* sex?

I dated a wonderful guy, Ralph, for an all-too-brief period in my youth. At the time he was totally unsuitable for me: tall, dark, handsome, sexy, successful, great sense of humor, sweet, smart, really fun to be with—you get the picture. There was no way I'd get serious with a guy like that. I preferred the unemployed, although the unemployable were particular favorites, too, in those days. But anyway, Ralph also happened to be Jewish. I am not, and he made constant witty references to this shortcoming on my part, referring to me as a "white woman." When he would say it, he would affect this really thick drawl and stretch it way out, with a very long, flat "eye" sound in "white." On one occasion he made the mistake of making an ill-timed pass; he was normally a brilliant tactician. Upon being rebuffed, he commented, "Ever'body knows, whi-I-ite wimmin don't li-I-ike to be pestered."

The True Magic Words

Yes, indeed. Blow jobs make the world go 'round, just in case you still thought it was love. Everything that happens, good or bad, in the entire world, can ultimately be traced back to a blow job, either given or withheld. Men have two states of mind that can be best illustrated with two crude drawings: one of a big, smiley, happy face; the other of a big old scowl. The accompanying captions would read "Blow Jobs" and "No Blow Jobs." Properly timed and executed, blow jobs given to the right personnel on a regular basis would no doubt bring world peace. Perhaps we should unleash all those beauty pageant contestants who are always clamoring to work for world peace. Put 'em out there where they can do us all some real good. Save the whales, the children, the rain forests, the oceans, the ozone layer, the owls, the beach mice—everything! Save 'em all! They've got to organize! A union is what they need.

But we know the secret truth: The Promise of a blow job works just as well as the real thing, at least from our perspective. We deduced this important principle from a tip I read some years ago in "Hints from Heloise." One clever mom had discovered how to avoid the sticky mess that always occurred when she gave her children ice cream. She swore they were just as happy with an *empty cone!* I recall thinking those must be some serious dumbass kids if they couldn't tell the difference between ice cream and no ice cream. Turns out she was 100 percent correct. And so it is with the utmost confidence that we recommend The Promise to you. According to Tammy, Queen and Inhouse Counsel, the Promise is not enforceable in any court of law. Believe me, if it were, with as many lawyers as we've used it on, we'd have heard about it by now!

The Best Advice Ever Given

IN THE ENTIRE HISTORY
OF THE WORLD

For the most part Sweet Potato Queens prefer the *giving* of advice over the *taking* thereof, with a few notable exceptions. The following story from my childhood represents advice I am proud I was given. Naturally I want to pass it on to you. My father's people (in the South, your family is called your "people") were from a "suburb" of Kosciusko, Mississippi, called Ethel. Kosciusko is also Oprah Winfrey's hometown, but you're not likely to see her at the Piggly-Wiggly on a regular basis. The town did have a big deal honoring her some years back. I was prevented from attending by the advanced state of my pregnancy—that time that used to be called "the confinement," when you are just too huge to be seen by the unaided human eye and it requires a panoramic lens to take you all in. I have always regretted that I missed getting to see her in my daddy's hometown, since Oprah is one of the few celebrity types I really admire.

Other than Oprah (who is no longer there), woods and red dirt roads were, and still are, the dominant features of the area. This is not to say that those characteristics would differentiate Ethel from any of a jillion other little hamlets in the South. We mostly sort of lump them all together under a few generic names for the sake of shortening the telling of tales. "Podunk," "Bumfuck," and "East Jesus" cropping up in a story would indicate to you one of these places with not much else but woods and red dirt roads. Graveled roads in some of these vicinities are considered to be newfangled ideas. As are teeth.

But anyway, we went to see my grandfather in Ethel a lot when I was a kid. He was deaf as a post for as long as I can remember. I also remember that he didn't seem to mind in the slightest being deaf as a post. Most likely that was because he was a lot more interested in monologues than dialogues. We all referred to him as "Harvey" since he couldn't hear us say it. Seems he didn't like to be called that, and since the beginning of time my grandfather had told everybody his name was Philip. Harvey was, in fact, his name, but this did not become known until Daddy was a full-grown man and named his own son Philip after my grandfather. Only after the naming did my grandfather 'fess up that his true name was Harvey. This irritated Daddy to the extent that he refused to call the man anything but Harvey ever again. My uncle fell prey to the same ruse. Somewhere in Pennsylvania I have a cousin Philip who was named for his grandfather, Harvey. Normal family.

But then, maybe not quite as "normal" as some other families in the Attala County area where my people lived. There was one guy who was called by all who knew him "Hoe Handle"—only the *d* in Handle wasn't pronounced. It was "Hoe Hannel," or more often just "Hannel," on account of him stepping on a hoe once, probably forty-five years earlier, and whacking himself smartly between the eyes with the handle. He apparently never quite succeeded in living it down. Then there was this other guy who was universally addressed as "Big Dick." Even his own mother called him "Dick." This was unusual because his name was Charles or something. I can't imagine how that got started. So, all things considered, I guess the Philip/Harvey thing was pretty tame.

Granddaddy Harvey always wore the same thing: gray wool pants, black belt, white long-sleeved shirt buttoned to the neck, black hard-soled shoes, and gray felt hat. Winter or summer, it never varied. He was old, always old, and thin as a rail, with skin like parchment paper. He rolled his own cigarettes from a little cotton pouch he kept of Country Gentleman tobacco. He smoked the entire thing. There was no cigarette butt, ever, not even so much as what would be called a "roach" today. It was simply gone. Ecologically sound, I suppose, in a twisted sort of way. I once brought him some strawberry-flavored papers I'd bought at a head shop in Atlanta. He looked like a really old, skinny Jerry Garcia puffing on a joint. He could squat for days, his skinny little butt just grazing the ground. He would sit like that for hours watching me ride my horses in the lower pasture. When he got tired, he would simply rise. No groaning. No pushing with his hands. He would simply stand straight up and walk away. I did not inherit his knees.

When the time came for us to leave, he would walk us out to our car. "Us" being my parents, my older sister, and me. We would be getting into whatever model Ford Daddy was driving at the time—that is, until he got mad at Ford for something and started buying Buicks. He was like that. Totally brand loyal until the manufacturer did something he didn't like, and then he would quit them forever, never to reconcile. He quit Gillette and Falstaff and took up with Schick and Old Milwaukee the same way, just for spite.

My grandfather would walk us out to the car, and he would always say the same thing as we were leaving. He'd never use any of the usual ones, like "Be careful," "Be sweet," or "Be good." Mama used all those on a rotating basis. Daddy's parting shot was always "Don't fuss with your mama." No, Harvey would wait for Daddy to roll down his window, and then he'd prop those skinny elbows on the ledge and stick his whole head, hat and all, in through the window. And he would say, "Y'all come when you can," which was of no substantial pith or import, but then he would add, "Be particular." Except he pronounced it "p'ticklar."

Be particular. That is, without a doubt, the Best Advice Ever Given in the History of the Entire World. Consider, if you will, the profound effect that following advice would have on, say, your diet, your love life, your financial situation, your decision on whether to have that next drink. I mean, what do those two words not cover?

The times when one has not heeded this sage advice will stand out with alarming clarity. Huge amounts of pain and money are frequently associated with such times. Just to show you how awry things can go when one is not particular, I offer this personal testimony from one of the Queens, Tammy. Whenever the subject of sexual escapades presents itself—and in a group of women it presents itself fairly often—Tammy always offers this as her most bizarre sexual experience to date.

The Redheaded Man Who Would Not Move

"Whenever I think of him to this day, some twenty years later," Tammy says, "I always think of him in capital letters—THE REDHEADED MAN WHO WOULD NOT MOVE.

"It was like this: I had been dating this guy for a couple of months. Somehow, don't ask me, it happened that I had been dating him all this time and hadn't gotten around to sleeping with him yet. Anyway, we had a relationship by this time that was based on stuff like friendship and companionship, and I really liked the guy a lot. So it got real weird, real quick once we Did It.

"This guy had the most bizarre approach that I have ever even heard of, let alone experienced. If there was any of what is commonly referred to as 'foreplay,' I totally missed it. I swear to this day, it never happened. The way I remember it, there was no activity between the time that we got our clothes all the way off and the time that he lowered his entire—and it was substantial—body weight onto me. There was no customary propping-up-on-the-elbows stuff—I got the full load. And there it remained, parked, dead still, motionless for what seemed like an eternity. During which time many probing questions entered my mind, as you may well imagine. Things like 'Huh?' Come to think of it, that was probably the only question that came to me at that particular time. But it got repeated over and over.

"Every time I tell this tale, somebody will ask me why I didn't just take over the situation. There are at least two answers to that question, which did occur to me at that time. The first one was that I was doing good—with all my effort—to maintain airflow to and from my lungs, squashed as I was. What most people, I think, would consider the 'normal' movements associated with the, ahhh, missionary position cannot, for the record, be generated solely by the party in the lower position without the full cooperation of the party in the upper position, if the party in the upper position outweighs the party in the lower position by a good seventy-five pounds. And this, I'm afraid, is the unhappy position in which I found myself, with no help in sight.

"The second thought that came to me was this: 'He obviously does not think that you are supposed to move during this procedure and thus would be shocked, horrified, if not outraged, by any attempt at movement on my part.' I imagined him saying to me, through gritted teeth, 'Ladies do not move!' And as I was in no position to argue the point, I let the moment pass without comment.

"But this, I am so sorry to report, was not the end of it. I rationalized the situation to death. I concocted I don't know how many 'reasons' to explain away the event, or nonevent, as it were. I guess, in retrospect, I must have come up with something satisfactory, because I fell for it—again. Yes, indeedy-do, a few nights later found me in the same predicament as before. Only this time it was much, much worse because I knew what could happen—or in this case, could not happen. And danged if it didn't. A repeat performance of the nonperformance.

"Well, let me tell you, it was a difficult situation I found myself in, and I knew if I allowed myself to think even one thought about it, it would be all over. I'd start laughing, and I'd never be able to stop. So I thought about dead dogs. It was the first thing that came to mind that was not funny, and I just honed in on it and thought about it as hard as I could. Until it was over.

"After that I told him I thought we ought to just be friends, and he moved away. All's well that ends well. No blood, no foul. No tickee, no washee. A rolling stone gathers no moss. I don't know what clichés would fit this particular situation best, but I do know, at the very least, I've never forgotten the Redheaded Man Who Would Not Move."

The moral of this story should come as no surprise: *Be particular!*

4

Be Prepared

ON ACCOUNT OF YOU JUST NEVER KNOW

The first rule of being prepared is, of course, *always shave your legs.* In a perfect world we would not even have to mention armpits, but sadly, even in the rarefied atmosphere of the Sweet Potato Queens' domain, the hairy armpit issue has materialized. We have one Queen—she's the youngest, and she missed the whole hippie thing when it was original, and she's being forced to live through it now, when it is so over, since she chose to move to Boulder, Colorado, where it is apparently the height of chic to be an ugly woman. At any rate she has not grown up and out of it sufficiently yet to begin—or I guess *resume* would be more accurate—shaving her underarms, and so we have to do a pit check on her when she comes back to Jackson every year at parade time. (It should be duly noted that she's so beautiful and queenly that, even with hairy armpits, she's a knockout and thus has become a tourist attraction in Boulder.)

Shave everything that needs it, and by all means, *always wear pretty underwear, on account of you just never know.* I know your mother said you should always wear clean underwear, but at this stage of your life, you really should not need to be reminded of this one by anyone, including yourself. Clean is a definite given. And clean would be sufficient if the only unexpected aspiration you have is something along the lines of a car wreck. However, it would seem to me that if you've just had a head-on collision with a Peterbilt or a Mack truck, chances are excellent that the clean factor has been torn asunder anyway.

So let's look on the bright side of things and hope for something unexpected of the tall, dark, and handsome variety. The mood will be destroyed if you are wearing orthopedic underwear. It must be pretty. It must also be tiny. How many of James Bond's girlfriends have ever shown up in big underpants? Pretty and tiny are both readily available ready-made; however, the Queens do not like to buy off-the-rack. We prefer instead to travel to the West Coast, where we can camp out at our friend Ned Walton's house in the Hollywood Hills, which is the most serene spot on the planet and we wish we could live there all the time. From our campsite at Chez Ned, we can go to a little place on La Cienega called, aptly, Trashy Lingerie. Owned by the incomparable Miss Tracy, her helpmate, the ineffable Mitch, and their devoted son, Randy, Trashy Lingerie is a delightful little shop wherein they custom-make—what else?—trashy lingerie. And I do mean custom-make, too. In the course of your fitting, you will be measured in ways your dressmaker never dreamed of. Nipple to nipple. Cheek to cheek. But, hey, your underwear will fit.

A good fit in underwear is a definite advantage when you're wearing the pretty stuff—"single underwear" is what I call it—because otherwise it can be miserable. Bras crawl up your back or down your belly (if they're strapless). Slips ride up and stick to your dress. Straps fall down. And panties—Lord, deliver us from pretty panties. You just put them on, and they immediately wedge up your butt, you don't even have to move. Thongs were a perfectly natural progression—why not save all that extra material, they all end up in the same place anyway.

My friend Gayle, the one who's so good looking and not only knows it but tells us about it all the time, and her husband were in Florida for a romantic getaway. They had retired for the night, and he commenced fondling her loins in that way and commented, huskily, that he loved that new thong she was wearing, to which she snappily replied, "Oh, John! Don't get all excited; my panties are just up my crack!" Then they both laughed so loud, the people in the next condo complained to the management. Our Gayle can make a mood or break it just that fast, but it keeps ole John on his toes, let me tell you.

But answer me this—how come they don't make men's underwear so it goes up their butts, huh? Same thing with swimsuits. Even guys who wear those dreadful Speedos, they put 'em on and they stay put. The only women whose swimsuits don't crawl up their butts are the ones in beauty pageants, and that's only because they use Firm-Grip stuff on their butts. I call this unfair. I propose that they either make stuff for us that will stay down—or make all the men's stuff so it crawls up their butts. I don't care which—I'm just looking for parity here.

Actually, a good case can be made for "married underwear." "Married" may be a misnomer; it may be "postpartum underwear" I'm speaking of. Perhaps women who have never had children continue to wear beautiful underwear till the day they die. I'll have to verify that point. At any rate a big change occurs shortly after conception, and as far as I can tell, it is irreversible. For one thing they do not make pretty underwear for pregnant women. They make orthopedic underwear for pregnant women—big, sturdy, serviceable, substantial Russian immigrant underwear. And it's indescribably comfy. This means that, once you've experienced it, you may never go back.

This brings us to another essential principle of preparedness: *Never Wear Panties to a Party*. This rule evolved quite by accident when I was severely pregnant. My erstwhile husband, the ubiquitous MoonPie himself, came in the room where I was struggling to clothe my behemoth body for some festive occasion. I had somehow managed to stuff myself, sausagelike, into a very tight casing of maternity pantyhose. Those and one of those gigantic bras, the cups of which would fit on my head, were all I happened to have on at that moment. What a vision.

The truth was, I had long since outgrown anything resembling what you would normally call panties. What I could fit in at this point looked more like pillowcases. I had to hide them from MoonPie; whenever he would find a pair of them, he would throw them away. I knew what he was thinking: If he could just get rid of all the big ones, I'd be forced to buy new—and small and sexy—undies. Typically male in his thinking, he never looked at the big picture—that's how we ended up pregnant to start with. I bet if you researched it, you'd find out that all the pretty underwear factories are owned by gangs of obstetricians. Everything's a plot, I swear.

But anyway, I wasn't wearing any panties of any kind in order to avoid that pesky visible panty line. Now, why on earth I thought anybody would be looking at my butt—well, pregnant women are not always rational. Anyway, Pie walked in and was surprised that I wasn't wearing anything under my tights: "You're not wearing any panties?" I didn't hesitate, nor did I even look up at him. I just said, real offhand, "Oh, you never wear panties to a party," and kept on doing whatever. He just stood there, slack-jawed, for a full thirty seconds, considering the implications, I suppose. I had moved on, forgotten about it, and he was still standing there, gaping. "You don't? Nobody does?" "Nobody does what?" I asked him. "Panties to a party—doesn't anybody wear 'em?" He was looking sort of dreamy and clearly thought he was being let in on some big secret of all womankind: that every party he'd ever been to or would ever go to—there wasn't a pair of panties in the room—and he was the only guy who knew.

He was so highly entertained at the prospect, the Queens tried it on some other husbands and fiancés with comparable results. So we made it a rule: Never wear panties to a party. But there's no point in not wearing panties if nobody knows you're not wearing panties, so be sure to tell someone. You will know instinctively with whom to share this information.

Sometimes you just don't know how much preparedness will be required. A girlfriend of mine went to the Y to work out. Feeling rather sporty in her workout gear, she sauntered out to the front desk area to chat with new arrivals. After a surfeit of small talk and gooning guys, she was ready to hit the track. Since it was still a bit chilly outside, she put on her sweatshirt. Somehow, in one of those flukes that you could never recreate in a million years, a pair of pantyhose that had been lurking in the depths of the sweatshirt somehow contrived to thrust themselves up and out the neckhole and fly fifteen or so feet across the crowded lobby, landing smack on the counter in front of some unsuspecting guy just standing there waiting for some towels. Great little ice-breaker, I thought. (I must remember it—odd we hadn't thought of it before.) For years women have been hurling their underwear at rock stars on stages all over the world. Why not bring this time-honored tradition down to a more day-to-day application, where it might actually accomplish an introduction, at the very least?

Actually, come to think of it, I did already think of it. Many moons ago, long before the advent of postpartum underwear, when MoonPie was still ardently earning his name and thought that the sun shone from various orifices of my person, we happened to be in the Paradise Café in Grayton Beach, Florida. MoonPie got his name because you know when you fall in love and feel so great and act so goofy and mushy—that's being moonpied. (A Moon Pie is a gigantic, gooshy, chocolate-covered-marshmallow-graham-cracker deal that we are inordinately fond of in the South. Moon Pies are often consumed in conjunction with either a cola-type drink or an orange-flavored soda—as in a "Moon Pie an' a Ah-ra-Cee-co-cola" or a "Moon Pie an' a Big Ahrnge.")

So anyway, he was moonpied bigtime, and I, of course, found this gratifying. So at some point, after the salad and before the entrée, I excused myself to the powder room. When I returned, I leaned across the table and pressed something into MoonPie's hand. It was, of course, my panties—which, at that particular juncture in my life, were very small, pink, and lacy—completely unlike the aforementioned "married" variety. Needless to say, it was a very short meal. I recall go-boxes being ordered forthwith. So as I ponder this memory, I can assure you that lingerie-flinging can have felicitous results, and I recommend it to you highly. There is a lot to be said for timing and technique in this business of preparedness.

A good case could also be made for carrying around with you your toothbrush, a change of underwear, a large supply of your chosen method of protection, your favorite pillow, and perhaps even a small canned ham. Our good friend Larry Bouchea showed up at a Queens' gathering recently and pulled out of his pocket the tiniest little canned ham we ever saw. "Oh!" we cried in delight, "it's a *pocket ham!*" We were so taken with the idea that we've included it in our Be Prepared Kit. You can, and we hope you will, visit our website at www.sweet-potatoqueens.com and order your own Be Prepared Kit. Some may feel that a pocket ham moves one beyond simply being Optimistically Prepared and into the realm of Predatory Anticipation. We feel that this is a matter of personal conscience and we would come down hard on the pro-choice side. After a pretty bad streak of men, we even considered amending the list to include carrying some sort of weapon, also because you just never know. If there exists in this universe anything more infuriating and crazy-making than a man, I don't know what it is, thank you, and I don't want to know. Of course, on a good day, I would also have to say if there is anything in this universe *better* than a man, I don't know what it is; and I don't think it would even be healthful for me to know at this stage of my life.

But if you've decided to go out on a limb and kill one, for goodness' sake, be prepared. We all read, with dismay, the sad story of a good woman wronged in south Mississippi who took that option and made a complete mess of the entire thing. See, first she shot him. Well, she saw right off the bat that that was a mistake because then she had this enormous dead body to deal with. He was every bit as much trouble to her dead as he ever had been alive, and he was getting more so all the time. So then she made another snap decision to cut him up in pieces and dispose of him a hunk at a time. More poor planning. First she didn't have the proper carving utensils on hand, and hacking him up proved to be just a major chore, plus it made just this colossal mess on her off-white shag living room carpet. It's getting to be like the Cat in the Hat now, only Thing Two ain't showing up to help with the cleanup. She finally gets him into portable-size portions, and wouldn't you know it? Cheap trash bags. Can anything else possible go wrong for this poor woman? So the lesson here is obvious—for want of a small chain saw, a roll of Visqueen, and some genuine Hefty bags, she is in Parchman Penitentiary today instead of New Orleans, where she'd planned to go with her new boyfriend. Preparation is everything. However, if you have been particular, you shouldn't need to be prepared to this extreme. Try to avoid getting involved with somebody who's gonna need killing before it's over. It may seem to you that that narrows the field somewhat, but be diligent.

So moved were the Sweet Potato Queens by this woman's plight that we swore a mighty oath that it would never happen to us, no, not to us nor to any of our people. Since that time, whenever one of us gets married, which seems to be a pretty regular occurrence for some unfathomable reason, we make sure that all the basics of preparedness are covered at the bridal shower. Chain saws and garbage bags are only the beginning. The centerpiece is traditional: an extremely large (I'd say about three feet tall, and a foot or so in diameter) inflatable penis. This lends a festive air to the occasion. Many Fat Mama's Knock You Naked Margaritas are prepared and cheerfully consumed. The bride is presented with the catalog from our favorite store, The Pleasure Chest, whose Los Angeles location we frequent whenever possible. The Queens are quite Clampett-like in their wide-eyed wonder at the incredible array of exotic devices on display. We had never even heard of a butt-plug, and here we were, faced with an entire butt-plug department in a retail establishment. We were quite carried away with the assortment of tit clamps available as well. Tammy's favorite was actually the cheapest model available—seven dollars—an old-fashioned wooden clothespin—painted black!

The bride (and whoever else needs one) also gets the Good Vibrations catalog. This is actually a very educational book, and the Queens feel *very* strongly about education. We learned, thanks to our dear friends at Good Vibrations, that the vibrator was invented in the late nineteenth century—in America, of course—by doctors for treating "female disorders." It seems that genital massage was SMP (standard medical practice) at that time, to induce what they called "hysterical paroxysm." We like to call it "orgasm" today. The vibrator was invented to be a labor-saving device for the doctors! And quite the little time-saver, too, I expect. You got twenty women in the waiting room who want to get off before you can play golf—you got to come up with a better way. We were not in the least surprised to hear that men were in too big a hurry to fool with us, even in that slower era. That one of the greatest boons to womankind was actually invented to make life easier for men is okay by us.

According to the Good Vibes folks, it didn't take long for this handy-dandy new apparatus to show up for sale in women's mags and mail-order catalogs. It was touted as a cure-all for headaches, asthma, "fading beauty," and tuberculosis. We would like to offer our personal testimony as to the efficacy of these happy little machines: Our headaches are gone, our asthma cleared up, our beauty actually *needs* to fade a bit to make it safer for us to go out in public, and not one of the Queens has ever had TB. We must say, those vibrator manufacturers are some creative little buggers.

We pass the catalogs around, and everybody gets a chance to pick out the models she finds most intriguing. There is a lot of reading aloud. There are a few consistent crowd pleasers: the Auto-arouser, which plugs into your car's cigarette lighter and promises to add a whole new dimension to road trips, and the Butterfly, which is apparently a little deal that you can actually wear under your clothes, say, to work, to keep you vibrant during those wretchedly boring staff meetings. We think these butterfly devices should be standard issue for all postal workers—indeed, all government employees, and anybody else who has to deal with the public. On reflection, wouldn't the world be a better place if we all wore one? In fact, if we all wore them long enough, could we not expect some natural form of butterfly vibrator to evolve into our species? And isn't it strange that with all the attention He/She devoted to detail (strawberries, for example—who but God could have come up with those?), we are not already so equipped? The only possible explanation we can come up with for this glaring lapse is that not even God could have predicted at Creation just how far over time we humans would stray from the path.

But anyway, we provide the bride with the means for obtaining whatever marital aids she personally feels will aid her the most, and we do not force her to share with the group what exactly those might be. We restrict our gifts to things we know for certain she will need: the smallest, most beautiful lingerie ever created, and high-heeled satin slippers with marabou trim.

There will be those days, however, when none of these items of preparedness are sufficient. Not pretty panties or married panties or no panties. Shaved legs won't matter, and even butterfly vibrators will do you no good. And even if you have a chain saw, you won't be able to get to it. Sometimes the only thing that will work is your own ingenuity. And this brings us to the last and most important rule: *Be creative.*

Before Xena, There Was Curtisene

The very essence of creative preparedness is contained in the person of Curtisene Lloyd, and for this reason she is the unchallenged winner of the Sweet Potato Queens' highest award: *The Most Prepared Woman the World Has Ever Known.* (Every word of the story I am about to tell you is true. It is authenticated in court documents.) Curtisene Lloyd is a mild-mannered, sweet-voiced little Sunday school teacher of a lady, middle-aged, a nurse. She lives, with her very old deaf aunt, in a nice house in a little town not far from Jackson, where she works at a large hospital.

February 1990. Late one night Curtisene awoke to discover a man in her bedroom. And he was definitely not there at her invitation. This intruder advised her of the various and sundry obscene things he planned to do to her before he made up his mind whether or not he would kill her. "I might kill you," he said, "but I'm gone git me summa dis fust." And with that he removed all of his clothing and climbed up on the bed. He situated himself on the headboard somehow and began giving Curtisene some rather detailed instructions concerning the performance he expected from her.

Now, our Curtisene, she was paying real close attention. She had taken note right off that this guy did not have any sort of weapon with him. And then she did something that never in his worst nightmares had he dreamed she would do. She just reached out and took *aholt.* She did. Our Curtisene grabbed a hold, and then she commenced to twisting. She got both hands on his merchandise, and she twisted—in opposite directions at the same time with as much force as she could muster.

Apparently it was sufficient. Her attacker beat her about the head and shoulders and struggled frantically to get free of this death grip, but Curtisene was on him like all those time-honored phrases you've heard all your life—white on rice, duck on a June bug, and so on.

So, still holding fast, she drags him, now sniveling and crying, through the house, where her little old deaf aunt is sleeping in peaceful oblivion. He's begging her to let go:

"Let go and call the po-leece! Just let go!" He's swearing he's dying.

"No, you ain't dying," she says back to him. "I'm trying to kill you, but you won't die."

He promises he'll leave if only she will, please God, let him go.

"Fine," she says, "go on then. Leave."

He's crying and saying he *cain't* and how can he when she won't let him go?

To which our Curtisene casually replies, "You broke in, didn't you, sumbitch? Break out!"

He is wailing to beat the band, and she is dragging him to the front door. She tells him there are three locks on that door that he'll have to open in order to make good his escape. He is pretty much a lifeless heap by now, except for the bawling. She hoists him up to open the first lock. He gets it open and falls back to the floor. "He was starting to wheeze a little by this time," Curtisene reported.

He's crying and saying how much she's got him suffering, to which she snappily replies, "How 'bout all that suffering you were fixing to put on me?" She tells him he's got two more locks, if you please. She hoists him up, and he thinks he's out.

"Nope. The screen's latched," Curtisene tells him.

And up he goes again. And he's sure he's free now. At this point, she later confessed to the jury—in the shyest little voice you ever heard, like she was letting you in on a little secret—"I kinda worked on him a little bit." Meaning, if it had been possible to twist his genitalia completely off his body, she would have accomplished that feat at the end of her front porch.

And then she repeated to those assembled her final words to the man: "I'm takin' you to the end of the porch, and then I'm gon' go back in the house and get my gun, and I'm gon' blow your m——f——g head off, you slimy, stanking, low-down piece of shit, you!" As she repeated those words, clear as a bell, in open court, you could feel, in every living soul in that courtroom, an almost overwhelming desire to stand up and cheer.

What happened to the rapist wannabe? Well, he limped off through the bushes, but he wasn't hard for the police to find. Especially since he departed buck nekkid and left all his clothes in her bedroom—with his full name written on the labels inside. He was also pretty easy to spot in the lineup: He was the one who didn't stand up straight. He may never stand up straight again, actually. And don't you just know he was a big man in jail, after the truth came out. Little-bitty Sunday school teacher just waxed his ass.

Curtisene Lloyd did not get the standing ovation that her testimony so richly deserved—courtroom decorum and all that—but every single person in the courtroom that day went up to her afterward and said, "Miss Lloyd, I just want to shake your hand."

Curtisene Lloyd, my hero. I love this woman, the Most Prepared Woman the World Has Ever Known.

Educating Our Young

IN A MANNER MOST BEFITTING A QUEEN

I have a preteen daughter who was nicknamed BoPeep by the Queens' Official Consort, Lance Romance, while she was still incubating inside my spacious midsection. His theory was that as a child of the Sweet Potato Queens, she should not have a name overused by the masses. As far as we know, there's been only one other female with this particular name in the history of the world. My daughter doesn't have to worry about which Sarah or Amanda or Melissa they're calling because she ain't one of 'em. Bringing up 'Peep in a manner befitting the daughter of a Queen has been no small task.

Understanding pageants is an essential part of the curriculum. The Queens have a love-hate relationship with pageants. First the hate part. We hate the thought of females of any age—but certainly the younger they are, the worse it is (their mamas should be clubbed to death with cans of Aqua-Net)—posturing, preening, groveling, if you will, for meaningless titles with no accompanying power and appallingly cheap crowns from crass promoters with dubious agendas. It's too embarrassing for words. But we do love to watch them do it. I mean, we really love pageants.

Whenever there's a pageant of any kind on TV, we all gather at my house for the Pageant Party. This means the standard many margaritas and large quantities of food. I have a personal arsenal of rubber dart guns, and everybody selects the weapon of her choice and gets a pile of darts. Then bring on them beauties! Our favorite part is the opening cattle call, especially when the contestants wear some sort of costume representative of their home base. In one state pageant we got to see two grown women dressed, respectively, as a recliner and a small aircraft. In the year that will forever dwell in our hearts, we got a hula dancer, a marimba player, a clogger, and one girl who danced barefoot on broken glass to "The Battle Hymn of the Republic" as performed by Elvis Presley. Pageants with talent competitions are obviously preferred.

The darts fly as the spirit moves us. Sometimes the TV will be one solid mass of darts, and sometimes only a solitary missile will be launched, but we have a wholesome good time at the expense of the trick-dog contestants locked in mortal combat for those scholarships. I'm personally grateful they'll do anything for a crown.

Growing up in a house where Pageant Parties are a regular occurrence was confusing to young 'Peep in the beginning. She would sit, observe all this frenzy from the sidelines, and ask, in her sweet little-girl voice, "Why are y'all making fun of 'em, Mama? They're so pretty, and I like those sparkly dresses, Mama." We took this as our opportunity to begin educating her properly, hoping to nip the bud of this pageant thing, at least in our own home. We explained to her that yes, they're pretty. We're all pretty, thankfully. It is a good thing to be pretty. But we are not *just* pretty, and pretty all by itself is not worth much since it lasts only about an hour, relative to the rest of your life. In addition, pretty is just a major accident of birth, and nobody can take any personal credit for it (except when it's bought and paid for at the plastic guy's office, but never mind that). They shouldn't be handing out awards for being lucky enough to not be born a dogball, I tell her.

Life holds few pleasures, if any, more exalted than riding on a float in a sparkly dress with a crown on one's head, I admit to her. What matters, however, is *how* you *get* that crown. We're not about to do tricks on national TV for a crown. In life, I tell her, it's vitally important that you buy your own crown and declare yourself Queen, and then spend the rest of your life living into that. Pretty will last a short time, at best, but stupid can last forever. Fortunately, so can smart.

Are You Quite Certain You Have the Upper Hand?

The Sweet Potato Queens Educational Program extends far beyond beauty pageants and crowns, however. As with all good mothers, discipline is important to us. We are against hitting children. My father always said this really annoying but true thing to my mother, and it always pissed her off because it was so true: "If you can't control yourself, you can't control a child." We think it takes craft and wiles to raise children effectively without creating a mutant race of sheep-kids who will meekly comply with any command from any adult. Spare us those mealymouthed little "yes ma'am, no sir" robots. We know that they've been literally beaten into submission. We also know that they are inwardly seething, and there will be hell to pay one fine day.

What I always did with BoPeep on the extremely rare occasions when she was acting buttheaded in public: I'd squat down right beside her and get right in her little ear and say, real low and contained, often through clenched teeth (I've found that just about anything you say through clenched teeth takes on an added tone of pith and import), "You are acting awful, and it's embarrassing me, and if you don't stop on a dime, then in about two seconds *I* am going to do something that will embarrass *you* so much, I doubt seriously you'll ever completely recover." Presto! She would immediately revert to being the perfect child. I never had to *do* anything and actually never had any idea of what exactly I would do, if she called my bluff. It's never happened. I figure that, having grown up watching me doing any number of things she considered humiliating when I was in a good mood, she was so terrified when I was in an angry one that the prospect was unthinkable to her.

But witness what can happen to you when discipline goes awry. This is, sadly, a true story. An unidentified mom is attempting to conduct a banking transaction in a downtown bank, during lunch hour, on a Friday. Only a few thousand people are in there. Her kid is running all over, being your basic four-year-old asshole. Mom loses her place in line about fifty times chasing the little beester down. Finally she's almost up to the teller's window, when she looks around and sees Beester on the far side of the bank on top of a loan officer's desk, rummaging, pillaging, and stomping around. So she shrieks across the bank, "*Beester!* If you don't get down from there and get over here *right now,* I am gonna *blister your bottom!*" To which Beester retorts, at the top of his little lungs from his highly visible vantage point atop the officer's desk, "No, you won't neither! 'Cause if you do, I'm gonna tell Meemaw that I saw you put your mouth on Daddy's weenie!"

Talk about your slam-dunk. I have no idea what the fate of the hapless Beester was, but Mom dissolved on the spot into a little greasy puddle and evaporated into the air. What else could she do under the circumstances? But doesn't this kid have leverage forever? I'm talking bulletproof for life.

Regarding Prejudice and Religion

When my sister, Judy, was in the first grade, they had those double desks, and her desk mate was, of all things, a boy. This in itself was hardly to be tolerated, but to make matters worse, he smelled "funny." In the forty-some-odd years I've known my sister, I've never been able to ascertain what "funny" meant, and so I have no idea what he smelled like. Well, it seems that he also had red hair, and since he was the only redheaded person she had ever encountered and he smelled funny, little first-grade Judy extrapolated that redheaded people smell funny—all of them. And she is now, well, she's a lot older than she used to be, and she still believes that. It's a basic corollary of life for her. Until the day she dies, she will maintain that redheaded people smell funny, and she can't be persuaded otherwise.

I, too, had a vivid prejudice-forming experience as a small child. There was a family on the street where I grew up who belonged to some off-brand of church that called itself Baptist. These folks were four-plus crazy, in my opinion. They had all these bizarre rules for all aspects of life, such as: Nobody may wear shorts on Sunday. Now, I couldn't have been over six or seven years old, but I distinctly re-member thinking that that was the stupidest rule I had ever heard. With all the terrible things going on in the world—the only ones I can remember being well informed on were the starving children in China and World Communism, but I was properly horrified by both of those—all God's got to worry about is whether or not Lindy and Mindy are wearing shorts on Sunday? I thought if that turned out to be true, my opinion of God was gonna drop a notch or two. So I asked the fount of all wisdom, Daddy, what he thought about it. He pursed up his lips and twinkled a bit around the eyes and replied: "Some people must think God's stupid."

So growing up, I just knew I might become a lot of things, but I knew I never wanted to be a Baptist. Then I grew up and could fully understand that all Baptists didn't believe such nutty things; but a trace of my old prejudice lingers still, and I'm always on guard in the presence of known Baptists.

The point of all this is to demonstrate how easily lifelong prejudices can be formed by the silliest of circumstances. Therefore we feel it is important that our children be taught this simple tenet: Hate people on an individual basis only—you must actually get to know someone at least slightly before you can properly hate him or her.

My daddy told about an old man who lived in Kosciusko when Daddy was a little boy. This man was locally famous for his favorite oath. Whenever he told a tale that was particularly unbelievable to his listeners, he would end it by saying, "And if that ain't so, then God's a possum!" Devout members of his audience would gasp and step back to avoid the lightning they felt sure was about to strike the man. It never did, of course, and this demonstrated definitive proof to me and my daddy that God has a great sense of humor. We Queens always feel lucky in that regard since we make fun of everything.

In the Jackson neighborhood where I grew up, not only was the Baptist count high, there were also some off-brand cult types—all ultrareligious. When tempers would erupt during a game of chase or hide-and-go-seek, the children of these off-brands would splutter and stammer in anger, too young and inexperienced to know how to cuss each other out properly. When matters finally really reached the boiling point, right before blows were to be exchanged, one would yell at the other, *"You don't know your Ten Commandments!"* It always came out sounding like one word, *"Tinkamandments."* And the battle would be on. I'd watch all this and muse, "Now, I wonder what God thinks about this?"

In trying to provide some spiritual guidance for your kid, I swear, weeding out undesirable elements—or garbage, as I like to call it—

takes almost as much energy as dispensing the good stuff. There have been a number of religious groups in recent years that I've found wildly entertaining. One of my preferences was that woman who claimed her body would be sporadically taken over by the spirit of a 35,000-year-old warrior. She made about a gabillion dollars with this. I'm sick I didn't think of it. I saw a video of her. Considering myself to be pretty open-minded about spiritual matters, I sat down to watch, casting aside any judgment about the probability of a 35,000-year-old warrior randomly inhabiting the person of a middle-aged woman from Montana.

The woman on the video came out quietly, almost demurely, in flowing white pajamas, and stood before a big wicker papasan chair. The audience (a couple of hundred believers who had paid about $750 each) sat in rapt silence. She addressed them briefly, in the softest little voice you ever heard. Then she sat down in the chair, took a couple of deep breaths, and slumped forward in a "trance." All of this took no more than eight seconds, I swear. Then, in the "trance," she sprang up out of the chair and began striding forcefully about the stage, pausing every now and then to strike a pose that looked not a little like Yul Brynner in *The King and I*. As a matter of fact, everything she said and did, right down to the pajamas, was a straight rip-off of Yul Brynner in *The King and I*. Her pronouncements, delivered in Yul Brynner's voice, were on a level of profundity with "The book is brown" or "Potatoes are good." I don't know whatever became of that woman, but my guess is she is somewhere, rich as all get out and pretty happy about it.

Then we had those Heaven's Gate people. I never did really understand their deal completely, but it had something to do with them all killing themselves and hitching a ride to Heaven on the Hale-Bopp comet when it swung by. Who came up with this theory? Whoever it was put in some interesting details for the group to follow. Apparently they were to kill themselves because they wouldn't be needing their "containers," or bodies, as we laypersons call them. Despite the fact that the "containers" would not be needed, it was imperative that all "containers" look exactly alike—same clothes, same goofy haircut, and so on. When all the identical "containers" were discovered dead as nails, each of them had a big sack of quarters nearby. Let me understand this. In Heaven we don't need our bodies, but we do need quarters? If Heaven turns out to be a place governed by a bunch of folks who demand that not only must all people look alike and dress alike but also have exact change, forget about it—I'm hereby canceling my reservation. Sounds suspiciously like Hell to me.

Regarding people who endlessly pass judgment on others and proclaim loudly, as if they know, who will and who won't be in Heaven and why, my daddy always said, "Last time I checked, your name wasn't listed on the 'range-mints [arrangements] committee." Meaning thank God, you're not the boss of anything. One of our very dearest Baptist buddies told us one morning that she'd never go to a nude beach on account of the rapture might come, and there she'd be with a bunch of naked people! I said, Well, if it comes anytime soon, I hope I'm sleeping; everybody looks innocent when asleep. If God wasn't mightily amused by our humanness, I figure he'd have wiped us out a long time ago.

Making Mama Proud

"How yew gon' ack win yew git sumware?" is a question often asked— or "axed," depending on your neighborhood—of all Southern children—or "chirren." Knowing and then cheerfully doing the right thing in all social situations is a burden that weighs heavily on the children of Southern mothers. Any failure on our part to know and do the right thing is no reflection on us, personally, even if we happen to be fifty-five years old and our mamas have been dead for thirty years at least. No, if we commit some unspeakable social faux pas (often pronounced *foo paw* here), the blame for it will be placed at the door of our mamas. It's not bad enough that we actually threw up in the azalea bushes in the front yard of the Governor's Mansion; the truly bad thing is that someone saw us and told not only our mamas but our mamas' friends. And it's no help to tell Mama that the only reason that rat saw us throwing up in the azalea bushes in front of the Governor's Mansion was because he nearly ran over us making his exit via the governor's flower garden in an erratically driven automobile. He's the one who got arrested. Does that help our cause one speck? It does not. Let *his* mama suffer that particular shame; we're discussing our own. And now, thanks to us, our mama cannot look anyone in the eye, so shamed is she by our behavior.

Being a source of embarrassment to your mama is just about the worst thing that can happen to you around here, unless, of course, whatever you did happens to make a whole lot of money. The wish for fortune is the only reason I'm able to sit down and actually write this book. I can assure you that my mama and all her friends will be properly horrified at its contents, except for the parts that they won't understand. I told the other Queens when I started this book, "Well, girls, it looks like it's time we explain to our mamas that we've been promising people blow jobs for the last twelve years." Most of us then had to explain what a blow job was and, furthermore, why men find them so desirable. As predicted, all the mothers were indeed horrified. However, they are somewhat mollified by the prospect of profit. It's okay to humiliate the family if it pays well—sort of an extension of the beauty pageant notion "anything for a crown." If I fail to make sufficient money from the sale of this epistle, however, I'll not only become the poster woman for immoral scum who have embarrassed their mamas. I'll no doubt be targeted for special visitation by the Jehovah's Witnesses. (A good pal of mine loves for the Witnesses to come to his door. He graciously ushers them inside, prepares refreshments, and bids them to tell their story. But first he'll say, "Write down your name and address for me because tomorrow I'm gonna drop by your house and tell you what all *I* think about religion." They can't get out of there fast enough.)

Two Tough Tests for Etiquette

My dear departed friend Beth Jones, a college English professor, related to me a story that is fraught with etiquette dilemmas. Beth swore to me that the star of this show was not Beth herself but a friend. I've always had my doubts, but as Beth is not here to defend herself, we'll grant that this happened to someone else. Beth's friend had to travel to another city on business. As it happened, Beth had other friends living in that particular city, so she arranged for her friend to stay in the home of these other friends. Beth's Jackson friend arrived at the other friends' house in time for dinner, and a jovial time was had by all.

By and by, after dinner Beth's friend was shown to her quarters for the night, the guest room. During the night the guest was awakened by a call of nature. Now, if memory served her correctly, the facilities adjoined her hosts' bedroom, which in turn adjoined *her* room. This meant that she'd have to go through their bedroom in the middle of the night to reach the potty. She was in a fair quandary, Beth's friend was. She didn't want to walk into these people's bedroom unannounced in the wee, wee hours. Nor did she want to knock on the door. She didn't want to wake them if they were sleeping, much less walk in on any late-night activities. What was she to do? By this time, she was practically dancing a jig, she had to pee so bad. Out of utter desperation, an idea came to her, and she went into the other room that adjoined hers, the kitchen. She felt around in the dark for a very large bowl she had earlier noticed sitting on the counter and found it. And yes, she did just what you're afraid I'm going to tell you she did. And with great relief, I might add. But alas, her relief was to be short-lived. For just as she was comfortably midstream, all the lights blazed on, and there stood her hosts, staring in bewildered disbelief at this grown woman squatting over and urinating into their very large mixing bowl.

Suffice it to say that nobody concerned knew quite how to respond to the situation they found themselves in. What can you, the hosts, say to a houseguest whom you met only a few hours ago and have just discovered whizzing in your dishes? What would Emily Post say? Miss Manners? What can you, the houseguest, say to your hosts, to whom you were introduced only hours ago, who have found you whizzing in their dishes? Her heart had been in the right place: She truly did not want to disturb them, no matter what they were doing. We think, however, they were perhaps a tad more upset by what resulted. Given the choice of having her knock on their door, barge right in, or weewee in the Wedgwood, I'd bet my money they'd pick hands down one of the first two options.

There are just some situations—I don't care how vigilant your mama was about teaching you manners—that will throw everybody's learning for a loop.

One time one of the Queens, Tammy, and I were out for our early-morning walk around the track at the Y where we work out. Tammy was in a major funk about something, and I'd been practically tap-dancing around the track, trying in vain to perk her up. I was pulling out all my best stuff, and nothing was working. And then I glanced off to the right, behind Tammy, into the parking lot of the hotel at the other end of the track. Under the brilliant beam of the streetlight stood . . . a *nekkid* man. Now, I say nekkid because that's what he was. There's a profound difference between naked and nekkid. Naked is proud, noble, graceful, without shame or the need for it. Nekkid is, on the other hand . . . well, it's nekkid.

And so I said to Tammy, "There's a nekkid man." We paused momentarily while she turned to look.

She nodded in agreement. "There certainly is."

He was just strolling along, not a care in the world, not a stitch on. He made no effort whatsoever to conceal his parts, although I saw nothing worthy of so ostentatious a public display. About this time he looked our way. Tammy said cheerily, "Hi!"

"Hi!" he said. "How are y'all this mornin'?"

"Oh, much better now, thank you," she replied, the absolute soul of politeness. The nekkid man seemed to appreciate her gracious attitude.

You see, in this very small verbal exchange, Tammy upheld not only the sacred doctrine of Southern hospitality but the very highest standard of the Sweet Potato Queens. She spoke kindly to the man, regardless of his race, creed, color, religion, social status, or appearance, which was nekkid. I was proud to call her my friend. I hope BoPeep turns out so well.

6

He Ain't Nothin' But a Man

YOU BETTER HAVE A GOOD DEFENSE

Once upon a time I was passing through Carthage, Mississippi, on my way to the Neshoba County Fair, which is held near Philadelphia, Mississippi. The Neshoba County Fair is called the "Giant Houseparty." That is somewhat misleading, but the truth would take too many words, and it doesn't really matter because no new people can come to it anyway. Here's the deal with the Neshoba County Fair: A hundred-some-odd years ago, for reasons long lost in the mists of time, a bunch of people went to the county fairgrounds in Neshoba County and built themselves a whole passel of shacks that they would then go live in for one week once a year when the fair came. That particular week always happened to fall around the last week of July, first week of August, depending. Depending on what, I have never figured out. Loosely translated for people in more temperate climes: Fair Week is hotter than the hammered-down hinges of Hell. Somehow it caught on, though, this week of shack-dwelling, and it has continued unto this very day and time. It has become a part of my life, and I can't even remember how or why.

Once a year, for a couple of weeks in July, I am driven by unseen forces to cook like a fiend the most fattening casseroles I can think of, freeze them all, and cook more. Then I'm forced to load all the food and BoPeep into the car and head for the red dirt hills of Neshoba County to live in a two-story, unair-conditioned shack with about thirty people and one bathroom. Once there I unload all the food and discuss with Lallah Perry, the owner of our particular shack, what dishes should be thawed for dinner that night. Eating is the primary fair entertainment for those who don't favor alcohol poisoning.

Whether you are an eater or a drinker, the drill is the same: You do all you can stand to do at one sitting in your own cabin. Then you go sit on the porch until you can recover enough to walk. After that you go to another cabin and repeat the drill. Sooner or later you usually wind up back at your original cabin, where you go upstairs to your assigned bed and rest up for the next day's activities, which are identical to the ones you just completed. Sometimes it happens that folks don't make it back to their home cabin and assigned bed. Sometimes they end up wedged behind a door for the night or underneath a stranger on the infield of the racetrack or the ninth hole of the golf course, which is not even close to the fairgrounds. But these would be exceptions to the rule, and hey, it's Fair Week, so it doesn't really count. Everybody is *so* laid back and friendly, you'd really have to go out of your way to piss somebody off.

Two years ago I wandered up in one cabin, not knowing a soul, and struck up a conversation with the lady of the shack and somehow worked into the conversation that I wished I had a whole bunch of deviled eggs, and did she happen to have any? She said she didn't have any but she'd be happy to whip up a couple dozen if I didn't mind going to borrow some mustard since she was out of it. So I said I wouldn't mind a bit, and while she set about boiling a big ole pot of eggs, I headed out to go door-to-door of other cabins in which I didn't know a soul, asking could I please borrow their mustard so Sylvia Mars could make me some deviled eggs. I'll have you know that the folks in the first cabin that happened to have some plain old yellow mustard were just thrilled to loan it to me, and they never even asked if they could have some of the deviled eggs, too. I trotted back with the mustard, and Sylvia made me those eggs. I ate a fair bait of 'em and bid her a fond farewell and didn't see her again until the fair the next year.

When I stopped by her cabin to say "Hidee!" she sort of looked blank, and I reminded her that she didn't really know me but she had made me a batch of deviled eggs last year, and she said, "Oh, of course, come on in, how are you?" And we sat and visited like old chums. I certainly do consider Sylvia Mars to be one of my best friends on account of those eggs. Do you have any idea how much trouble it is to make deviled eggs? A lot, which is why I hadn't already made them myself. Well, that's just the kind of stuff that goes on at the fair. And that's why people have been going for a hundred-some-odd years.

And as I was passing through Carthage on my way to the fair one year, I stopped for a Little Something at the Crestview Dairy Bar. That is the ice cream store that looks for all the world like a bank. I went in and placed my order for a Little Something. I happened to be wearing one of my favorite T-shirts. I have one that says, "You Are Dumb." I love that one. I have one that says, "Men Are All Idiots and I Am Married to Their King." That's a real favorite, too. But the one I had on that day read, "My Next Husband Will Be Normal." Well, the little old lady behind the counter just about fell over laughing at my T-shirt. She was walking up and down back there, laughing and talking to herself. "I don't know what in the world all these girls are thinkin' of these days, gettin' married; they must just like changin' their names—you cain't make nothin' but a *man* out of 'em. And I don't care *who* he is when you git 'im home, they's somethin' *bad* wrong with 'im!"

Really, we Queens love men. They taste just like chicken. Well, we can't really say that for a fact. The ones we've actually bitten were not only not cooked properly, they were alive and kicking. Shrieking, as it were. In our defense I would have to say that they deserved it, and in retrospect I imagine even they would agree. But anyway, we do love men. In theory at least. I mean, they do sound great on paper, don't they? And we are quite the eternal optimists, we are. Even when there are no serious contenders in the game, we like to have a number of men on hand. Just to play with, you know. We think of them as cat toys.

We've had a lot of experience with men who were looking for Barbie and the Dreamhouse. All men want Barbie. It's certainly easy enough to see why—I mean, her feet won't even go flat. She wears spike heels, more commonly known as FMPs, all the time. (That's F—— Me Pumps, for the undereducated.) Even if she has on tennis shoes, Barbie's feet are standing on tiptoes inside the tennis shoes. Show me the man who claims to be unmoved by the sight of a woman in high-heeled shoes, and I'll show you a liar—and a fool, too, if he thinks anybody believes him.

Look at Barbie's body. No, really *look* at it. Notice that impossibly fabulous shape. Then become aware that it is only a shape—she has no actual body parts that could possibly require outside attention. She is like a 3-D centerfold. She cannot see, hear, feel, or, best of all, speak. Another big plus is that permanent pleasant expression on her face. (Alas, even Barbie has a drawback. You'll notice that Barbie, perfect as she is, could not perform a blow job on a bet.)

And so here is the universal male fantasy: He is sitting—make that *lying*—on the couch, watching [insert appropriate sport] on the biggest big screen TV ever made. You are in the kitchen, wearing an outfit that amounts to Band-Aids and high heels, while cooking obscene amounts of extremely fattening food for him. You serve this food, along with buckets of beer, in the TV room. You bend over a lot in your little outfit. When all the food and all the beer is gone, you give him a blow job. He falls asleep, and while he is sleeping, you clean up the house and iron all his clothes, including his underwear, and then you leave. You have performed all of this without ever uttering a word. You appear, unbidden, as if by sorcery, on a regular basis to perform this little ritual. His level of participation is strictly that of happy, passive recipient. This is what is known as Barbie's Dreamhouse.

Men get all pissed off if you accuse them of wanting Barbie. This is only because they can tell from your tone of voice that you perceive this to be a negative character trait in them. They haven't the foggiest idea why this would be a negative character trait—I mean, we're talking Barbie here, what's not to like? Right? But you are frowning when you say it and looking at him like he just crawled out from under a rock, so he instinctively knows that this is a bad thing, and his knee-jerk reaction is to deny, deny, deny.

Not that any of us would disparage a defense based solely on denial. We are all in favor of it and have used it satisfactorily on many occasions ourselves. In fact, Tammy, our own personal Queen of Mean, has taken it one step further. She has taken your basic denial defense, which pretty much states that, even if you are caught in the act of whatever, red-handed, as it were—just look 'em in the eye and de-ny, de-ny, de-ny: "Who are you gonna believe—me, or your lying eyes?" Tammy's twist on that is she doesn't stay too long in the denial mode. No, our Tammy makes her denial statement with a look that says, "No, not me. I would never," moving almost simultaneously into "Why would I?" and then, looking just as wide-eyed as you please, into "How could you even think such a thing?"

At this point something just comes over her. That sweet look of wounded innocence is gone so fast, it makes you woozy. In its place is the Tasmanian Devil. She gets all fuzzed-up and wild-looking, you can feel it coming from her toes, you can see it behind her eyes, and then she just explodes. "You m——f——r!" she screams at him. This catches him off guard, as you may well imagine since, if you'll recall, *she* is the one who just got caught. He had been seeing himself as the injured party in all this. What is she yelling at him for? In that split second—when he's distracted and his thoughts are racing, trying to figure out if, in fact, he has done something and forgotten about it and now she's discovered it and what the hell could it be?—in that nanosecond the wind changes. The tide turns. Advantage Tammy.

She just lets fly. None of this makes any sense—doesn't have to. It's just like yelling at your dog. He has no earthly idea what you're talking about, but he does understand that he is in big trouble. This is known as the "you m——f——r" defense, and it should be used only in dire emergencies. It is not for the faint of heart. To achieve maximum effectiveness with this approach, you have to be prepared to pull out all the stops and pitch a major hissy fit.

Here is how well it can work. There was this girl, a mere acquaintance, not a Queen—"Jennie," we'll call her. Jennie had a boyfriend she'd had for so long, the novelty had worn off, as will happen. So she had a few auxiliary boyfriends. She and one member of the auxiliary decided to take a week-long retreat, and she told the old-timer that she was going somewhere with a couple of girlfriends, namely me and my sister. Now, she did not ask us up front if we were willing to participate in this subterfuge, but we didn't think it would require any actual effort on our part, and so we reluctantly agreed to keep quiet. That was all we agreed to do.

Well, as it turned out, the spot the two of them chose for their week of debauchery also happened to be the very place that my sister and I were going to be for a day. One day. Then we were moving on. Jennie said that we should meet them "for a drink." We foolishly agreed. At the appropriate hour she showed up with her camera and a whole bundle of film. We were then cajoled into going with her to any number of locations and putting on different clothes at each and posing for pictures with her at every stop—to make it look like we'd spent the week with her. It was pretty funny. So we did all that, and then we left and forgot all about it.

When Judy and I returned home on our appointed day, we learned that Jennie had come in a day earlier and gone to a movie with the auxiliary boyfriend, only to discover the old boyfriend sitting smack in the middle of the theater. Did she skulk out furtively? Did she make any attempt whatsoever at hiding? She most assuredly did not. Our Jennie, she marched herself right up to the unsuspecting chump and demanded (in explicit and extremely loud terms) just what in the hell he was doing in that movie. He was, as Elvis Costello would say, bobbing and squinting just like a nitwit, and dared to ask her the same thing, adding that he'd seen my boyfriend and learned that Judy and I weren't coming back until the *next* day.

He was sorry he asked that; he was very sorry, real quick-like. She gave him the full frontal attack, leading off with a resounding "You m——f——r!" and moving swiftly along with how she had had enough of me and Judy and was missing him so bad, she couldn't stand it, and so she just got on a plane and came back early to see his sorry ass; and not only was he not at home or at work to receive any of her "messages," she had to track him down in a f——ing movie in the middle of the dang day, and she really believed he must have done it on purpose; she knew he got all those "messages" and just ignored them and came in this movie to hide from her. And with that she burst into tears.

The guy who said that the best *de*fense is a good *off*ense was no dumbass.

The Five Men You Must Have

IN YOUR LIFE AT ALL TIMES

A very wise woman told us this once, and we really took it to heart: There are five different kinds of men that you must endeavor to have in your life at all times in order to have the equivalent of one completely satisfactory man. She explained that it is clearly not possible to find all the required attributes in one single man, and we should not expend needless energy by even looking for him—we'd be damn lucky to find the five separate men. Once in a blue moon, she told us, you might come across a man who has one and maybe a half of the attributes or maybe even two. Finding and maintaining convivial relationships with five very different men, all at the same time, in order to have one's basic needs met—it will not be easy, she cautioned. But it's at least possible. In her valued opinion, trying to live one's entire life without, say, dancing just because your man doesn't like to dance—well, you might be able to manage, but is this really something you want to spend the next fifty years doing, or in this case not doing?

The Basic Five are these: (1) a man who can fix things, (2) a man you can dance with, (3) a man who can pay for things, (4) a man you can talk to, and (5) a man to have great sex with. As I said, this is the rudimentary team you need to form, according to our sage adviser. Certainly other functions can be added to suit your more refined tastes, but with this starting lineup, you can at least avoid abject misery.

Oh, the allure of a Man Who Can Fix Things. Is there anything more appealing? Well, yes, I suppose there is, but you won't be able to think of it when the toilet is overflowing. When you've got a flat tire, or your bedroom doorknob falls off in your hand, or your new stereo is delivered in its various unconnected component parts, or your neighbors are threatening to barbecue your dog the next time he pops through the hole in your fence into their garden party—then the Man Who Can Fix Things will be the hottest fellow you've ever seen in your life. You will breathe harder when he gets the toolbox out of his trunk. He is your dream boy. But, you know, once the pieces are assembled and the wires all connected and the music is playing on your new stereo and you realize that he claps on one and two, Handy Andy's out. It's time for a Man You Can Dance With.

Dancing Jones comes to your side, and the two of you dance a hole in your shoes. But now the hunger's creeping up. Fred Astaire's younger brother would love to take you out to dinner, but he left his buy-one-get-one-free coupon at home, and so you either have to pay or cook. You'll have a lot more choices with the Man Who Can Pay for Things.

There are plenty of compliments we could pay to the Man Who Can Pay for Things, but by far and away the best one is that he can pay for things. And he will. Loves to. It's what he lives for; so for God's sake, humor him. Order everything on the menu, and he will smile indulgently. I don't know about you, but being smiled at indulgently is just way up there on my list of favorite stuff. I'm especially fond of being smiled at indulgently while being dandled on his knee. A good knee dandle is just hard to beat. And a good knee dandler is hard to find. Try and remember the last time you had a really first-rate knee dandle. Finding a Man Who Can Pay for Things and who will do so while smiling indulgently and providing excellent knee dandlage might tempt a girl to overlook the other four categories. This could prove to be disastrous.

Money and knee dandling are fine, but they do not a life make. If you say to this man, for instance, "*Here's* something!" meaning "Listen to *this!*" and his initial response is "Where?"—you've got a problem. If you say to this man, in exasperation, "I ain't taking you *to raise!*" and he says, "Where's Ray's?"—he is a dullard of the first water and in grave danger of screwing up sack lunches, should any be in order. You cannot talk to this man, and you must have a Man You Can Talk To. One who will understand things without exhaustive explanations. High dramas cannot be played out with someone who always misses not only his cues but the punch line, too.

The Man You Can Talk To must be able to fully grasp the meaning of loyalty. Here's what is wanted: You call him and tell him you hate Joe, his best friend since the first grade and your lover. The only acceptable response from him is "I hate him, too. I hope he dies." He should not ask any questions—it is not necessary that he know *why* you hate Joe, only that you do. He should simply fall in line. Any embroidery he adds at this juncture about how much he hates Joe and how long he's hated him, while only pretending to like him for your sake, would be welcomed. If, for reasons best known to yourself, you find that five minutes later in the same conversation, you suddenly decide that Joe is, after all, the apple of your very eye, your darlin' sugar lump, he should immediately, without hesitation or question, say, "Joe is my very best friend, has been since the first grade, I love him like a brother, and seeing the two of you so happy together just tickles me to no end." Now, if you should decide after another brief interval that you were right in your first estimation of Joe—he's a lyin', cheatin' sack of shit—this man should not even miss a beat. "Hot-damn! I hate that guy!" should be his snappy rejoinder. He should be prepared to do this repeatedly and without end. This is the true test of loyalty. He should acknowledge, willingly and without prompting, that yours is the only dog in this hunt.

Now, let me see, what do we need now? By and by, I expect we'll be wanting to have sex and plenty of it. And that is something that is surely hard to find—the "plenty of it" part. I don't know about other places, but in the South we're big feeders. People come to your house, and you trot out more food just for lunch than they and all their kin can possibly eat in a month—all in the name of hospitality. The guest is expected to rave endlessly about the quantity and, of course, the quality of this feast. The hostess is expected to disparage the whole thing as absolutely pitiful: It was all she had time to prepare, and not even close to what all she *would* have prepared if she'd had an ounce of human decency and another thirty minutes or so. This little dance should be repeated frequently throughout the duration of the visit.

According to a story my father used to tell, my grandfather was the guest of the most acclaimed hostess in Attala County. You could drop by her house at any hour of the day or night with a school bus full of people, with no notice whatsoever, and she would lay out a spread that would feed and significantly raise the cholesterol level of the entire county. The table groaned with the sheer weight of all the food she had prepared for my grandfather, and so as to be polite and not hurt her feelings, he dutifully sampled all of it, in no small way. He ate and he ate and he ate. She waited graciously for him to begin the praise cycle. He never did. He just kept on eating. She waited as patiently as she could, and still he said nothing. The whole rhythm of the meal was being thrown off.

She tentatively began to make brief unsolicited sallies into the denial/disparage/denigrate cycle of the thing. "The beans were a little mushy, I thought." "And the biscuits were hard, weren't they?" "I just dried that chicken out, I'm always so afraid it'll be red at the bone, I just overdo it, I never could fry chicken like my mama." He would dutifully refute all her unwarranted and untrue statements as just that, but he would not follow up with the culturally appropriate and desperately sought hymns of praise for her food. She grew more distraught by the minute until finally she could stand it no more and she broke the cardinal rule of Southern hospitality: She just flat-out asked him if he liked the food. Being entirely cognizant the whole time of her horrendous discomfiture, he leaned back (back being the only direction he could lean, so engorged was his belly), gazed about the table at the ruins of the feast, and said, "Well, yes, it was pretty good— what there was of it." Knowing at last that she'd been had, she began beating him about the head and body with a wooden spoon.

This saying, "It was pretty good—what there was of it," became the accepted code in those parts for the highest possible praise for a meal. And here's the point I intended to make when I started all this: If something is really good, there is no such thing as too much of it. Indeed, there hardly ever is even *plenty* of it. This applies to food, and it most certainly applies to sex.

A congenial partner for sex is highly desirable, and although many partners may theoretically be available, don't kid yourself, missy. Mr. Congeniality is not likely to be waiting around every corner. No, ma'am. Finding him will probably involve more looking than finding. But suppose after exhaustive, not to mention exhausting, research, you do find him—whose glance starts the smolder, whose touch sets off the towering inferno. Now, what do you reckon the odds are that he's also a plumber, a fabulous dancer, or a really rich guy with an uncanny knack for conversation and excellent listening skills?

So as you can see, five is the absolute minimum number of men you can make do with. The great news is that four out of the five can be gay! As a matter of fact, it would be a plus if they were gay. Because then they'll not only carry out the functions of their position extremely well, you can also get fashion and makeup tips, not to mention get your house featured in *Better Homes and Gardens.* Gay men are fabulous, perfect for us in every way except one; but you have to be careful not to fall in love with them because there is just no changing their minds on that score. Believe me, if it could be done, I would have done it.

Boyfriends and Fiancés

GETTING THEM AND GETTING OVER THEM

*B*oyfriend*—any and all heterosexual male persons who buy you dinner, take you to movies, etc. We do not have physical contact of any kind with a "boyfriend."

Fiancé—any and all heterosexual male persons with whom you are currently having sex. Fiancé status does not have any bearing, real or implied, on the ultimate future, if any, of the relationship. Fiancés must be in constant compliance with both the Four-Hour Rule and the Twenty-Four-Hour Rule.

It is just so important to understand the distinction between Boyfriends and Fiancés and keep it clear in your mind at all times. Do not be hasty about elevating someone into Fiancé status prematurely. A Boyfriend can have all manner of habits and characteristics that would clearly signal danger if he were upgraded to Fiancé but that would not be an impediment of any kind in a mere Boyfriend. Since all the Boyfriend will get to do is pay for stuff, he can be a hound from Hell and it won't matter one whit. You'll find that you can painlessly have lunch with just about anybody. And keep in mind, nobody ever murders a Boyfriend. Fiancés, now, are another matter altogether.

Here's an important point to remember: "Never" does not really mean "not ever"; it doesn't even mean "hardly ever." What it actually means is "whenever you feel like it, for whatever your reasons." The man of your choice should never be able to predict when the tide will turn in his favor. He should know definitely that it is a *favor*, one that you can bestow or withhold at your whim.

Let's just say, for the sake of discussion, you have been particular and selected a guy. And let's just say that, for reasons best known to yourself, you have decided at this particular time and space to have sex with him, or at least to allow him to have sex with you. He's your fiancé. Two rules apply.

The Four-Hour Rule. This means that before you make him the happiest man in the universe and cause the earth to move beneath him and blood to seep from his ears, he must spend at least four hours demonstrating to you exactly how overwhelmed he is at the prospect. This should include rafts of compliments about everything from your eyes/face/hair/outfit and legs to the unbearable sweetness of your disposition. There should also be gifts and refreshments.

The Twenty-Four-Hour Rule. Assuming that he has complied suitably with the Four-Hour Rule and you did, in fact, participate on some level—any level at all—in some sexual act with him, then it is absolutely mandatory that he be in full compliance with the Twenty-Four-Hour Rule. The Twenty-Four-Hour Rule states flatly that within (well within, if he has any sense and/or hopes for the future) the first twenty-four hours following said act of sex, he must telephone to repeat all of the pre-sex compliments that he paid you regarding your eyes/face/hair/outfit and legs, and the unbearable sweetness of your disposition, plus, he should have thought up at least fifteen minutes' worth of new and additional compliments about the act itself. These compliments should contain glowing references to the smallest efforts you might have made on his behalf.

Graphic compliments regarding specific body parts not included in the previous listing are also nice. As a general rule, he should keep in mind that women prefer that some body parts be praised for their amplitude, while others should be lauded for being the tiniest thing he ever saw. The latter would apply most especially to our butts, if we are white girls, and also our legs. White girls do not love to be told that they have "such pretty big legs." That is a black thing. If you tell a

white girl that she has a butt like a little ole butterbean, she'll probably marry you. Tell that to a black girl, and she'll poke out that bottom lip so far, she'll trip on it and you'll never see her again.

Now, the Four-Hour Rule can certainly be waived at your complete discretion. If you've decided that he deserves a random act of
kindness from the universe—or more important, that you do—and
you greet him at the door wearing nothing but your biggest smile, that
is certainly acceptable. But it does not exempt him from the Twenty-
Four-Hour Rule. There are virtually no exemptions from this mo-
mentous decree; only death or prolonged coma are even considered.
Failure to comply must result in his being cast into outer darkness for
an extended period of time—certainly never less than forty-eight
hours, although a longer sentence would be more effective. During his
time in that outermost dim and murky realm, you should not acknowledge his existence on this planet. Should you eventually decide,
in your boundless mercy, to allow him to emerge from darkness and
resume his place in your life, he should find that the Four-Hour Rule
has been extended somewhat, so he has ample opportunity to reassert
his worthiness.

Just remember, as women, we are just like ice—they ain't no substitute, honey.

Tammy's Rule

Okay, so you are now in a relationship. How particular you've been
will become apparent soon. One former Queen, Tammy, meanest little woman you ever saw, has one rule and one rule only, and it serves
her well. Works like a charm, as it were. Tammy's rule is: *Treat 'em like
shit and never give 'em any.* She swears if you do this, men will follow
you around like dogs. She continues the canine comparison by re-
minding us of how much dogs love to chase cars; they are not, however, particularly interested in catching them. I've been watching her
work this magic for about twenty years now. I've seen her make any
number of grown men bawl like babies, using only venomous words,
spoken through clenched teeth, accompanied by a mean and squinty-
eyed look.

The next day, those suckers are sending flowers, buying jewelry,
cooking dinner—happy as pigs in the sunshine that their precious
Tammy is speaking kindly to them again. But she's never nice to them
for too long a stretch.

We're admittedly dubious about the "never" part of Tammy's Rule. Our friend in Connecticut (who likes to call himself "the Duke" and sometimes Tom, even though his name is John) told us about a study that demonstrates that "never" may not always give the best results. This scientific investigation was conducted to determine why some men would rather play golf than just about anything. They did the research using (what else?) rats. It's fascinating that they would experiment with rats, as opposed to just asking a bunch of guys, "What's the deal with golf?" I figure there were at least two good reasons for it: (1) They got a federal grant to do the study if they used rats. (2) They discovered they could get a straight answer from the rats.

So what they did, of course, was put a bunch of rats in cages with food-releasing levers. (A lab rat's idea of Heaven must be a place with no food-releasing levers.) One group's levers would release food every single time the rats pressed them. The second group's levers never worked. I guess they all starved slap to death—big turnover in these rat studies. The third group met with success and failure in a completely random pattern. Sometimes they could pump away on the doohickey all day long and never get a bite. Then other times they could just look at the thing right, and big wads of food would come tumbling out. The first group was fairly bored with the process: A steady diet of immediate gratification apparently palls quickly. The second group was not only bored with endless failure; they were withering away to nothing. The third group, though, was fairly obsessed with its levers.

Then the lab guys cut off everybody's supply. Nobody's levers worked at all, ever. All the rats were now starving. The group that had been completely successful on each try gave up pretty quickly when the source dried up. They had taken it so for granted that they were unskilled in working for it and not interested in learning. The rats that *never* got any at all had already given up and were just lying around waiting to die. But that third bunch that had met with inexplicable success, they kept at it twenty-four hours a day, seven days a week. They had calluses on their little ratty hands from slapping that lever, just knowing that the next time was gonna be the charm.

I can see with total clarity how this explains men and golf addiction. Most guys are not great golfers. (This is the most charitable way we can put it.) But even the lousiest golfer will go out there on a given day and do something unbelievably great. He has no earthly idea how or why it happened, and so he'll just keep on trying to re-create the magic. It was, in fact, just a random act of kindness by the universe, but he'll pursue that fantasy to his death. If he *never* has any luck, however . . . well, we see a direct correlation to Tammy's Rule here.

Jay at the Desk

Okay. Worst case: All the rules have flown out the window, and you're madly in love with the guy. You've been eating shit, running rabbits, and howling at the moon—all of which clearly should be his job. He's been participating—whether fully or marginally doesn't matter—and you are completely around the bend. In your mind the china's picked out, the honeymoon planned, the children named, and then what happens? It's squirrel time. He has gone to that all-time favorite guy place—Outta Here. And you are what is commonly referred to as In a Hole. If you could find an actual hole, deep enough and dark enough, you would happily crawl off into it and sever all ties with life as you know it. Life is just bleak, and nothing, with the notable exception of food, holds any appeal for you. (The hole would need to be large enough to house a refrigerator and a microwave.) All you want to do is cry and eat.

But don't you do it. Snivel a little and have a fair-sized medicinal snack, and then get over it. Here's why. One of the Queens, Tammy, had a guy just absolutely rip her very heart out and use it to fix a flat, right before her very eyes. And she crawled through life for months and months and spent all kinds of money on therapists trying to figure out what happened (he dumped her), and why (he was a squirrel), and what she could do about it (not a damn thing). Then one day he called her again, out of the proverbial blue. And she felt . . . *nothing.* Shortly after that, as soon as she realized that she felt . . . *nothing,* she got real excited. She felt really good. Now, all this happened while she was at work, naturally. If there's the slightest chance that a guy can turn you into an emotional wreck during the course of your normal nine-to-five, he will take it every time.

Well, as it happened, there was a young man who worked in her building. A nice enough young man, although she didn't know him personally at all. His name was Jay, and he sat at the front desk. When she was relating the story to me of how the asshole had surfaced in an attempt to weasel back into her life and how she had lived and breathed and prayed, waiting for this very moment, dying to have him back, and when he finally called her to make all her dreams come true, she felt . . . *nothing*, she squealed delightedly into the phone, "Nothing. I felt NOTHING! He could have been Jay at the desk for all I cared!" And so "Jay at the Desk" became synonymous with being totally over somebody. They become Jay at the Desk.

Another Queen, Tammy, had a hideous relationship with a squirrel that lasted literally years. None of us thought we could survive it. It was a toss-up as to which was worse, when they were on or when they were off. It was just awful all the time. And then finally one day it really did end. No one knew why it was different this time, but everybody knew it was. Tammy took up permanent residence In the Hole. Chain-smoked. Took mood elevators that did little to differentiate her from a bug stuck on its back. Cried all the time. All the time. The swelling in her face never went down. She was just hoping he would come back. She was well along in that aspiration, when one day he approached her from the opposite end of a large parking lot, and he called out solicitously, "Hey! Tammy!" She smiled and waved and thought to herself, "Who is that fat guy hollering at me?" Not only had she not recognized him, she perceived him as "that fat guy." He had become Jay at the Desk. And the good news is, no matter how bad you feel, sooner or later they'll all become Jay at the Desk.

My friend Fran works in a building with its own employee dining room. Fran's had her share of ups and downs with men, and one of the ladies who works in the dining room has been there long enough to read the faces of the folks she serves. Fran came in one day, and the lady took one look at her and said, "Git another one." Fran was confused, since she had not spoken a word. "What?" The lady laid her hand on Fran's arm, looked her squarely in the eye, and said, "You don't have to say a word. It's a man, I know it is. Git another one. This one don't do right. Git another one." As my daddy used to say whenever he thought too much of a fuss was being made over something lost or broken, "They makin' them thangs ever' day."

So dispense with all the weeping and wailing. Let him be Jay at the Desk sooner rather than later. They're making men every day. Just get another one.

Men Who Love Us

and the Incredible Lengths to Which They Go to Demonstrate Their Love

Many men give us money, as you may well imagine. Not us individually, you understand, but collectively—to support our efforts. Believe me, being a Sweet Potato Queen is no cheap deal. The outfits alone cost a fortune. And then, of course, we have to have new hair and accessories every year. Naturally we have corporate sponsors to whom we are deeply indebted, and they are, in fact, the only men we have ever loved. Our dear friend Skippy bought us all new fishnet stockings one year, the only stipulation being that he got to personally straighten all our seams. This was a win-win situation all the way around.

But there is one man who shall remain nameless, who really went to extraordinary lengths to prove his love for us. Naturally this man, who is a prominent and very successful man, would be proud and honored to be identified, to have his name bandied about in connection with us. Now, there's only one reason he's remaining anonymous. If I were to tell you who he is, every woman in this country would be trying to lure him away from us, and we intend to keep this one all to ourselves forever.

It was late in the afternoon of parade day, and the Queens were taking their only break from pleasing the crowds. We had gone into Hal & Mal's, previously identified as the official restaurant of the Sweet Potato Queens, chosen a table, and advised our doting waiter that we would be having everything fried on the menu, plenty of it and plenty quick. He scurried off.

Just as we were beginning to relax from the strain of making sixty or seventy thousand people happy, the cutest man we ever saw came over to our table. By way of introducing himself, he plopped down on the floor, on his back, and slid himself underneath our table, amongst all those legs and gold majorette boots. We all squealed girlishly and yanked him up, then situated him in a chair at our table. No other man in the whole establishment was invited to be seated in our presence. He was pretty pleased with himself.

After a bit, though, he obviously felt compelled to give us something of himself that could be acceptably presented to a large group of large women in a public place by a lone man. He calmly, with immense grace and dignity, unwrapped a single pat of butter, and removing his cap, he smashed it, the single pat of butter, on his totally bald head.

More girlish squeals and clapping. And so it went for the rest of the time we had together. Every few minutes another pat of butter would take its place on his dome. "Generations of men in my family have proven their love for their women in this way," he said. "Men with hair cannot do this." We assured him that men with hair are highly overrated in our opinion, and we, personally, would not give you two cents for a man with hair. He beamed with joy and applied more butter.

By this time we had consumed all the fried stuff we could stand, but there remained on the table a few french fries, a bit of a cheeseburger, and a couple of odd hot tamales. This, alas, also went on his head, a bit at a time. And so it was that his cap became a cornucopia of delight.

Now, if we can only get him to give us money.

Gifts ~ Fit and Unfit

Presents, too, are always welcomed by the Queens, although some items will not be well received. Take, for example, jewelry. It falls in one of those dangerous gray areas, but let us clarify that. *Expensive* jewelry is profoundly appreciated. Wildly expensive jewelry, quite naturally, would be wildly appreciated, and your basic good jewelry should not be ruled out for everyday gift-giving occasions. Cheap jewelry, however, is worse than no jewelry at all, and there are very few things in life that are worse than no jewelry at all. Any item of jewelry that contains pink or lavender stones that do not actually exist in nature itself is grounds for immediate dismissal. Antique estate jewelry is good. Gold nugget jewelry is bad. Anything available by the gross from a discount house is bad.

But guess what—you can spend big old wads of money on jewelry and still go wrong. One of the Queens, Tammy, received as a gift from one of her fiancés the worst-looking piece of jewelry any of us had ever seen. And it had cost him a bloody fortune. She could have bought a BMW with that amount of money. It was one of those giant gold coin pieces mounted in about a pound of gold, with big gold stems shooting out all the way around and about five pounds of diamonds stuck grotesquely on these stems. This monstrosity was suspended on the center of her chest by a gold chain that you could have moored a big-ass motorboat with. "Oh my God, you aren't gonna have to wear that hideous thing, are you?" She sadly said yeah, she had to because he was so proud of it. Picked it out all by himself, don't you know.

He wanted her to wear it all the time. She'd have on this fabulous Armani suit or something, and smack in the middle of it would be this *thing*, just hanging there. It was depressing, but Tammy was a good sport. She wore it day in and day out. Then one day, after it had been insured for a decent interval, it was stolen!

Now, it probably really had been stolen, and I'll go straight to Hell for even implying that Tammy would've flung that precious gift out her car window. She certainly has never admitted any such an act, but she has expressed the fond hope that the person who did find—my mistake, *steal*—her favorite necklace has profited from it handsomely. A sweet-spirited, forgiving girl by nature, our Tammy never could hold such a grudge.

Do not *ever* give a Queen a home appliance as a gift. Period. The end. Now, an exception can be made in the event she just happens to mention in passing that she wishes she had, say, a full Viking kitchen, and then she goes out of town for a few days; and when she comes back, her entire kitchen is renovated with fabulous Viking appliances. She will just be touched. On the other hand, if it is her birthday and you, all on your own, select, purchase, and present her with a Crock-Pot, well, you are over.

The Queens also do not want anything that can be described as "cute country." Talk about your oxymoron. And don't bring us any kind of wreath for our door unless it's Christmas. Under no circumstances are you to buy us one of those home vacuum cleaner disguises that we first saw at crafts fairs but that are now appearing on the much-revered home shopping channels. These are not intended to transform a person or a thing into the guise of a vacuum cleaner, but rather to disguise the vacuum cleaner itself as something else—like a giant duck, cat, or doll. At a crafts fair you can buy one that will disguise your vacuum cleaner as a giant Mammy, but that is way too politically incorrect for the enlightened souls at the home shopping channels. Someday I hope to meet a person who actually owns a vacuum cleaner disguise that he or she personally bought on purpose. I want to know: Why don't they just keep their vacuum cleaner in the closet? Why would they want it sitting out in the middle of the living room looking like a four-foot-tall duck?

Is this present-day obsession with disguising everyday household items a purely Southern thing? My friend Allen Payne, who grew up in Philadelphia, Mississippi, and now lives in New York City, assures me that vacuum cleaner disguises are simply not seen in New York. He also swears you cannot buy a lacy phone book cover or a crocheted cover for that extra roll of toilet paper. Why does anyone feel the need to dress up a roll of toilet paper in a little frilly outfit and set it on the back of a commode? You can also buy tiny aprons to dress your two-liter bottles in. They look just like real cooks' aprons—the little loop around the neck, the pocket, the strings that tie in back—and they come in the most festive colors and patterns. So now, even though that empty bottle of Pepsi is only going to be there on the counter for a few hours, while it is there, it can be appropriately dressed.

I guess naked soft drink bottles in the kitchen and bar could be jarring to one's sensibilities. Maybe they should wear clothes until garbage time. There's probably some crafty individual, right at this very moment, creating appropriate burial attire for used toilet paper, empty Pepsi bottles, vintage phone books, and broken vacuum cleaners. The landfills would be so much more attractive if all the garbage were dressed up in little outfits. I bet Lady Bird Johnson would have a fit over this idea.

If, however, we should happen to mention to the Man du Jour that we are considering having our own Queenly selves disguised somewhat—or as we say, *altered*—in some fashion, his immediate and vehement reaction should alternate between swearing that we will only do such a thing over his dead body and begging us not to change a single thing about our most perfect selves—he cannot even bear to think of it. He should go to considerable lengths to convince us that the way the crepe of our eyelids actually hangs down far enough to distort our vision is adorable and that the way our chest is completely devoid of anything titlike—well, that's just the way he always dreamed tits would be. Whatever it is we have determined, after endless hours of scowling into the mirror, to have fixed—that should be his very favorite part of us.

I mean, you know you're a mess and something needs to be done and soon—you know this—but you don't want the man in your life to agree that you do, in fact, look like a dog-faced Al Capone. He should swear that any alteration to your perfection would be a shameful waste of good money, money that could better be spent buying you jewelry and Caribbean cruises. He should acquiesce only to please you. Then he should, of course, pay the doctor and smile indulgently as he writes that big ole check. After it's done, he should for a very brief time mourn the change; then he should forthwith endlessly extol your beauty. And he should never, *ever* mention the procedure again. Disparaging comments about your previous state will result in an immediate loss of playground privileges.

The Man We're All Looking For

There is this woman I know and love—I named my daughter after her, for crying out loud (my daughter's real name is Bailey; surely you didn't think I'd actually put "BoPeep" on the child's birth certificate?)—who has all the best men. If you are wondering why you can't find a good one, call Joan Bailey; she's got them all to herself, the bitch. She's married to one, she gave birth to another one, one is her brother, one is her son-in-law, and then on top of all that, she's got the Amazing JB. For years she'd been regaling me with tales of the Amazing JB and producing all manner of obscene cards and letters allegedly sent by same—with return addresses like "Treasurer, PTL Ministry, Trust Me Lane, Big Lick, South Carolina."

Finally I could stand it no more. I demanded to be put on his mailing list, and thus I, too, became the pen pal of the Amazing JB. He and I, although total strangers to one another, began sending stuff through the mails that required the traditional plain brown wrapper (sequined jock straps, crotchless running shorts, personal pleasure devices disguised as vegetables, and the like). Joan and I would compare atrocities received several times each week. MoonPie and Joan's husband, Buster, were at times appalled by the trash sent to us, but they didn't see the trash we were sending out.

Well, starting one January, JB began threatening to come for a visit. Said he was gonna get on a Greyhound bus and come to Jackson in September. Every correspondence we received for the next nine months made reference to his coming to town on the 'Hound. In the spring he named September 23 as his arrival date, and we began getting several cards a day, ranting about his long-awaited arrival at the downtown 'Hound pound. This barrage continued for months. We were starting to get nervous.

On September 22 I received two cards, "See you tomorrow." Joan did, too. We didn't know whether to shit or go blind. All day we were on the phone: "Is he really coming?" Buster, who was obviously in on it through JB himself, swore to God it was true. At 9 P.M. on September 22, Joan got a phone call from some official-sounding guy saying he was the national president of Greyhound in Denver, Colorado, and he was just calling to confirm that the Amazing JB would, in fact, be arriving on the 12:15 bus tomorrow. (The thing is, JB is the kind of guy who could actually get the president of Greyhound to make such a call.) Joan hung up the phone, and Buster confirmed that the headquarters for Greyhound are actually in Denver. We were perplexed. See, if he was really coming, we wanted to dress up real trashy and go to the bus station to meet him. But then again, if he wasn't, then there we would be at the bus station in gold lamé shoes, for goodness sake.

Six A.M., September 23: Buster was leaving town. Joan gave him one last chance to tell the truth. "Look at me, Buster," she said. "If you lie to me about this, do not come home ever." Chuckling, Buster took a solemn vow that really and truly at 12:15 that day, a Greyhound bus would arrive in Jackson, and on board would be the Amazing JB, and

"Y'all damn well better be there to meet him; he's coming all that way from North Carolina on a bus just to see you!"

We vacillated, but then we decided to take our chances. We met at 11:45 and went to the store to buy Tootsie Rolls to black out our teeth with. They didn't have any Tootsie Rolls! I went nuts. "What do you mean, you don't have any Tootsie Rolls? What the hell do you have in here? What are we supposed to put on our teeth?" The clerk was confounded. I bet they have Tootsie Rolls from now on, and everyone will have me to thank for it. I mean, really, whoever heard of a squat 'n' gobble-type store that doesn't carry Tootsie Rolls? Off schedule now, we raced to a nearby drugstore, which fortunately did have Tootsie Rolls. On to the bus station.

We parked right in front and proceeded to dress in the car. We didn't do as elaborate a job as we would have liked because we still didn't wholly believe JB would materialize. Joan put a big Tootsie Roll over her teeth, and BoPeep put on her tiara, which, because of her hairless condition at the time, had to be secured with surgical tape. I put on my "Barq's Root Beer with Metamucil" cap, my red sunglasses with the flashing lights, my T-shirt that reads, "Eat Me Raw at Fud-drucker's" (a gift from JB), and a liberal coating of Tootsie Rolls over my own front teeth. 'Peep at this time had no teeth, so she was set.

We pranced into the bus station like we had good sense. The bus arrived. A man alighted from the bus wearing a priest's robe, a base-ball cap, and a button that said, "Drop your drawers and then I'm yours." He knelt, in the middle of the bus station, as if in prayer. *As if,* is right. This would be John Burress.

We whisked him off to lunch at the Mayflower Café, a great old, funky diner-type establishment in downtown Jackson. The Mayflower is a place to which we could go dressed as we were, Tootsie Rolls and all, and we would be given the exact same service as if we were dressed to the nines—surly. The customer service at the 'Flower is a sort of insider's joke. You go there your whole life, and it seems nor-mal for the staff to be crabby. Sort of like your mom: She's *willing* to wait on your sorry ass while you just sit there, perfectly capable of doing if for yourself, but she's pissed off about it anyway.

The Mayflower also has one of the most bizarre rest rooms in the entire world. First you have to go through the kitchen, and if you think the wait staff is crabby—it's hot in the kitchen, and the cooks are having to slave over a stove in the heat while you just sit out front laughing and talking and eating in air-conditioned comfort. You walk a little faster through the kitchen. Next you have to go up a really steep, really narrow flight of stairs, unlit except for a single naked lightbulb hanging from a cord in the ceiling at the very top of the steps. It looks like the kind of place one would go to have an abortion with a coat hanger. It's the scariest place I've ever been. I only went once. After one trip up those stairs, I vowed my bladder would burst and flood the place before I'd go back again. I know lots of individuals who feel so strongly about it that they'll go out in the parking lot behind the place, rather than face the stairs, and seek relief behind parked cars. And these are not all guys I'm talking about here. We made JB go to the scary bathroom, and he was visibly shaken for some time.

Anyway, JB had shown up with presents—two huge matching duffel bags full of them. We sat in the back booth of the Mayflower in our outfits, shrieking with pleasure over each new trinket, gadget, or marital aid to come from our goodie bags. And then out of the blue—or bag, as it were—came this gorgeous string of pearls, obviously very real. Joan and I didn't know what to say about it. JB spoke up and said, "Those are for BoPeep." Well! Tell me this isn't the most wonderful man in the entire world, living or dead. Here is a guy who takes almost a full year setting up an elaborate joke for our amusement. He gets on a plane in Winston-Salem, flies to Jackson, takes a cab from the airport to a nearby hamlet so he can get on a Greyhound bus and arrive as promised on the bus. He's obviously devoted a great deal of time and energy assembling his outfit, not to mention these enormous goodie bags, and he's been up since four o'clock in the morning just anticipating it all. And he brings my baby pearls! I love this man. Make me laugh and buy me sparkly things, and I am yours.

JB is truly deserving of his title, Amazing. He told me that this bus trip was one of those things-that-you-think-about-and-talk-about-and-they-sound-great-but-you-somehow-never-do-them. He had a number of such plans, he said, some funny like this one and some serious, but starting right then, he was going to actually *do* one of them every ninety days. John Burress is so alive and so glad of it and so willing to do something about it. I wish there were a hundred of him, but there is only one. He is fit for a Queen.

Men Who Signal Danger

BE ON THE LOOKOUT
FOR THESE RED FLAGS

Experts tell us that all the warning signs of a bad relationship are there for us to see in the first ten minutes after meeting. I am here to testify to that, although it's never deterred me in the slightest. But perhaps my experience can benefit others who are more willing to pay attention.

Wild About Hairy

I have personally found hair to be a pretty fair index for future problem potential. Here are some examples—see if you can spot what the problem will be. Consider these first two guys, both of whom have what I would consider to be some of the world's best hair. Or rather they did have, until they started jacking with it.

Guy Number One had this really thick, slightly wavy, salt-and-pepper thing going—truly some of the best hair I've ever seen. Everywhere he went, people would comment favorably on his hair. Stylists would positively salivate over its texture and sheen. Not for any amount of money could any stylist anywhere duplicate those subtle shadings. His hair was one of those perfect flukes of nature. *Was* is the operative word here. He decided it looked "gray," and he got some yay-hoo to bleach it for him. So instead of white streaks that really looked more blond than white, he now has orange streaks through a gold background. It is the worst hair travesty I have ever witnessed. The stylist should have her license revoked for malpractice. From a distance now it looks like a football helmet—either Tennessee or Notre Dame, depending on the light. I was too undone over it to even make an attempt at being nice about it. He said he thought it made him look younger. I told him it made him look like an old guy with a bad dye job.

Guy Number Two is my erstwhile husband, MoonPie, who had a really nice, well-groomed coif for the first ten or so years I knew him. Then one day, out of the blue, he showed up with that new look that is so ridiculous looking. You've seen it. It looks sort of like they put a bowl on the guy's head to cut it—almost no hair on the sides and back, shaved up, and then all this long, floppy stuff on the top. Totally undignified and nasty-looking, too. The Queens can't stand a guy, or a girl either, for that matter, with hair that's always flopping down in the face. So you've got all these guys who are constantly pushing their hair back, or even worse, they've learned how to *toss* it back, like a redneck girl in a boondocks bar.

I was not kind to MoonPie. For one thing I was once married to him; that relieves me of the normal societal burden of having to be nice to him. I might have made some effort except it was just such a shock. This guy is *always* dressed to the eyeteeth and groomed to perfection. I'm saying he wouldn't go buy a Sunday paper without a shower, shave, and ironed blue jeans. Stunning that we are no longer married. At any rate, the words just tumbled out before I knew it. Something like "What in the world have you done to your head? That's the worst-looking mess I've ever seen in my life! Who did this to your beautiful hair?" And I repeated things of this nature every single time I saw him for the next several weeks, to no avail. He actually seemed to be *pleased* with what greeted him in the mirror.

Finally I found the solution. A mutual friend of ours saw him at a function and reported that she had finally seen firsthand the new do that I had been ranting about, and she had the perfect description for it; but I had to swear I wouldn't tell him what she said. So I swore away and then promptly called him up and told him anyway. It was too good. She said he looked just like Moe in the Three Stooges. Let

me say that he could not get to the barber—or in this case, *stylist*—
quick enough, and that was the last we've seen of that mess.

We were all atwitter about the dye job and the Moe-do, and then
one of our friends, Cozette, had a semiclose encounter with a guy who
maybe had no hair at all. I say "maybe" because it was never determined for sure one way or the other, and the whole thing was just a
trauma for her. See, she had met him at the Olympics in Atlanta. Cozette actually met quite a number of men there, from all over the
world. Of course, she is the type (read: little, blond, big tits—enough
said?) that men would notice from across a crowded stadium and
walk across the backs of all 350,000 people who have the misfortune
of being between him and her—just to be near her. The rest of us are
the type that the same men would ask us would we mind moving
down some so they can set their beer there.

So she met this guy at the Olympics, and when they met and he
fell hopelessly in love with her, he had on a baseball cap. Now, this
was not the guy from Sweden who owns the equivalent of, say, Mer-
rill Lynch over there. And this is not the guy who lives in New York
and is the most handsome man in this hemisphere. No, this was the
other guy she met, the one who just sold his company, which wasn't
Microsoft but a reasonable facsimile. Get the picture? If I had gone to
the Olympics, I would've been damn lucky to catch the eye of the
peanut guy if I was starving and waving hundred-dollar bills at him.

At any rate, post-Olympics, the baseball cap comes to Jackson to
call, only he ain't wearing the cap. He's wearing, she's pretty sure, a
rug. It was all she could think about over drinks and dinner. She felt
her eyes irresistibly drawn to his head. She was mesmerized, as it
were, by his hair, or rather what purported to be his hair, but she was
pretty sure it had been *somebody else's* hair up until recently. She
found herself positively obsessed with divining the truth—turning her
head this way and that, trying to view it from the angle that would be
most revealing. At one point she even tried to walk behind his chair
and sort of bump into him, stumbling, thereby allowing her to grab
hold of his head in order to steady herself—and still she couldn't be
certain. The uncertainty plagued her. We raised the question of
whether perhaps, just *perhaps*, it wasn't a rug after all but he'd actually grown that fine head of hair.

We don't understand the theory of toupees. We don't know one
solitary female who would refuse to go out with a guy with no hair.
On the other hand, nobody can take a man seriously who wears a wig.

Or who perms his hair—can't you just see him sitting there in his little cape with all those tiny rollers in his hair? Wouldn't you get that mental picture at the most inopportune moments? And what about guys who color their hair? On the coloring issue it was a split vote among us as to who is more repugnant—the man who darkens his hair, the man who bleaches his hair, or the one who gets his hair frosted. (He would rank up there with the perm guy for sitting there with all those little hair sprigs pulled through that little cap.) Going to a beauty shop and getting your hair done is just not a guy thing. It's too creepy for words.

What are you supposed to think of a guy whose only gray hair on his head is about four white hairs on each temple, while the rest of it is a uniform shade of brown that does not naturally occur in living things among any of the various species that grow hair? And then he takes off his shirt (if you can stand to let him, knowing what you already know about his beauty shop habitudes), and you're confronted by a heavy thatch of snow white chest hair? Are you really expected to have no thoughts whatsoever about this incongruity?

Hairdos, coloring, perming, augmenting, and so on—all this is girl-type stuff. We're not interested in having any of our guys assume or usurp any of our girl-type activities. We find that we can't take them seriously as guys if they do these things. As a matter of fact, we don't like men to fuss with their hair at all. We can't respect a man who spends more time on his hairdo than we spend on ours. If he's paying all that attention to his hair, he's not paying nearly enough attention to us, and that's the rub.

Plastic Parts Won't Help

We believe this to be true: All people, including us, get better looking—or worse—the longer you know them, and it's got very little on earth to do with what actual physical attributes they possess. Some guys are gorgeous until they open their mouths, and then it is so over. By the same token, we know any number of men who are not only not classically handsome, they tend more toward plug ugly, but they are so smart and so funny and so charming and they pay so much attention to us that we think they are the most attractive men who ever lived.

This brings up the subject of plastic surgery. The rule is this: Women may alter any and all parts of their bodies repeatedly and forever. Men may not have any sort of plastic surgery whatsoever unless they've received third-degree burns over at least eighty-five percent of their anatomy. Implants masquerading as major muscle groups are unacceptable. If you're too big a weenie to work out and build some respectable pecs, you must go through life with the chest of a wren and everyone must know it. We know a guy who got calf implants, and now he wears shorts even in blizzards.

It cannot be emphasized often enough—if a man is paying too much attention to his own appearance, he is not paying nearly enough attention to ours. The only looks that are important are ours.

You Can't Put a Saddle on a Clothes Horse

This clothes angle with men is a tricky one to read. We're certainly not suggesting that you seek out men who wear cheap clothes. No, they don't even register on our radar. If a man wears cheap clothes, it's for one of two reasons—it's either a freewill choice (not a good sign) or he has no choice (also not a good sign). If he can afford whatever he likes and he likes cheap clothes, he will more than likely want you to wear them as well, and this, of course, is not an option. If he wears cheap clothes because they're all he can afford, we're certain that he's a very nice man with many wonderful qualities, but he can't afford you, dear, so don't toy with him; it isn't nice. It doesn't take long to ascertain whether he's truly cheap or just poor.

The man who wears expensive clothes is another matter altogether. We want him to look good, to complement us, naturally. However, the *appearance* of prosperity is not enough to make us happy. It is, in fact, just enough to make us mad. Not just angry-mad either; it can make a person crazy-mad. If you date this man, he will dress up in total-body Armani, take you to the finest restaurant, order everything on the menu, and belatedly discover that he left his wallet somewhere, although it doesn't matter where the wallet is—there ain't no money in it anyway. Nonetheless, you've been successfully manipulated into paying the tab. If you end up married to this man, you will wear the same clothes for ten years while he struggles to find his new sixty-dollar pair of socks in the dark, because he didn't pay the electric bill.

Living with Mom is the same kind of deal. It's imperative that you determine posthaste if he's living with her to take care of her or if she's living with him to take care of him. If Mom is paying all the bills and doing all the work, neither of them is likely to be very interested in bringing another woman into the mix, unless Mom needs some help taking care of the boy, in which case, all I can say is *"Run away! Run away!"* If he's taking care of Mom, it can be a very good sign. Just make damn sure you like Mom before you sign on for this gig; she could outlive you.

Men who look good but aren't will cost you heartaches and tears, pain and money. My daddy would say, in the vernacular of Attala County, Mississippi, "He needs to git further or smell better!"

I've never seen a man wear ill-fitting expensive clothes. Expensive clothes are never too tight or too short. I've also never seen a man in a pair of custom-tailored slacks wearing a tool belt. I think this cannot be coincidental. Explain this theory to me: A guy with a sixty-five-inch waist buys size thirty-two pants and simply fastens them below the big belly. Then, since guys are hipless, there's nothing to keep the pants up; and since his T-shirt won't cover the big belly either, we, the general public, are treated to a view of his belly from the front and his butt from the rear. Perhaps he's confused by all the articles in women's magazines declaring how much women love to look at men's asses. This is true, we do love to look at your butts, *but*—and I think I speak for all women here—we have to know you really well before we are remotely interested in looking at your *actual* butt. Until such time, we all prefer—in fact, we insist—that you keep it completely covered up. When we're ready to view your butt, we'll let you know, thank you.

Don't Sweat It

Some men sweat more than others. The ones we're talking about here sweat a lot. And let's just clarify for the record here that we're not opposed to this. One of the Queens, Tammy, used to date this really fabulous-looking guy with a major sweat problem. He was in perfect shape and quite the sight to behold when he ran, shirtless, in those itty-bitty running shorts outside in the Mississippi heat, which is formidable. The sweat would simply run off him in torrents. However, our Tammy liked it. Tammy always was a fan of water sports. She said he was just like a great big ole Slip 'n' Slide. Now, all this is to illustrate that sweat, and lots of it, is not necessarily bad. However, as you can plainly see from this fairly graphic illustration, we're only interested in a body-to-body transfer of sweat.

There are few things worse than the sensation of lying down on a weight bench at the gym two seconds before you realize it's lathered in sweat from the inconsiderate asshole who just got up and didn't wipe down the bench before moving on. I hate him. I hope he dies and they bury him in that ratty-ass sweatshirt he's wearing that smells like he stopped on his way to the gym to roll in a dead squirrel. (If, in fact, I want to roll around in your sweat, trust me, I will communicate that to you privately.) A man who will do this is capable of God knows what-all in the personal hygiene department. Run away! Run away!

Adults Only on This Ride

The Queens are not interested in very young men. Even when we ourselves were very young, which we decidedly are no more, we preferred the charms of the older man. It's so odd that we are no longer numbered among the young. One minute, it seemed, we were young and cute, and the next thing we knew, we were all wedged up in front of a mirror pulling our faces up and back and wondering *how much it will cost to fix this*. We are one hundred percent in favor of fixing anything and everything by whatever means possible, and damn the expense.

I don't know when we crossed the line into ma'am-hood. I wasn't paying attention and never saw it coming. But now, whenever they hire new men in the weight room where we work out, they always call us "ma'am"—at least until we threaten to rip their tongues out and feed them to our cat. But then, seeing as how they are so all-fired young and energetic, we leave all our weights out for them to put away for us. We only want to be called "ma'am" if it is preceded with "wham bam" and a polite "thank you."

I don't feel like a ma'am. But apparently, I look like one, and that's worse. I totally agree with that guy who used to say, "It's better to look good than to feel good." However, I know I would *feel* a whole lot better if I didn't look like Whodunit. All of a sudden, when I take my hair down, I don't look like a flower child anymore. I look like Loretta Lynn. This is not a good look—for Loretta or me. Not to mention that there are big streaks of gray everywhere in my hair, but the last time I checked, Loretta was still using boot-black on hers.

When we go out dancing, usually at Hal & Mal's, the crazy old ladies up front who dance every dance are *us*. We do take much pride and satisfaction in the fact that, old and crazy as we are, at least we're out there. We haven't relegated ourselves exclusively to the TV. And according to our exhaustive research, we can still outdance and definitely outlast any twenty-one-year-old in the place. We find our youthful sisters and brothers to be either hopeless weenie people who cannot hang or limp-dick dead people who will not hang. We're proud to be of the generation who knows there used to be two Allman brothers and the first time we saw them play, they were playing warm-up for a band called Pacific Gas and Electric. Yes, we're old and getting more so all the time. Try to imagine how little we care.

And as I said, we've always preferred the company of older men. One of the main attractions here is that we will always be young and cute to old guys. This is a big plus. As a general rule, older men have more money to spend—on sparkly things—for *us*. Our ideal man at this point would be around seventy. His cataracts should be almost totally opaque. Remember that TV show *Moonlighting*, with Cybill Shepherd? They shot the whole show normally, but whenever the camera was on her, it had a cheesecloth filter over it. She always looked a little hazy and back-lit—therefore, fabulous. That's how we look to old men with cataracts. Once he's paid for our plastic surgery, we'll allow him to get his cataracts removed.

We also love to talk to men at least our own age or older so we have a common view of the world based on common experience—stuff to talk about. We've never understood the older guy-practically teenage girl thing. We've tried. We've belabored the point with our friend Randy, who, while in his forties, was dating a girl who was still in high school. He and his date—or, as we liked to call her, his "little friend"—would be late to everything. Randy would explain that she had band practice. When she was out of earshot, watching *Saved by the Bell* or something, we would berate him endlessly. We demanded to know what they could possibly talk about. When he wasn't immediately forthcoming with that info, we declared we could guess what they talked about, and we bet him a million dollars we'd be right, and we would know we'd hit it when we saw his face. "You talk about her hair and what happened on *The Young and the Restless*." Bingo. He had the decency to blush slightly.

There was much discussion about what a date would entail, since bars and some movies would be off limits. "Omigod! Randy! You have to go to the *mall!*" It took a while before he admitted it. Her dad had the presence of mind to voice some objections over this "relationship."

The two of them—the dad and Randy, who graduated from high school the same year—met to discuss it man to man, over a beer. Somehow Randy convinced the dad that this was a good thing for his baby girl. We gave up. If it was okay with the dad, we figured, what the hell. We told him flat-out, though, that when summer rolled around and the Spice Girls were in concert, he was on his own; we were not going with them. Neither were we hosting a party to watch Nickelodeon's *Kids' Choice Awards Show.* We predicted that when she got old—like when she had all her molars—he would dump her. Which, of course, he did. It took a couple of years for him to realize that he missed his Friday nights at the high school football stadium.

Tammy had to double-date one night with such a couple.

Tammy said she tried to be nice to the girl and include her in the conversation, but within a five-minute span the youngster disavowed any knowledge of the Vietnam War and did not know who Jackie Onassis was. That was the end of the conversation for Tammy.

Here's the deal. People in their twenties and thirties should date each other, as should people in their forties and fifties. The only acceptable exception to this precept would be if *we* happen to be the younger women. Actually anything we do, anyone we want to go out with, is fine. We're only interested in passing judgment on the behavior of others. This is because we are so good at it, and we always want to excel.

11

Men Who May Need Killing

Quite Frankly

It's sad—but even sadder, it's true—that a disproportionate number of men who you will be temporarily enraptured with throughout your lifetime will turn out, rather sooner than later, to warrant killing. It's just almost never a good idea to follow through—although, I swear, it seems like the only way to get rid of some of them. In our experience the more incorrigible the guy, the more deeply in love he is with us; and his tenacity is like that of one of those unrelenting Boston terriers that will bite the end of a rope and then you can swing the rope, dog and all, around over your head a hundred miles an hour all day long and the brute will never let go.

He will, however, never demonstrate that perseverance toward positive matters, such as paying the bills, giving up drugs and other women, or not farting loudly in movie theaters. He'll continue his objectionable behavior of whatever persuasion until such time that you, having reached your saturation point, declare closure. Then he'll pause in his objectionable behavior of choice long enough to attach himself to your ankles, sobbing, where he's prepared to remain until you forgive. It doesn't occur to him to go ahead on and find himself a woman who would count it her joy in life to support his sorry ass just to have the pleasure of his company night and day. He doesn't *want* a woman who wouldn't care how many other women he had because she has another half-dozen men on the string. If he finds a woman as cute as he is, that will steal his spotlight. If he finds one who's a bigger deadbeat than he is, who will feed them? No, he wants *you*, and you need to look out for yourself, or you'll be spending a lot of time hoping for zippity-do-dah, let me tell you.

Zippity-do-dah is our secret code for widowhood. Well, it's not exactly a secret anymore since one of the Queens told her husband about it. Shortly after she leaked this, he was at a men's church group meeting, and they were doing something sappy like standing around singing songs, and some poor oblivious guy requested that they sing "Zippity-do-dah," which they did, all except Tammy's husband, who went into hysterics and nearly had to be sedated. He kept ranting, "That's their *theme* song! Don't you know that?" What Tammy had revealed to him was this: Being a widow is way better than being a divorcée. It's better in every way. Financially, definitely. And it has to be far less damaging emotionally. Plus, everybody feels sorry for you and wants to help out. Nobody takes sides after a funeral the way they do with a divorce; there's only one side left standing. Widowhood is so much easier on the friend pool.

So what we like to envision is this: See the crowd at graveside. See the grieving widow in a smart black Ungaro suit, great shoes, heavily veiled but smashing hat. See the low-hanging clouds. See the mourners pay their last respects. See the solitary widow being helped into the ebony limo for her long ride back home alone. As the limo pulls away, see a break in the low, black clouds, allowing a single, brilliant shaft of sunlight to shine through. Behind the darkened windows of the limo, from deep behind the veils of the very smart hat, hear halting tones of the very small voice, "Zipp-i-ty dooooo-dah. . . ."

If you've waited a decent interval for him to expire, and it appears he won't, divorce is the only sensible avenue open to you. We've acknowledged the absolute folly of killing him your ownself, no matter how abundantly he deserves it. It will only result in further contrivance for you. As terribly inconvenient as divorce may be, it's not nearly so confining as capital murder. You can get an old friend to safely handle your divorce proceedings for free, *pro bono* as it were, but if you're on trial for your life, you're going to want to invest in the best defense available; and this is money that could be better spent on plastic surgery.

One of the Queens, Tammy, was going through a divorce a few years back, and her old high school sweetheart, a lawyer, bless his soul, handled the whole nasty business for her. He even paid her filing fee, the darlin' thing. When she got the first draft of the legal papers, we all congregated and read through them to be certain he had covered the important facets. We found him to be very thorough indeed. We were just reading along, one paragraph after another, just regular old d-i-v-o-r-c-e lingo, and then we came to a paragraph called "Optional." It read:

> It is agreed by and between the parties that the husband shall not procreate nor sire any further offspring by any means presently known or to become known in the future to man or science, to include but not limited to, normal intercourse, artificially manipulated mating, cloning or any other form of reproduction or sibilance thereof.

We're reading, and shouting, "Can we say this? Is this legal?" We read on:

> To insure compliance with this, the parties agree the husband shall, within thirty days from the date hereof, admit himself into a qualified hospital or clinic of his choosing and undergo the proper and necessary surgical procedure and/or procedures to fully remove all genitalia from his person and erase all evidence of maleness from his waist down. The husband shall be under no compulsion, obligation or court order to "take this as a man." Within fifteen days of said surgery, the husband shall deliver to the wife all items removed from his body during said procedure and/or procedures, properly preserved, hermetically sealed and suitable for inspection, identification and exhibition.

Never mind that this was an affectionate hoax. Tammy's lawyer-friend belongs on the U.S. Supreme Court. We declare his words to be the ultimate final decree of divorce.

Is That a Wedding Ring in Your Pocket— or Are You Glad to See Me?

And then there are the Men with Nice Wives. I've found it hard to address this subject without my words having an *edge* to them, and so I gave up trying to eliminate the edge. The edge is there because so many of the Queens—indeed, we are but a microcosm of all womankind—have been Nice Wives, and man, does this piss me off. Of course, all the Queens were brought up as Aspiring Brides. As such we were counseled to obtain our teaching certificates so that in case we married football coaches, we'd be able to teach when their coaching careers were ended. For the same reason it was also acceptable to become a nurse. You could be a nurse or a teacher, but only if you *had* to work because your husband turned out to be a worthless piece of shit, but even if he did, he was still your husband for life, the king of you, and you were damned lucky to have him.

And so the young girl grew up to be the Nice Wife by doing everything her family and husband told her to do. She has been faithful and true, a cameo of abject perfection. She has borne and brought up children, often with exceedingly little help from the other parent. She has kept herself and her home in good working order. Meanwhile her husband is at a bar trying to pick up Bambi, and by way of explaining that white circle on his left hand where a wedding ring obviously resides most of the time, he says that, yes, he's married—*miserably so*—but he can't do anything about it because his wife has never done anything wrong; she is a very nice person! Somehow, in some convoluted way, it was not as infuriating when they used to say they were not understood at home, or they were married to the ditch witch but couldn't leave because of the children. (Speaking of whom, don't you know the kids would be proud of Dad now?)

It was just this sort of behavior that caused the Queens to search the Scriptures for guidance. After much deliberation we think we've come up with the first correct interpretation in around two thousand years. Remember that line that says, "It is better to marry than to burn"? Well, after centuries of theologians, most of them men, screwing around with it, the meaning got garbled. The true meaning is just exactly what it says: Being married is better than being set on fire. But they didn't say how *much* better; and from our own experience, it might not be such a clear-cut choice.

One of the Queens, Tammy, in the throes of divorce proceedings, sought advice from a close friend, Shirley. Shirley looked at Tammy with compassion and said to her, "You know, Tammy, if your husband was living according to the Scriptures, ya'll wouldn't be in this mess." Tammy said she didn't know what that meant. Shirley explained, "Well, the church folks just love to spout all that about wives submitting to their husbands. First of all, that presumes that the husband has some sense and perhaps more than an ounce of human decency. But the main thing they leave out is that the husband is supposed to be as Christ was to the Church." Tammy was still confused. "Christ died for the Church," Shirley explained. She went on to say that if this man was willing to put you absolutely first in every single decision he ever had to make, the whole matter was a guaranteed success. "Yes, I see your point," Tammy exclaimed. "If he would *die*, we wouldn't have to suffer through this awful divorce!" Shirley looked for an instant like the little boy whose bread was stolen by the chicken, and then she collapsed laughing. We do so love our sisters whose spirituality does not eclipse their sense of humor.

Anyway, the next time a Man with a Nice Wife tries to hit on you, promise me that you'll make a scene large and loud enough to alert all other women in the vicinity to his location. Try to involve as many of them as you can in the scene; a cast of thousands would be excellent. If he could later be found, bound hand and foot with women's panties, with a big red A indelibly painted on his forehead, wouldn't that just be gravy?

I think I kept most of the edge out, don't you?

No Peace for the Wicked

I spent a splendid weekend in Pittsburgh with a man who seemed too good to be true, and as it turned out, he *was*—but I get ahead of myself. I'll spare you the details of the fabulous weekend, as you'd no doubt throw up from sheer envy. Things deteriorated somewhat rapidly upon my arrival home, which I guess is to be expected. Never, however, could I have anticipated the particular turn that events would take within a few short hours.

I was exhausted. Being adored just flat wears me out. You? Being waited on hand and foot for days is taxing. Got home to Mississippi by 9:30 P.M. In bed by ten, asleep by 10:03, with my daughter, BoPeep, beside me. I'd had about six hours' sleep the whole weekend, so being awakened at 2:30 A.M. was not exactly what I had in mind. Nonetheless, promptly at 2:30 A.M., I heard a noise. A very small noise: *ch-ch-ch-ch-ch* . . . It sounded exactly like my mother shuffling down the hall. (She's been enjoying ill health for the last year or so and lives with me and 'Peep.) Poststroke, Mama never picks up her feet when she walks. It's like living with Tim Conway's little old man character; I hear her coming for ten minutes before she gets there— drives me up the wall. So it's 2:30 A.M., and I was getting this *ch-ch-ch-ch* business. There were no lights on. I thought, not only is she up wandering around the house, she's also completely lost her mind trying to navigate in total darkness when she can hardly do so in broad daylight.

"Mother?" I call out. Again, "Mother!" No answer. I fling off the covers and stomp out into the hall, turning on lights everywhere. The hall is empty, and there's no sign of Mother. Her bedroom door is shut, and not a sound emanates from within. I crawl back in bed, putting my glasses on the night table. Only I miss the table and I hear them fall to the floor behind the table. I decide to worry about them later. I try to get back to sleep.

Again, the *ch-ch-ch-ch* noise. I'm livid, at what I don't know. I roll over to turn on the bedside lamp so I can begin the hunt for my glasses. On their own my eyeballs could be considered purely ornamental. I cannot see jack without major optical assistance. I'm not at all expecting to look down and see, sticking out from under the side of my bed, no more than a foot and a half from my very face, a long, hairless tail attached to a round, gray, furry behind. Having spent the last forty-five years trying to grow up in Mississippi, I know, instantaneously and beyond any shadow of a doubt, that tail and behind belong to a full-grown possum. Geezloueez! There's a possum under my bed! All I could say out loud was, "Oh!" but I said it real loud and over and over, with profound feeling. I can tell you, I was *completely* surprised.

I briefly contemplated calling The Man in Pittsburgh, thinking how interesting this would be to him at 2:30 A.M. since I bet this almost never happens in Pittsburgh because (a) I don't think they have possums up there to begin with and (b) if they do, they probably call them opossums and even pronounce the o, which everybody knows is silent and so why bother putting it in there? But I thought better of it and mustered the nerve to retrieve my glasses, which had landed approximately three inches from the nose of the possum. I sat there, on the edge of my bed, gazing at that possum butt and asking myself what in the samhill was I gonna do about this possum under my bed?

Everyone I've told this story to has butted in at this juncture, if not before, and wanted to know how the possum got in the house to begin with. I explained, as patiently as they deserved, that at 2:30 A.M. when you wake up and discover a full-grown possum under your bed, you aren't particularly interested in how he got in. You are, however, vitally interested in how he's going to get out.

Okay. I've got to have a plan. So I get up and go off in search of materials for constructing a possum trap. What would my daddy do? He would know, without the slightest hesitation, what to do when you wake up at 2:30 A.M. and find a possum under your bed. Daddy picked a fine time to be dead for fifteen years. Well, I'm nothing if not his daughter, I say to myself. I'll instinctively know how to deal with this situation. And so I'm led by some intuition into the kitchen—to the garbage, to be precise. (That possums love garbage is an irrefutable truth.) I select a suitably aged chicken package, containing some nicely ripened chicken skin and fat—manna from Heaven, if you happen to be a possum. I grab a large empty liquor box with a sturdy lid. Now hideously wide-awake, I return to my bedroom. I set the box in my bathroom, the delicate scent of the rotten chicken skin already permeating the air and, I hope, delighting my rodent roommate. I get back in bed and wait.

I have to do this in total darkness. Possums are nocturnal, and they don't like it when you turn the lights on. So I'm pretty happy. Just home after playing Queen for a Day all weekend. I'm trying to sleep a little so I can resume my real life as Mom to half the free world tomorrow, but instead of sleeping, I'm sitting bolt upright in the dark waiting for the possum under my bed to make a move on the chicken skin. Along about now I start to see the humor in all this. Now I'm sitting there, and I'm laughing fit to kill. This is too good, I'm thinking. I'm going to phone somebody. But who?

When it comes to calling somebody at 3 A.M., to report the presence of a possum under your bed, however, you are working from a very short list. I rule out The Man. I'm crazy about him but not certain that our relationship has progressed to the point that he's on my 3 A.M. Possum Report List. I think you probably have to be at least engaged for that. I decide that my sister, Judy, who lives in New Orleans, would probably want to hear about the possum situation.

I turn on the light momentarily to dial her number; then I perform a quick possum check. Still there, not a hair out of place. I get her voice mail. I'm talking really low to avoid awakening the slumbering BoPeep beside me, who is still blissfully ignorant of the fact that we have a possum under our bed. I swear, I barely spoke above a whisper, but somehow my voice reached into her sleeping brain. She catapulted straight up and began to shriek loudly, in staccato, "GET-IT-OUT-GET-IT-OUT-GET-IT-OUT!" And with that she fell back on her pillow, apparently still asleep. She lay still for a few moments and then sat up again, demanding to know if she had dreamed it, or was there in fact a possum under our bed? I've made a rigorous policy of honesty in her upbringing, and I could make no exceptions now. She demanded to know what I planned to do about it. I told her about the trap. She was dubious.

"Why don't you call Dad?" she asked. *"Dad?"* I can't convey to you the scathe in my tone as I repeated that word to her. "Dad? Darlin', Dad grew up in *north* Jackson, and I can just tell you, he doesn't know squat about a possum under the bed." MoonPie had lived practically forty years, all of them in Mississippi, before he accidentally stepped on a slug with his bare foot for the first time in his life. He let out a scream that was so loud, so piercing, and so prolonged that, hearing it from the back of the house as I did, I could only assume that a panther had bitten off his arm and was devouring it before his very eyes. He flew past me—if a large, grown man hopping on one foot and squealing could be said to fly—toward the shower. I fell on the floor in helpless guffaws. Who, born and bred in the South, doesn't know that you cannot wash off a smashed slug? I'll tell you who: MoonPie, that's who. He wanted to go to the MinorMed and have his foot amputated. From this knowledge I judged, and I think accurately so, that he would be utterly worthless to us at this time.

'Peep announced that she couldn't remain long in a dark room with a possum, and so off she went to the kitchen. On her way there she made a discovery. "There's possum poop on the dining room rug!" she shouted down from the hall. Well, now, that mobilized me. I hadn't considered the possibility of possum poop. Being a lot more familiar than I'd care to be with the offal of kitty cats, I could only imagine what the effect would be if this possum had a full *bladder.* I would probably have to burn the house down to get rid of the smell. Action was called for, and I was the only one on call. As I've always told BoPeep in times of crisis, "I can handle this and I will handle this because *I* am the great and powerful *mother!*"

Men Who May Need Killing

I turned on the light and checked out the possum. Sound asleep he was, sawing big ole possum logs, right there under my bed. Not the slightest bit hungry, it would seem. That did it. I sprang up and got my great-great-granddaddy's walking cane that he'd carved by hand from a sassafras tree. I poked that possum with it until he woke up. I proceeded to try to herd him into my bathroom, hoping he wouldn't move farther up under the bed. He ran under the bench at the foot of my bed. I was down on all fours, nose to nose with this thing, jabbing at it with my cane, cussing all the while. I don't know if he was scared of me, my stick, or my profanity, but he ran into the bathroom. I followed him and slammed the door. I was now sealed off, alone, with the possum. I sprang into the bathtub, where I could reach him with my stick and prod him out into my exercise room. This having succeeded, it was simple enough to climb over the NordicTrack and onto a ledge, push open the door to the outside, and secure freedom for the possum.

A little while later I was on the walking track at the Y with Gail. I told her of my weekend as the Queen of Pittsburgh and then about the possum. She concluded there was a moral to it all. "That's all well and good for you to run off up there to Pittsburgh and carry on with that handsome man, little missy, just so you remember that when you get back where you belong, there's gonna be a possum under your bed!"

As it turned out, it was a portent of things to come as well. The whole Pittsburgh relationship went from magical to mythical pretty much in one histrionic swoop. What seemed one minute to be a rapidly developing mutual admiration turned swiftly into something else altogether. After many multihour phone conversations, flowers, plane tickets—all of which indicated a certain level of interest—The Man suddenly said to me, "I am not interested in pursuing a relationship with you at this time." I said, "Excuse me?" And he said it again: "I am not interested . . . in pursuing a relationship . . . *with you* . . . at this time." I was particularly struck by his emphasis on the words "*with you*," clearly suggesting that a relationship with anybody else on God's planet would be given thoughtful consideration. *Nonplussed* pretty much sums up my feelings on the thing.

Of course, I immediately shared this information with my fellow Queens, who had been following the whole involvement quite closely, as you might imagine. All of them insisted that I had either misunderstood him or just blatantly twisted some innocent statement into something sinister. And so I repeated, for each of them in turn, the exact words, swearing on a stack of the holy items of their choosing that these were his precise words: "I am not interested . . . in pursuing a relationship . . . with you . . . at this time." They were just as taken with the "with you" part as I was and repeated his words to me frequently, as an aside to whatever we might be discussing at the moment, which had quickly ceased to be *him*. They forgot all about The Man from Pittsburgh but retained his parting words as some sort of mantra.

The big surprise came a month or so later when I heard from him again. He called my house, and my mother told him where I was, which happened to be a Queens' gathering at Tammy's house; he called me there. I answered the phone but failed to recognize his voice, and he apparently didn't recognize mine either. I handed the phone to Tammy. She said, in earshot of all the Queens, "Oh! Hi [his name here]! Yes, she's right here," and handed the phone to me. All the Queens shouted in unison, "We are . . . not interested . . . in pursuing a relationship . . . *with you* . . . at this time!"

He was calling because his latest very young thing had just dumped him unceremoniously, and he wanted to get on a plane at that precise moment and fly down for me to make him feel better, carefully adding that he was still "not interested . . ." This was what we call your slap in the face with a wet squirrel. I was so flabbergasted, I had to ask questions to be sure I was hearing what I was hearing. "You're telling me that this little girl hurt your ego so bad that you don't think you can survive it and you want to get on a plane and fly down here and you want me to drive all the way out to the airport at midnight to get you, whisk you off somewhere, and knock myself out consoling you for a day or so, and then you want to fly out of here and forget the whole thing? Is that what you're asking me to do?" He indicated that, yes, that was pretty much what he had in mind, did it sound okay to me? He was deadass serious. I replied that it certainly was tempting, but I didn't think I would be "interested at this time."

I walked back into the room with all the Queens, who, of course, were about to have a stroke wanting to know what he wanted. Once again none of them would believe me when I told them. "You are lying!" was their reaction. They all wanted me to call him back and tell him I'd reconsidered and I'd be happy to help him out and then not go to the airport to get him and, when he called, say, "I am not interested . . ." A lengthy discussion ensued at this point as to whether he just had brass balls or whether I did, in fact, have *chump* tattooed on my forehead and we had just never noticed it before.

I really must take some of the blame for this debacle. I've readily confessed that more often than not I'll see those red flags flapping in the breeze at first glance and willfully ignore them, plunging headlong into sorrow. In this particular case I'd blithely overlooked at least two sure signs that this was a man who might need killing: I had been duly apprised of his predilection for girls much younger, and I had personally observed the unmistakable tint of Grecian Formula. The words "I told you so," while so gratifying in application to others, are a serious irritant when directed at oneself. I'm curious. Wonder what FedEx would charge to deliver a live possum to Pittsburgh?

My senseless disregard in this instance of the red flags, and the consequences that followed, eventually reminded me, however, of pithy counsel from that wise old granddaddy of mine. He would look off thoughtfully and declare, "As you walk down life's pathway, you may chance upon a turd—don't kick it!"

12

What to Eat When Tragedy Strikes

OR JUST FOR ENTERTAINMENT

A ll tragedy is relative, of course. It could be anything from a car or plumbing failure to the death of the only woman in the world who has ever been able to give you a really great haircut. If you're in any way upset by something—it's a tragedy. A tragedy demands food, and lots of it. We Queens try to include items from all four major food groups—sweet, salty, fried, and au gratin. Balance is very important to us. You'll also want to have friends on hand for the tragedy-thwarting feast. Under no circumstances, however, should you invite any of the assholes who refuse to acknowledge the depths of your misery. They can stay home and fill up on water for all we care.

Chocolate is the main staple of sedative food—the undisputed queen of all the comfort foods. I know this in my deepest heart. I frankly don't understand how people who are genuinely allergic to chocolate manage to put one foot in front of the other, day after day; I'd have to throw myself in front of a bus. I thrive on chocolate. My system requires an abundance of it every day, just to function normally.

CHOCOLATE STUFF

The Sweet Potato Queens' drug of choice is clearly my famous Chocolate Stuff. I got the recipe from my mother, who called it something like "fudge pudding." None of my friends could remember the name, however; they'd simply beg me to make them "some of that chocolate stuff." The biggest problem with the recipe is that it doesn't make very much. I'd recommend that you automatically double the ingredients. Doubled, it will make three pans. This has proven to be just enough.

Unfortunately it has to bake 40 to 50 minutes, which is a helluva long time when you're suffering. Good news: It's really just as fine— some factions argue *better*—eaten raw as fully cooked! We've been known to eat entire batches of it right out of the mixing bowl, skipping the baking altogether. Usually we're content with leaving copious amounts of the precious goo in the bowl and sticking our faces into the bowl while the oven works its magic on the major portion. When you make your personal judgment call, keep in mind that the recipe contains eggs, at this point raw, and you may be risking your very life in pursuit of instant gratification.

I've reduced the amount of flour by half and cooked it in the microwave for just eight and a half minutes, but you sacrifice texture this way, and I don't recommend it. One of the most important qualities of Chocolate Stuff is its unique texture: really gooey on the bottom and sort of chewy, crunchy on the top. Nuts are optional. We take our desire for nuts by spells, and this carries over into many aspects of our lives.

I'll tell you how to make my Chocolate Stuff, but your best option is to kiss my ass six ways to Sunday and get *me* to make it for you, because it's always better when I make it myself. I don't know why, I swear to God. The recipe I will give you does not omit any ingredients or instructions to sabotage your efforts. It just seems to know me, and it performs better in my hands. I even make it better than my mother does, and it was her recipe to start with.

Here's the deal: Beat two eggs with a cup of sugar and ½ cup of flour. Add ¼ teaspoon of salt. In the microwave melt together one stick of real butter (I never use unsalted; I think it tastes flat) and 2 fairly heaping tablespoons of Hershey's cocoa. Get regular Hershey's in the dark brown box—anything else is different and will screw it up. Dump the butter-cocoa mixture into the other things, and stir it up good. Then add a running-over teaspoon of vanilla. I use real vanilla, but the grocery store kind won't ruin it. Stir that up, too. If you decide to go for nuts, use a whole bunch of pecans, chopped up fine.

Pour the Stuff into a greased loaf pan, set the loaf pan in a pan of water, and stick the whole business in the oven set at about 300 degrees. Depending on how your oven cooks, it needs to stay in there for 40 to 50 minutes. You can reach in there and tap on the top of it at 40 minutes. If it seems crunchy, I'd take it out. You can't really undercook it, since it's good raw, but you don't want to overcook it and lose the gooey bottom so crucial to the whole texture experience.

Trust me. This will be the best thing that has happened to you in a very long time, possibly ever. From now on, for as long as you live, just the simple act of getting out the bowl to make Chocolate Stuff will have an incredibly assuaging effect on your psyche. I can say, without fear of contradiction, there is virtually *nothing*, not one situation, that can't be faced with calm and grace and serenity if you have Chocolate Stuff. You can eat it and feel better *fast*, and when it wears off, you can just make another batch. Believe me, in no time at all, you'll be grinning like a mule eating briars.

The Queens have found what we think is a very effective eating pattern. *Sweet and salty.* For us this combination works equally well whether we're eating simply for recreation or if we're engaged in your true therapeutic wolfing. In our exhaustive testing of all the programs suggested in this book, we found that if we had sufficient quantities of satisfactory sweet and salty foods, we could eat for approximately seventy-two hours straight, with maybe the odd nap thrown in here and there. And you can appreciate, I'm sure, that there's healing value in this. The concept is that when you've sufficiently met your body and soul's requirement for sweet foods, your salty needs are practically screaming for attention. By the time you've gratified the salty, you'll be happily ready for sweet again. We're particularly fond of regular Ruffles and the original version of Fritos for some quick and effortless salty foods.

Armadillo Dip

Sometimes a life event is just too catastrophic for quick and effortless remedies. You'll need Armadillo Dip to go with those Fritos. New Allison gave us this recipe, for which we're eternally grateful, and as a token of our gratitude, we've allowed her to be a Sweet Potato Queen Wannabe. (New Allison is called New, by the way, because we already had an Allison. So when this one appeared, we had to have New Allison and Old Allison. If that wasn't enough confusion, we then got yet another Allison Wannabe. Since she's at least twenty years younger than the youngest one of us, we call her Baby Allison. We aren't currently accepting any further friends by this name.)

When New Allison introduced us to Armadillo Dip, being more fat-conscious than any of the rest of us are willing even to think about, she made it with ground turkey. To say the Queens are fat-*un*-conscious would not be accurate at all; we're actually fat-obsessed, always seeking to increase the number of fat grams we can cram into any meal. As soon as New Allison moved to Chicago, we dropped the ground turkey and went for ground chuck.

You brown a pound or so of ground chuck. Pour off the grease; this is done purely for the consistency of the dip and should in no way be construed as a fat-saving measure. Dump in a bunch of taco seasoning, hot picante sauce, and hot Cheez Whiz. It's like a fancy Rotel tomato-cheese dip, a staple at all Southern gatherings—only hotter and more fattening. Armadillo Dip is great on Fritos and Tostitos, as long as they aren't the baked kind, which we're against.

New Allison's Mambo Margaritas

Occasionally, in order to feel adequately soothed and mollified, you're going to need some alcohol. The Queens are partial to margaritas, and New Allison's are hard to beat. You may think these sound weird, if not awful, but I promise it will become your favorite margarita recipe. You pour in one big can of frozen limeade; that's 12 ounces. Then add one bottle of Corona beer, 12 ounces of 7-Up (never Sprite), and 12 ounces of really good tequila. Don't attempt to mix this in a blender. We've all done it, trying to make them frozen, and blown the top of the blender and sprayed this sticky mess everywhere. (You'd think that would be so obvious, wouldn't you, what with the beer and the 7-Up?) A brisk stir in a fair-sized pitcher is the way to go.

Fat Mama's Knock You Naked Margaritas

When we want our margaritas frozen or we're too lazy to mix up New Allison's, we have another plan: Fat Mama's Knock You Naked Margarita Mix. Tammy, who owns our favorite gourmet store in the entire world, called me one night and said she had a new product she was thinking about stocking, but we needed to test it first. Always willing to consume about anything in the name of research, I said, "Bring it over!" She arrived with two tiny bottles of Fat Mama's Mix and proposed that we commence the test. I said fine, but each of these cute little bottles makes 48 ounces. If we tested that much, we'd be sure to fail. We mixed up one bottle and found that 48 ounces was just exactly the right amount for the two of us, thirsty as we were and all. And I must say, the forty-eighth ounce was every bit as tasty as the first one. Plus, we *love* the name. We find that just saying the name makes us feel festive, which is, of course, a favorite Queenly feeling. Fat Mama's is made right here in Mississippi, and you can order it, no matter where you happen to live, simply by calling The Everyday Gourmet, a Queen-owned and -operated establishment. Call 1-800-898-0122, and Tammy will be so happy to send you some of your very own.

Absolut Fredo

Sometimes the Queens like to get all buffed up and go out among the grown-ups. Our favorite venue for acting grown-up is an Italian restaurant in Jackson called Bravo! We prefer to have martinis here— nothing makes you feel more grown-up than a martini—but we hate the regular kind. When Jeff Good, the proprietor of Bravo!, served us the Absolut Fredo, our lives took a couple of turns. It instantly became our favorite adult libation. Nobody else makes the Fredo in town, so we persuaded Jeff to disclose the ingredients, just in case we needed to feel grown-up somewhere else. Here they are: three parts Absolut Kurant, one part Triple Sec, and one part Rose's lime juice, all this shaken over ice and served exquisitely in a chilled martini glass. We've been unsuccessful in duplicating this drink at home. We whipped up a batch of them for watching the last Miss Mississippi pageant on TV, and they were singularly potent. Jeff didn't indicate what size the parts should be, and so we surmised them to be cup-sized. They were tasty, indeed, but we had trouble sitting up after just one.

Oh, God!

We like to augment our sweet supply sometimes with fare that's not made with chocolate. One of our favorite supplemental sweets is a chocolate caramel pie that's come to be called "Oh, God!" I'm sure it originally had another name, but every single person, without exception, who's ever tasted this luscious concoction for the first time has exclaimed, "Oh, God!" It doesn't come out clear like that; it sounds all moany and, frankly, sexual—"Oh-h-h-h! Gaw-w-w-wd!"—clearly indicating extreme pleasure. There is absolutely no way to cram any more fat into a single food item. I got the recipe from my mother's friend Estelle, who is so sweet, you want to squeeze her guts out every time you see her. She has this hug-eliciting quality and comes up with recipes like this one.

First you make a pie crust, with 1½ cups of flour, a stick of butter, and 1 cup of finely chopped pecans. You mash all that into a couple of pie plates and bake it for 10 minutes or so, at around 350 degrees, until they get tan. Then, in a pretty big bowl, mix together—this is so fattening, I can't even write it with a straight face—8 ounces of cream cheese, a can of Eagle Brand Sweetened Condensed Milk, and 16 ounces of Cool Whip—my three favorite ingredients. Pour this mixture into the tan pie crusts.

Meanwhile, mix together 7 ounces of coconut, a half stick of melted butter, and a cup of chopped pecans, and spread it all out on a cookie sheet and toast it. You'll have to really watch it and stir it a lot, or the coconut will burn slap up. Spread the toasted coconut combo on top of the pies. Then take a 12-ounce jar of caramel sauce, and pour it over the pies. That is it. Freeze them for a little while before you try to cut them, or you can just sit down in the middle of the floor with a pie and a spoon and have at it—our preferred mode of serving.

COME BACK SAUCE

We've figured out why so many people in the world have eating disorders. Therapeutic eating works! I don't care what's happened, a caramel-turtle-nut-fudge sundae the size of my head from our favorite ice cream parlor, Swenson's, will fix it. Follow that sundae with a bottle of Come Back Sauce from Hal & Mal's on several baskets of crackers, and you can be happy for a while.

If you're feeling industrious, you can whip up some sacred Come Back Sauce in your own Cuisinart. You'll need the following ingredients: 3 cloves of garlic, 2 cups of mayonnaise, ½ cup of chili sauce, ½ cup of ketchup, 1 cup of salad oil, 2 tablespoons of black pepper, the juice of two lemons, 2 teaspoons of yellow mustard, 2 teaspoons of Worcestershire, 2 dashes of Tabasco sauce, and half an onion, grated. Dump it all in the Cuisi, and whirl away.

Come Back Sauce is an all-purpose dressing, good on everything as far as we can tell—salad, of course, and black-eyed peas and even pizza. A number of Jackson's local restaurants feature their own variations of Come Back, but Hal & Mal's version is the Queens' favorite. If you're a hopeless slackass, you can call Hal & Mal's at 1-601-948-0888, and they'll ship you out some for a modest fee.

DANGER PUDDING

For the uninitiated, Danger Pudding is made with a can of sweetened condensed milk. I don't know about you, but I can get happy just thinking about eating an entire can of Eagle Brand, just as it is, right out of the can. Malcolm White says when he was little, his mama used to give him a whole can of sweetened condensed milk to eat, all by himself, on his birthday; it was basically what he lived for every year.

To make Danger Pudding, you take your can, and without opening it, you boil it for an hour or so. Now, the people who make sweetened condensed milk are hip to this, and they say flat-out you shouldn't do this, ever. They feel so strongly about it, they actually print this warning right on the label: "Danger! Do not heat unopened can!" So be forewarned: You're risking your life and assorted kitchen parts by doing it. In my opinion, however, it's worth the hazard. All that sugar caramelizes, and it has about nine jillion fat grams, and this is why it's such strong medicine. You can actually make Danger Pudding with the fat-free sweetened condensed milk, and this will do if you're artery-conscious. But you shouldn't do any of this yourself because you could be killed. Come by my house, and I'll make it for us. I'm very brave.

MIMI'S BUTTERFINGER COOKIES

A surgeon general's report ranked Mississippi really high—in the fat demographics, that is. We finally get at the top of a national list, and look at what it is. The rest of the country is praying that we don't fall off and smash them. I personally have done my part to maintain our high standing in this regard. I generally eat like there's no tomorrow, or at least no lunch tomorrow. We can't just rest on our big fat laurels and hope to keep this high rating, however. We'll all have to participate. Here's a little something for anybody having trouble keeping those precious pounds on: Mimi's Butterfinger Cookies.

I wouldn't have thought it possible to improve on a Butterfinger candy bar, but danged if Tammy's mom, Mimi, didn't figure out a way. I think it's the combination of sweet and salty that makes this dish so completely irresistible. You need 1½ cups of sugar, 1⅓ cups of dark brown sugar, a stick of butter, 4 eggs (Mimi used just the whites, but when you read the rest of the ingredients, this seems laughable, like ordering everything on the menu but putting Equal in your tea—to save calories), and 3 running-over teaspoons of vanilla. Mix all that up. Then dump in 2½ cups of chunky peanut butter, and stir that all up also. You need 2 cups of flour, a teaspoon of baking soda, and ½ teaspoon of salt. Work those into the mix.

Now it's Butterfinger time. You can either use the BB's, which are really easy to deal with, or you can get just regular Butterfinger candy bars—20 or so ounces' worth—cut 'em up, throw 'em in, and blend together the whole wondrous conglomeration. Drop teaspoon-sized blobs on a lightly greased cookie sheet, and bake them at 350 degrees for 7 to 9 minutes.

Funeral Food—
The Brighter Side of Death

When someone dies in the South, it's not altogether tragic. We always like to think that death has its advantages for the departed one—journey's end, sweet chariots, unbroken circles, and all that. For everyone left behind after the untimely passing, there's the unmistakable comfort of funeral food. When there's a death in a Southern town, everybody who has ever known anybody in the family has to take food to the home of the bereaved. It is practically a law. One of the Queens, Tammy, said there was a lady in her hometown who got up every morning of the world and fried a chicken first thing so that just in case somebody died that day, she could be on-the-spot with first-class funeral food.

Most of us are not quite that obsessive about fixing funeral food, but it's a tradition we have no plans to give up. Granted, it's a pain in the butt to have to stop whatever you're doing and make a casserole to give away, but we always remember that sooner or later some of our people will be departing, and all the funeral food will come home to roost with us. "The smaller the town, the better the food" is a pretty good rule for assessing funeral fare. In your bigger towns and cities, you might get the occasional ready-made cold-cut platter and once in a while a store-bought pie might slip in. But in a small town it's like a baking competition. Everybody who brings something will be checking out what everybody else brought—and talking about it, so one doesn't offer anything not homemade.

Even the most anguished, devoted family member can find some shred of consolation in funeral food. If there's a balm in Gilead, I'd be willing to bet it's made with cream of mushroom soup, Velveeta, or Cool Whip. Nearly all funeral food contains at least one of these staples. I don't care how fancy a gourmet cook you might think you are—you may not even allow Velveeta in your own personal kitchen—but I've yet to meet the palate too sophisticated for funeral food. In fact, I've observed that the snootier they are, the higher they pile those plates up. Everybody loves funeral food; it's a universal truth, and this is easy to explain. There's hardly anything quite as soothing as a warm casserole—especially a warm casserole that someone else made. That is, after all, one of the primary qualifications for good food: Someone else prepared it.

When one of my very favorite mamas, Hazel Rubenstein, mother to two of my favorite sons, Michael and Ted, died in Booneville, way up in northeastern Mississippi, we were all transported to a celestial apex by the staggering quality and quantity of the funeral food. And let's face it, as I've earlier suggested, quantity is at least as important as quality. If it's the best morsel you ever put in your mouth but there's just a little dab of it, it will not satisfy as intended, but rather will serve as a major annoyance.

Well, at Hazel's last hurrah, not only did we have a delightfully embarrassing abundance of food at the house, there was funeral food at the funeral home as well. The funeral home had a big room with long tables in it, and all the friends of all the bereaved families could bring their food there for the solace of the mourners. This way you can mingle with everybody and not have to interrupt your grieving in order to have a snack. A fabulous innovation; I hope it spreads. As I recall, they also had a TV room, and this enabled the male mourners to grieve continually without missing a single major sporting event.

MISS LEXIE'S PINEAPPLE CASSEROLE

One of the very best things to come out of Hazel's funeral—and it's an ill wind, after all, that blows nobody good—was an extraordinary pineapple casserole brought by Hazel's friend Miss Lexie. This is truly one of nature's perfect foods, not just combining, as it does, sweet and salty, which would be enough of an accomplishment right there, but also having cheese in it. Not many foods can satisfy the sweet, salty, and au gratin requirements at the same time. This is a very special dish. We stood around the table like vultures (albeit Queenly vultures) and ate it straight out of the casserole dish until it was gone. You couldn't risk putting some on your plate and going off somewhere to eat it before coming back for more. It was too good. We knew it would soon be gone, and so we just made sure that it went to its rightful diners, namely us. And since we were among family and our closest friends, we could get away with wolfing down an entire casserole ourselves and simply whisking the empty dish away out of sight before the other mourners arrived.

When you make this dish, I strongly urge you to double or, better, triple it; otherwise I can assure you there won't be enough. You want to drain a 20-ounce can of pineapple (in its own juice) chunks or tidbits. Save 3 tablespoons of the juice, and mix it with ½ cup of sugar and 3 tablespoons of flour. Stir that mixture in with the pineapple and a cup of sharp grated cheese. (I've never tried making this with fat-free cheese and consider that blasphemous, but I have used some reduced-fat cheese when it was all I had, and it came out okay.) Dump all that into a greased casserole. Melt a stick of butter, and stir into it ½ cup of Ritz Cracker crumbs; put all that on top of the pineapple mixture. Bake it at 350 degrees for 20 to 30 minutes, and prepare to be comforted.

Making the Best of a Bad Situation

Another occasion for substantial gatherings of people and mammoth feasts of fattening foods is the family reunion. There's very little on the surface to distinguish a family reunion feed from a funeral feed. There's an overabundance of food and family at both of them. At a family reunion, however, there's usually not a dead body, and there's virtually none of the relief from the icky family members, immediate and extended, that's provided by friends and comparative strangers at a funeral. All in all a funeral is much to be preferred over a family reunion, even if somebody *does* have to die for it. Most people I know would actually volunteer as designated dead guy at the funeral before they'd willingly attend a family reunion. Face it, at a family reunion there will hardly be a soul you can stand to be around for five minutes, and hordes of people you've dedicated your life to getting away from, all vying for your share of the coconut cake.

The only redeeming feature of a family reunion is the food itself.

The Queens have come up with what we think is the best idea we ever heard in our entire lives. We're going to start having regular *familyless* reunions, complete with all our favorite foods, blankets on the ground, music, and games. And we're not going to invite a single soul from any of our families. We've entertained ourselves for several days just planning what-all food we'll absolutely have to have at the Familyless Reunion. Here's a fair summation of the A-list.

Fried chicken is mandatory, and it must be the skins-on variety. I can make excellent skinless fried chicken by marinating it in buttermilk for a few hours before flouring and frying it, but truly nothing on earth can compare to fried chicken skin. It's the very best part of the chicken, and we all know it. As a general rule, we're willing to give it up in day-to-day life, but this is, after all, a special occasion, and so we must insist on skin. BoPeep is truly the child of my heart and appetite. From the time that she had a tooth in her head, this little angel knew instinctively that the skin was the best part. I'd really hoped she'd have some inexplicable aversion to it; I pondered how much more chicken skin I could enjoy if my child didn't want hers. But this was not to be. If I were to leave a plate of fried chicken with skin sitting unattended for a nanosecond, I'd return to find a full platter of naked chicken. 'Peep would've picked all the skin off and sucked it down her greedy little gullet.

Deviled eggs—we can't have a Familyless Reunion without them. Someone else will definitely have to make them; they're a world-class pain to prepare. We've got to have the fried stuff—green tomatoes, okra, squash. It's all rolled in cornmeal before it's fried, so it's trouble, too, but so well worth it. One redeeming feature of cooking with okra is that when you cut the ends off the pods, you can stick them on your forehead and they will stay there all day, if you like. You can run down the street, and those okra tips will be sticking right there on your forehead. I once stuck them all over my face, including the tip of my nose, and wore them proudly while I cooked dinner for my guests. Of course, then everybody wanted some on their faces, too. I have a photo somewhere of this room full of people with okra stems on their foreheads—an intelligent bunch.

Foods that also made the A-list for the Familyless Reunion: chocolate pie, banana pudding, coconut cake, hot biscuits, corn on the cob, fresh lima beans, fresh lady peas, that awful green bean casserole with the onion rings on top that somebody always brings and we always eat it even though it's lethal, ribs, cornbread, Louisiana strawberries and homemade shortcake, blackberry cobbler, potato salad, sliced-right-off-the-vine tomatoes, homemade mayonnaise, and oceans of sweet iced tea.

What to Eat Before and After an Assignation

Well, "before" is a no-brainer; you can't eat a damn thing. If you do, your stomach will pooch out like you're twelve months pregnant, and it will ruin the lines of your trashy lingerie. And this is truly tragic. I don't think there's been any lingerie ever designed that will camouflage an engorged belly. A smock is all I can think of that would successfully conceal that you have eaten Chicago. Damn hard to look sexy in a smock. (If you've ever actually been pregnant, you can attest to this.)

You can get flat on your back as soon as possible—that helps. Your stomach always looks better if you're flat on your back. Of course, if it's so early in a relationship that reclining hasn't been considered, then this might appear unseemly. Location can also be a problem. I've found there are hardly any good places to lie down at the movies. Some bars are wisely addressing this situation and providing full-length sofas for overstuffed patrons. Encourage such attention to customer service by frequenting these establishments often.

Of course, as long as you're fully clothed, you can hide a lot—even if you just sit with your purse in your lap. If your companion becomes unexpectedly amorous soon after a large meal, stall him. Delay any activity that would necessitate the removal of any of your clothing until digestion has been completed. If you know in advance that this is to be his lucky night, then by all means postpone dinner.

After the fact anything is the limit. You can eat as much as you want of whatever you want. Even if he's still around, postfrolic, you can put on a big garment and look cute while you clean out the refrigerator with your own face. The very best eating, however, is to be enjoyed solo. Send him home, lock all the doors, pile up in the bed with a black-and-white movie, and have yourself a private smorgasbord. Two syllables: Hea-ven.

Queenly Entertainment

ROAD TRIPS AND THE
WFW LUNCHEON CLUB

The Queens are always searching for new entertainment, and so it was inevitable that sooner or later we'd venture to one of Mississippi's many casinos. Last time I checked, I think we had more casinos than gas stations or, as the indigenous folk would say, "fillin' stations." So far, in our esteemed opinion, the only one worth going to is the Silver Star in Philadelphia, Mississippi, on the Choctaw Indian reservation, and it's pretty fine. They have a world-class spa and a fabulous golf course that people, golfing types, fly in from everywhere to play. The very notion of all this is hilarious and ironic to anyone who has ever been to Philadelphia, Mississippi, pre-casino. You can drive through Neshoba County for miles, and you'll see nothing but red dirt, red dirt, red dirt—BIG CASINO—red dirt, red dirt, red dirt. Smack dab in the very epicenter of nowhere is the stunning hotel with golf course, spa, and casino.

But unfortunately we were late in discovering the Silver Star, and our first journey into the cosmos of Mississippi gambling was a jarring experience. There aren't any casinos in Jackson, where we live, because of some twisty-windy law that says that we can have gambling only if it's on a boat floating in a moving body of water or on an Indian reservation. At any rate I complained one evening that I was probably the only person on the planet who had not been to one of our state's casinos, and so one of the Queens, Tammy, and I struck out for Vicksburg. Tammy had previously been to casinos on the Gulf Coast, but she'd never tried Vicksburg's. I don't know what her expectations were for the evening. The only casinos I myself had ever been in were onboard big cruise ships, so my hopes were high. I expected that everyone would be beautifully dressed and well mannered, sun-kissed and sophisticated. It certainly never occurred to me to question whether our fellow patrons would have teeth.

I now realize that I have always taken teeth for granted in my everyday life. Most everyone I encounter in my appointed rounds has a full set of them. So accustomed have I become to people having teeth, and plenty of them, it comes as a shock to me whenever I find myself in the presence of an individual over the age of eight who is without them. I am taken aback somewhat by the sight of a snaggle-toothed adult.

The crowds parted wherever we walked, as if we were visiting royalty or movie stars. There must have been a large, perhaps national, convention in town, of men with no chins and women with fat arms. Our dress also set us apart from the misbegotten throng. As I recall, we had on skirts and blouses and stockings and shoes—things like that. You know, no ball gowns or anything, but like you would dress for some special event—such as being seen in public. We didn't wear skintight jeans wedged fetchingly up our butts or T-shirts with legends like "A Little Poontang Never Hurt Anybody." We didn't rat our hair up anywhere near enough for this crowd, and our makeup was on the tasteful side. We weren't even once tempted to spit on the floor. Our conversation was subdued, audible only to each other, and it was not punctuated by boisterous high-fives.

We did see three men of the type that I personally judge "normal." They were dressed in slacks and sports shirts, with room to breathe in both. They looked as peculiar there as Tammy and I did. The other 35,000 males there that evening were dressed in one of two prevailing shirt styles: (1) the nasty tank top, cut low enough on all sides to reveal an overabundance of body (especially back) hair, and stretched over the mandatory beer gut so tightly, they looked like huge hairy sacks of flour, and (2) the cowboy-stud shirt, a western shirt that belonged to one's little brother—so small that only the bottom two snaps can be fastened, and the hairy beer gut protrudes from the gaps. We likewise took note of the waitresses' outfits. It's been at least two decades since I've seen women dressed in such mortifying attire in the workplace. These waitresses have brought back the short-skirt-with-petticoats-so-you-can-see-their-ruffled-panties look, with the low-cut bodices that thrust their breasts out into the middle of the room.

We went to the buffet and thoroughly enjoyed it, I must say. Like all true Southerners, we consider fat a delicacy. We weren't disappointed. I can safely say I've never had a better meal at any pancake house in the country, and it was all-you-can-eat to boot. We didn't gamble. Not one thin dime. We were much too intimidated by the sweaty masses. We didn't try another Vicksburg casino since my friend Fran had recommended this one as having the best people. All I can say is, if those are the "best" ones, I can't imagine the lesser ones. If I can't have James Bond in Monte Carlo in a white dinner jacket, I'd just as soon be playing bingo at the church.

Out of Pocket

The Queens do love a road trip. Even if it's just for the day, our favorite thing is to be Out of Pocket. As soon as we get in a vehicle of any kind, headed anywhere, as long as the adventure pertains in any way to foolishness, we're Out of Pocket. As the doors shut behind each new addition to the passenger list, we exchange wicked looks and declare in chorus, "We're officially Out of Pocket!" And off we go.

Our most memorable trip ever was a trip to Graceland. One of the Queens, Tammy, had a guy friend who was coming to visit her, and for some reason he needed to be picked up in Memphis. So what we did, as if it made perfect sense, was to rent a big old tour bus. A real one, like the ones rock stars use on the road. We rented it for the day and went to Memphis in it. Two of the Tammys on the trip were in the Junior League. (I wouldn't have believed it myself; but they did emerge from the experience unscathed.) As it happened, the very day that we had chosen was also the day of some important event at the Junior League house, and as past presidents, they were expected to attend. One Tammy had declined weeks before, but the other Tammy had neglected to do so, and so she called the Junior League headquarters from the bus. Now, we had Delbert McClinton wailing on the stereo, the Tammys were all bouncing around dancing and squealing in that endearing girlish fashion for which we are famous, the bus itself was making a fair amount of noise, and Tammy, she just called them up and in a perfectly calm tone said, "I am so sorry I won't be able to be there today after all. A number of things have come up, and I'm out of pocket." At which we all fell on the floor, whooping and gasping for breath. And this was the genesis of "Out of Pocket" to designate both our destination and our mode of travel.

We were on our way to Memphis on the bus. Tammy had told her friend just to go to Graceland and wait for his ride. "You'll be picked up" is all she had said. All the way to Memphis, we tried on trashy lingerie. Everybody brought every article of pretty dritties she owned, and we tried them all on in every possible combination, selecting just the right thing to wear to Graceland. Even though Elvis would not actually be there, we wanted to dress appropriately. We decided that Tammy's high heels weren't high enough, and so when we got to Memphis a little early, we went in search of spikes for her. We happened to be in a neighborhood of Memphis that was filled with pawnshops. The sight of all those pawnshops got Tammy to thinking about handcuffs—the Queens love handcuffs—and soon everybody was clamoring for handcuffs. We stopped at a number of pawnshops and went in, wearing our carefully selected outfits under our fur coats. Nobody had handcuffs. All they had was some of the very biggest gold chains we'd ever seen. I don't think those chains exist anywhere outside of pawnshops—pawnshops in Memphis, for that matter. None of us has ever seen their likes anywhere before or since. Handcuffless, we continued the search for trashy shoes for Tammy. You just can't wear a sensible midheel with a black lace teddy. It contradicts the whole look. We finally found what we wanted. Then on to Graceland.

As we pulled into the parking lot of the souvenir mall across the street from Graceland, we sighted Tammy's guy, standing on the corner with his suitcase, watching the cars whiz by. He never so much as glanced at our bus, so totally unsuspecting was he that it was ours. We rumbled into the parking lot and debarked. As we strode across the parking lot with our high heels clicking on the pavement, we shrugged off our fur coats—despite the frosty wind—to reveal our outfits: black heels, black tights, and black lace teddies. We looked like we had escaped from a Robert Palmer "Addicted to Love" recording session. Tammy's fellow followed the gaze of the quickly accumulating crowd in the parking lot, and his little face just lit right up when he saw us. He seemed genuinely glad to see us. I guess the reasons were obvious: partly because he was freezing and sick of standing on the corner waiting for a ride, and partly because here was a whole big gang of women from Mississippi in black lace underwear walking across the parking lot with half of Memphis slamming on brakes to gawk at them—and they were there to meet him. I believe he walked a little taller that day.

Searching for the Wildest F~ ~ in the World

One of the Queens, Tammy, I believe it was, worked for a number of years with a very quiet little woman named Sandy. Now, our Tammy was always quite forthcoming with all the details of her dating life, but Sandy never said a word about her own. To the contrary, Sandy never admitted to even having dates. If Sandy had been named Goody, her last name would have been FourShoes—she was plainly that pure. Well, she was quiet anyway. So time passed, and Sandy moved away. But by and by, as circumstance would have it, a bunch of us happened to be having cocktails one evening in Jackson with a guy-friend of ours who's a well-known blabbermouth. This is one of his more endearing qualities. In the course of the conversations, which naturally included extensive discussion on the behavior of others, Sandy's name came up. Someone brought her name up as an example of a really boring person to go out with, should anyone be in the market for such. With this, the blabbermouth almost spewed beer out his nose, so anxious was he to blab what-all he knew. He said something like *"au contraire"*—he may have even used those exact words—he's that type.

At any rate he indicated that we clearly did not know jackshit about our friend Sandy. He said that he talked to this guy, Jack, who told him he had taken Sandy out for three whole months and never got the time of day from her. At this point we're all going, Yeah, that's the Sandy we know. "But *then*," he said, his tone dripping with portents of things to come. We were breathless, waiting. He toyed with us for as long as he thought it safe, and then he went on. Jack had reported to him that after the three months of dating, he somehow "cornered her one night." Now, we were real curious as to what that meant. Anyway, he cornered her one night, and in Jack's words, "She was the wildest f—— in the *world!*"

And that was all the blabbermouth said. He then just sat there, looking pleased with himself, like he had just performed something significant for the universe, and we just sat there looking back at him, waiting, obviously, for the rest of the story. He kept on sitting there, grinning. Finally, we demanded him to tell us the rest of it. He confessed that was all he knew. Jack said she was the wildest f—— in the world, and that was that. We were incredulous. "That's it?" we protested. "A guy tells you that some woman, whom you happen to know, is the wildest f—— in the world and then clams up, and you let him get away with it?" Surely he didn't expect us to believe that he hadn't immediately demanded to know details. Apparently that was precisely what he wanted us to believe. He swore up and down that when he heard the words, he was so completely blown away that he was at a loss for words; then Jack left.

So now here we all were—ravaged with curiosity about what specifically it was that Sandy did that prompted Jack, who was quite the hound, to rank her as the number-one wildest in the world. We were beating the blabbermouth about the head and shoulders with our purses and proclaiming him to be the most worthless piece of crap we had ever encountered in this life and insisted that he get up and go call Jack right then and get all the info we needed. "Jack doesn't live here anymore" was all we got for our trouble, and the blabbermouth got big welts all over from us whacking on him. No more than he deserved.

And so the Queens had a new mission in life: to be the Wildest F—— in the World (the WFW). But first we needed some outside assistance. We decided to hold focus groups—get a few luncheon speakers, as it were. We would call up a guy we knew who we thought had some sense, and we'd ask him to meet us for lunch. He, of course, would eagerly accept. When he arrived, he would find himself the only man at the table. This would initially please him, I think, and then we would notice just a trace of uneasiness creeping in. Good. (We read an Italian proverb once that said, and we believe it is true, "The fear of women is the basis of good health." We like that.) We'd sit close up to him and smile and pat a lot, and he'd start getting squirmy. Then we'd tell him, "You are our luncheon speaker." After his blank look we would explain that we wanted him to speak to our little group of Queens about something of keen interest to us, and he'd ask what was that, and we'd reveal his topic. "We want you to talk—

in great detail—about what, in your considered opinion, we—hypo-thetically speaking—would have to do in order to qualify as the Wildest F—— in the World."

His eyes would be rolling back in his head; I swear, delirium just comes on quick, doesn't it? We'd persist, "Is it clothes? Trashy lingerie? Props? Games? Talking dirty? Does it involve food?" He'd look word-lessly from face to face and make some muffled Porky Pig sounds, but we would not relent. Sooner or later, we'd wear him down and he'd give us some little shred of usable information.

The best tip we got was from our best buddy, Bob, who is this big blond bear of a guy who is more fun than just about anybody. What Bob told us was this: "You worry too much about how you look, what you wear, and it has nothing to do with any of that." He said that it didn't even matter that our bodies weren't perfect, although he was quick to say he was quite certain that our own personal bodies *were* perfect. He said all that mattered—*all* that mattered—was enthusi-asm. Enthusiasm! Well, in that case, we should be shoo-ins. We're nothing if not enthusiastic. We pressed him further. We wanted to be absolutely certain that if there was something to be done, we were doing it. He insisted that unbridled enthusiasm was our ticket to star-dom. We took him at his word, and that was the last meeting of the WFW Luncheon Club.

So You Declare Yourself a Queen

Now What?

Well, let me just tell you what life has been like for me since I became a Sweet Potato Queen. Some days I do not do jackshit. Now, before you scoff, let me tell you that not doing jackshit is not the simple act of sloth that it may appear to the uninitiated. On the contrary, not doing jackshit is, for some blighted individuals, next to impossible. They seem compelled, as if by some invisible force, to engage themselves in constant busy-ness. On vacations they must see everything in Europe in eight days. At home they're always running endless errands. At work they are always *working*. There's no end to it, and I do not, for the life of me, see how they can bear their lives.

Some years ago my sister, Judy, and I discovered our innate ability to not do jackshit. It was during our fifth trip to Cozumel that particular year that we noticed a pattern. Some guy in the airport in New Orleans struck up a conversation with us and was very curious as to why we would be going to Cozumel, or anywhere else, five times in one year.

"Do you snorkel?"

"No."

"Sightsee?"

"Certainly not."

"Parasail?"

"Do we look like we parasail?" (We're large women.)

"Do you dive?"

"No, but we like the look of all the macho housewives who hang around town in their diving shoes and wet suits with knives strapped to their legs, and we're considering getting our own leg-knives."

He pressed on: "Well, what *do* you do?"

In unison we responded, "We don't do jackshit! As a matter of fact," we said, "we're gonna start not doing jackshit as soon as we get on this plane, and furthermore, we can probably teach you to not do jackshit, too, and it will immeasurably enhance the remainder of your life."

And so we did, and he left us a much happier man for the whole thing.

Here's what a typical day of not doing jackshit back at home looks like: I rise early to greet the dawn, smell the honeysuckle as the sun first warms it, hear the mockingbird's earliest song, and begin not doing jackshit. I cause massive breakfasts to be prepared and shared. Calais—rice cakes like deep-fried bread pudding with pecans—blueberry muffins with lemon curd, cheese grits, regular grits with New Orleans grillades, waffles, and, of course, bacon—lots and lots of bacon. I think there's an unwritten law that should be written: You can never have too much bacon. And fresh-squoze orange juice by the bucket. (You say *squeezed* if you want to, my orange juice will be *squoze*.)

After breakfast it's necessary to lounge for a bit, waiting for the sun to get hot enough to bask myself. And I bask away—to Hell with the naysayers. Then it's time for cool, refreshing—possibly rum—drinks. Lying alternately in the sun and shade, I read novels that contain lots of descriptions of clothing and food. (Don't you just love to know what everybody was wearing and what-all they had to eat? I know I do.) Sometime along in here a light lunch will appear.

The gentlest of breezes blows across my terrace, making a nap in the shade irresistible. Then I drift awake to watch the trained yellow butterflies flitting about the backyard. When my sister, Judy, seeks a small diversion from not doing jackshit, she trains butterflies. Her tribulations with her first husband, the unsavory Ole Shep, sort of tired her out for dealing with people and dogs. So she trained a covey of yellow butterflies for my backyard. You've got to hand it to butterflies—they're damn quiet.

Sometimes, late in the afternoon, when the air would be unbearably heavy were it not for the breeze, there's music. A gospel choir might sing softly—or real loud, depending on my mood. Or maybe Etta James will drop by. Or Van Morrison. Or Aaron Neville. If I'm feeling sporty, Eric Clapton and Delbert McClinton might happen in, and if they do, they'll not be allowed to leave. Friends may come over to shoot dart guns at a beauty pageant on TV, and we'll eat Chocolate Stuff and fried chicken drummettes and drink margaritas.

Much later I take a big bath. Baths are real slo-o-o-ow around here. There's just no telling how long I might soak in that tub, but sooner or later I amble on off to bed, where I lie in the dark, listening to the sound of the breeze in the live oaks, high on the scent of the gardenias blooming outside my window, and wait for the moon to rise. Now, if you got a better idea of how to spend your days, I'd sure like to hear about it.

"Do what you will wish you had done when you are old." Everybody's heard this sage advice. Since I first heard it when I was still quite young myself, there aren't just a whole lot of things that I flat-out *haven't* done. Pretty much everything that came up required a choice, and I knew right off the bat, with very little pondering, what I would wish I had done. I'd wish I had done it all, and therefore I did it.

It goes beyond just the doing or not doing, though. If you decide in favor of doing and it turns out to be good, do a lot of it. You never know how short the supply might be. Some things in life are just so sweet—and sweet is really not strong enough—I mean, so soothing and delicious that sometimes the memory of them is all you need to get by. You can just close your eyes and put yourself there in an instant. Your mouth waters, your eyes tear up, your heart beats fast, and it's hard to catch your breath.

Kissing Bill French was one of those sweet things in my life. Bill French—and we always called him by both names, never just Bill—was, in my considered opinion, the Best Kisser in the History of the Entire World, living or dead. He just had a magic mouth. I could die happy right this minute if I could die kissing Bill French. We were never even boyfriend and girlfriend or anything like that, just good buddies. But somehow, for some reason, he kissed me one night. I knew he was *fixing* to; you can always tell, you know. I had my spiel all ready about us being just friends and all. But I let him kiss me that one time. And it just about melted the fillings in my teeth. I was like a dog eating peanut butter; I just couldn't qui-I-I-ite get through kissing him.

Anyway, kissing Bill French was one of those incredibly sweet things that, when times are really bad, I could just think about and feel better. I'd say to myself, "You know, if I wanted to, I could just get in my car and drive to Birmingham and kiss Bill French and feel a whole lot better." No matter that it wasn't actually feasible, that both of us were married to somebody else, that we'd had no contact in years, that I wouldn't even really know how to find him. It was just something I held out to myself. And I always felt like sometime maybe, sooner or later, our paths would cross again, and I could get me one or two of his kisses and no harm done.

And then one day on an impulse I called a mutual friend, Peter Binder, in Birmingham, and we were yakking away about old times and I mentioned Bill French. Peter was suddenly silent. Well, come to find out, Bill French had been killed in a plane crash a year or so before, and nobody knew how to call me. It hit me like an avalanche. I grieved and grieved over it. To find out that not only was he gone, he had *been* gone—just undid me. I will never again in this life kiss Bill French, and it makes it a little bit harder to go on.

And then they told me that Charlie Jacobs was dead. Charlie was a musician in a band called the Tangents that was popular all over the South in the 1980s. I couldn't go to the funeral. Call me a wuss. I swear I did it out of kindness to everybody else who would be there. I knew I'd be rolling around wailing if I went, so I didn't go. I did, however, find an old tape I had of the Tangents playing live at the George Street Grocery, a great old pub in Jackson. I put that tape on, and Charlie was singing "Love and Pain." I lay down on the floor between the speakers and closed my eyes. I was *there*. I could see him. Watching Charlie Jacobs perform was as good as hearing him, which is saying a lot. He didn't *play* the music; he *was* the music. The harp and the sax and that raspy, sexy voice of his—that's just how the music got *out* of him. His body contorted, face twisting, grimacing, grinning, eyes rolled up, fluttering, or squeezed shut tight, oceans of sweat streaming down his body, shining in the spotlight. And the music just carrying him—and me—away. I'd dance to every note he played, sweating every bit as much. I could not resist it.

I can listen to that tape, and as much as my heart sings with the sweetness of the memories, the knowledge that he's gone makes me feel like my whole body has turned to liquid and it's coming out my eyes—melting, melting. When it's over, I'll just be a pile of old clothes on the floor, like the Wicked Witch in Oz.

Here's the deal, though: One day, one day I'll get to Heaven, and when I do, the first thing I'm going to do is drink a cold one with my daddy and pet my old dog Randy, and then I'll get Charlie to play and sing, and I'm gonna dance till I drop. And in between sets, and on all the slow songs, I'm gonna kiss Bill French. Then I'll know for *sure* I'm in Heaven.

Some guy-type buddies of my youth lived for a time in a veritable garden spot that they lovingly, if misguidedly, referred to as The Ranch. If you've ever been to the South and taken a drive down a country road, you'd have spied out in the middle of a field an old abandoned shack. If you were somewhere in the western part of Hinds County, Mississippi, you may have seen the actual ranch. It was an absolute hovel. I have no idea if they even paid rent; there's an excellent chance they were merely squatting. However, back in the mid-1970s, it suited them just fine. They held huge wild parties, thinking themselves to be invisible out there in Podunk, as it were. I guess they didn't believe anybody would think it curious that there were a couple hundred cars parked around this shack in the middle of nowhere.

Anyway, a stranger came to their door one day. He was singularly unattractive—very little hair covering his hideous, sore-wracked skin, just generally ratty and nasty looking. But as is often said of the un-beautiful of the world, he had a great personality. He came to be known as "Funkdog," because he was, in fact, a dog, and he was really funky. He came around regularly, and the boys would feed him and talk to him, but no one could quite bring themselves to actually touch him. And so they started this thing of petting Funkdog with a small stick. He would come and sit at a respectful distance, I guess knowing himself to be unclean, and eagerly await being petted and scratched with his stick. That image always just made me want to bawl, and now I think I know why.

I think Funkdog being petted with his stick is a perfect metaphor for what can happen to any of us in this life if we don't pay attention. In any area of our lives, things can go from great, to not so hot, to downright unspeakable, and do it so gradually that we keep down-shifting our expectations to correspond with our current situation. We settle for less and less and tell ourselves "It's not so bad" until finally one day we wake up and we are, in effect, hairless and scabby, just hoping to get petted with a stick for a little while. You can forget what it used to feel like to feel good about life; feeling rotten—or just a low-grade funk—seems normal and therefore acceptable. I just don't believe that God intended for any of his creatures to be petted with sticks. If some area of your life sucks—do something else. Life is too short—and too long—to spend it being miserable. Life may indeed be short, but it is, for a fact, wide. It is high time we started settling for more.

The truth is that real life sometimes doesn't turn out to be exactly what we'd planned or dreamed. This disparity occurs with alarming frequency. But hey, you've got to do whatever's necessary to live, to take care of yourself and your kids. There are some pretty awful jobs out there, and real people are having to do them every day. My friend Scott told me about meeting a lovely young woman who worked, I swear to you, as a full-time chicken plucker. The girl stands by a conveyor belt and pulls the feathers off chickens all day long. He said to her, with intense emotion, "I can't imagine that. You must have *the* most boring job in the whole world." And do you know, she lit up like a lightning bug and responded seriously, "Oh, no. You get a brand-new chicken every thirty seconds!"

She has what is undoubtedly the most overdeveloped sense of optimism—or she is the most joyfully creative soul there ever was. If a chicken plucker is truly fulfilled in her work, I certainly applaud that. If, however, she has merely settled for less and is dissatisfied—if anyone is spending life toiling away at work you despise—I'd have to say authoritatively that God doesn't make chicken pluckers; people make chicken pluckers, and if you don't want to be one, then by God, don't.

But maybe your job isn't all that terrible. Your marriage is not really hideous; it's just sort of *beige*. Flat, dull, lifeless—these are not good adjectives when they refer to your hair; they are infinitely worse if they apply to your life. If you are stuck, sweating, on a sandbar in the river of your life, you've got to find a way back into those swift, effervescent currents of joy that are your birthright.

If you need to feel sexy, buy yourself a pair of high-heeled shoes or some trashy lingerie. If you need to laugh, I recommend that you order yourself a pair of fake teeth, as I did, called Dr. Bukk's Teef. They fit over your own teeth like a mouthpiece used in contact sports. They look utterly real, and they're the worst-looking things you ever saw in your life, unless you go to the Waffle House a lot. There are many styles to choose from, and I have two of them: Summer Teef—some 'r' here, some 'r' not—and Sole Survivor, featuring a single snaggly-looking tooth somewhat off center, bearing a gold crown with a heart carved in it. I just love the way that flash of gold catches the light. You can't fully imagine, without having seen them, the dramatic effect these teef have on one's appearance. And on one's disposition. I'm wearing mine right this minute, and every once in a while, I glance in the mirror and grin. Perks me up no end.

(If you want some, and I know you do, you can call Dr. Bukk right up on her toll-free number, which is 1-800-925-BUKK [2855], and you can have your teef by the very next day. When you receive them, you're officially a member of the Bukk Fambly, and as such you'll need a new name to go with your new identity. Choose one and send it in, and you'll receive the Bukk Fambly newsletter on a somewhat irregular basis. My Bukk Fambly name is "Gemi Moore." And when you order your teef, you be sure and tell them I sent you.)

You can wear your Bukk teef and your high heels and trashy lingerie to the grocery store if you want to, or you can just prance around in them at home and enjoy being a goose all by yourself. Or you can just not do jackshit. Sometimes that's enough. You don't have to move or change jobs or leave your husband or unnaturally alter your state of consciousness. We're not after an altered state; we're after our True State—unbridled joy. The adventurer Norman Vaughan, who's completed a dozen or so of those punishing dogsled races called Iditarods and, in his nineties, is still doing them, said, "The only death you die is the one you die every day by not living." And George Eliot wrote, "It is never too late to be what you might have been."

We thought all that is some mighty fine advice, and we turned out to be Sweet Potato Queens. It's working for us. I think you should give it a try.

Not ready to part with the Queens yet? Y'all come see us at our Web site,

www.sweetpotatoqueens.com
and bring your mommer 'n 'em.

Acknowledgments

There are a great many people to whom I'm deeply and proudly indebted. If I start naming at Crown Publishing, the list will be longer than the book—these folks have been so good to me. Of course, I'm fully aware that they all want to be Queens or to receive the Promise, but they've been nice nonetheless, and I appreciate it. Teresa Nicholas, Sue Carswell, and Rachel Kahan have exhibited extraordinary enthusiasm for the Sweet Potato Queens and this book from the very beginning, and I feel confident in promising them a fair shot at being Wannabes in the foreseeable future as a reward for their hard work and steadfast loyalty. Steve Wallace and Brian Belfiglio are definitely in the running for Consort. Everyone at Crown has a standing invitation to the parade, and on behalf of all the Queens, I promise you'll have a Big Time.

JoAnne Prichard, my editor, and her husband, Willie Morris, have gone so far out of their way to help me, it wears me out even to think about what-all I'll likely have to do to pay them back. Suffice it to say it will involve unseemly amounts of biscuits and fried chicken (with skin).

Acknowledgments

Malcolm White—what can I say? If there had been no Mal's St. Paddy's Day parade or *Diddy Wah Diddy*, I guess I'd have just joined the Junior League, and then where would we be?

Johnny Evans at Lemuria Bookstore and Roy Blount, Jr., have been so encouraging to me, I guess they'll have to go on the list for biscuits and chicken, too.

Not everyone has the good fortune that I had of being born into a whole family of funny people. My sister, Judy, is funnier than I am. My mother, bless her, has never had a boring day. The leader of the bunch was, of course, my daddy, who taught us the invaluable lesson of Simultaneous Reverence and Irreverence. Either without the other can be deadly.

All the Sweet Potato Queens, past and present, have my undying love and loyalty. As you read this list, please imagine the strains of the "Twentieth Century–Fox Fanfare"—it's only fitting:

Mona Britt Shumake
Cheri Anglin
Vivian Pigott White
Cynthia Hewes Speetjens
Lyla Gibson Elliot
Marsha McInturff

Carol Puckett Daily
Annie Laurie McRee
Annelle Primos Barnett
Elizabeth (Pippa) Perry Jackson
Donna Kennedy Sones
Sylvia Stewart

God Save

the

Sweet Potato Queens

It is with my deepest, heartfelt gratitude

that I dedicate this book to

JoANNE PRICHARD MORRIS,

gentlest of editors, dearest of friends, for her faith,

her vision, her guidance, her love, and to the precious

memory of her most beloved husband,

WILLIE MORRIS,

the best friend a fledgling writer could ever hope for, the

most unbelievably generous, uncommonly sweet man—

a gift, a blessing to my life.

CONTENTS

Contents

1

God Save the Queens!

I t is a warm, sunny day in the South—only March 18 in the year 2000, but already the azaleas have gone wild. At approximately one-thirty P.M. we are a half hour into the eighteenth annual Mal's St. Paddy's Parade in Jackson, Mississippi. The streets are thronged! Tens of thousands of people, all with a single mission: to see us, the Sweet Potato Queens! Nowhere is the crowd thicker or more urgent than in front of the Governor's Mansion (now again inhabited by a governor we like). Our float pulls even with the Buckethead Judges reviewing stand, directly in front of the Mansion, and stops. Silence. The crowd is hushed and positively quivering with anticipation. Out of giant speakers rolls forth the booming voice of Jackson State University's Dr. Jimmie James, but it sounds like the voice of God.

> Ladies and gentlemen! Fine-tune your sensory apparatus for the acme and pinnacle in the most incredible and exquisite sights and sounds found in any performance anytime and anywhere! For it's the utmost, the most impressionable, the

susceptible, the sentient, and the most acute performing aggregation you have ever witnessed.

Fans, judges, and slavishly adoring subjects—as you observe, this aggregation has reached the new millennium on time! You are witnessing the grace, the agility, the fluidity, the most perfected showmanship and the eccentricity of a most prodigious, immense, and outstanding bevy of buxom beauties that are a technological phenomenon in their own right. These precious, pert paragons of pulchritude have even given new direction to the Internet and the Y2K phenomenon! You are observing the pinnacle in showmanship with an exclusive show designed for only the superior in mind! It is filled with continuity, balance, flexibility, systematic planning, and relevance!

Mal's St. Paddy's Day Parade proudly presents for your ultimate viewing pleasure, the quintessence of contemporary sounds and maneuvers, the summa cum laude of womankind, Jackson's own titillating assets—the incomparable Sweet Potato Queens!

The crowd, including the Buckethead Judges and the mob on the mansion lawn, has gone completely mad. With the 20th Century-Fox fanfare blaring, the door to our float is slowly opened by our consort and love slave, Lance Romance, and out we come. Just when the fans think they are about to ascend directly unto heaven, Aretha comes over the mega-sound system—"R-E-S-P-E-C-T"—and our gyrations and pelvic thrusts push them over the brink into a frothing frenzy. We immediately blast into one of our hallmark performances, the song that asks the big question: "Who wrote the Book of Love?" To which everybody here knows the answer—WE DID!

Then we do something never before witnessed in the entire history of the parade: We get off the float. Our little boots touching the actual ground, we prance ourselves back through the lineup—past our children, the Tater Tots; past our mothers, the Queen Mothers and Used-to-Bes; past our best friends in the whole world, who we love more than life, but not quite enough to make them actual Queens, the Wannabes; all the way back to the newest stars in our ever-growing entourage, the Wannabe Wannabes, hundreds and hundreds of luscious ladies from all across the land, who flew, drove, hitchhiked, and chartered buses to Jackson, Mississippi. And Jackson has never been more proud.

Ever since the publication of *The Sweet Potato Queens' Book of Love*, we have been inundated with cards, letters, gifts, e-mails, and all manner of other beseechments from people all over this country and beyond, who believed that their continued survival might—but any hope for happiness did certainly—hinge on the possibility that they, too, might be able to partake of the Queenly life. The very first such plea came from a most surprising source. Kaye Gibbons, the widely known, much-lauded—and deservedly so—real writer sent to Johnny Evans, owner of one of the best bookstores in the entire world, Lemuria in Jackson, a handwritten fax marked, "URGENTO!" She had tried unsuccessfully to reach me personally and in desperation just fired off a fax to Johnny in hopes that he could locate me quickly to relay her frantic message, which, in the most plaintive tones, said, "I want her to make me a Sweet Potato Queen. My life used to re-volve around mounds of oyster stuffing at Thanksgiving. Now, having learned the true art of queenly living, my world is a vision of myself with big hair, waving, smiling, on the back of a convertible. . . . If I am not a Queen, I'll cut my throat." Her missive was only the tip of what is proving to be a very large iceberg indeed.

I began receiving what amounted to applications and résumés from supplicants. Ann from Baton Rouge, Louisiana, sent her list of credentials: "dropped out of a sorority before I ever got pledged, love to dance though rather spastic at it, fall into the category of 'those of us who have about four hairs on our head' so I would love to wear a big-hair wig, could perfect the queenly wave within a matter of hours if motivated and well-trained, can get over any trace of self-con-sciousness (necessary for the pelvic thrusting and other suggestive gy-rations) with just a small amount of alcohol, have a select group of truly succulent women friends whom I could mobilize into an SPQ chapter within a matter of moments, recently gave up a career as a lawyer (to be a realtor), because it allows me to sleep later and rarely requires panty hose, and have survived two failed marriages in the last nine years, proving great resilience (and now that I know about the Five Men I Need in My Life at All Times, feel quite prepared to shop for husband number three)."

The Million Queen March

The Wannabe Wannabes are women—and men—who had written to me after reading SPQBOL. I answer all e-mails, and when I wrote these wonderful folks back, I invited them to come to the parade in Jackson in March. More and more and more of them started writing back that they were indeed coming, so many of them, in fact, that we started calling it the Million Queen March. They came and they came and they came. They filled up hotels, they filled up restaurants—especially Hal and Mal's—for days. Jim Dollarhide, the official cinematographer to the Sweet Potato Queens, spent several days at the Edison Walthall Hotel in downtown Jackson, just riding the elevator up and down, interviewing and filming Wannabe Wannabes. (The video is available on our Web site—www.sweetpotatoqueens.com.)

We had a big party for them all at Hal and Mal's on Friday night before the parade. Saying we were unprepared for the numbers is, well—what would you do if you turned on the bathtub faucet and Niagara Falls spewed forth? They came from near 'bout everywhere—New York, Connecticut, Massachusetts, Maryland, West Virginia, North and South Carolina, Georgia, Alabama, Florida, Tennessee, Texas, Louisiana, Missouri, Arkansas, Colorado, California, North Dakota even. We think this is significant. I mean, it is one thing for someone in North Dakota to find, buy, read, and like a book about a bunch of crazy women in Mississippi—that's pretty special in itself. But for that person then to take time off from work; buy plane tickets, hotel rooms, and food; conceive, design, and manufacture costumes; and convince their friends to do it with them, just to come to Jackson, Mississippi, of all places, in order to dress up funny and walk down the street with a bunch of other crazy women, well, we think this tells us a whole lot about these folks. Namely that they are highly motivated, easily led to the better things in life, and have a disposable income, possibly too much time on their hands, and an unquenchable zest for living. And man alive, were we ever glad to see them! For one thing, it gave us great leverage and credibility here in our hometown: See? It's not just us—there are a lot of other crazy, fun-infected folks out there! And by the way, we have invited them all here, and whaddya know? They all came!

Everyone was invited to come dressed as the Queen of Whatever They Chose and march in the parade. We had the Queens of Crude, the Blue Margarita Queens, several factions of Turnip Green Queens (we feared there might be an altercation, but all went smoothly), the Pink Flamingo Queens, the Florida Navel Orange Queens (they threw oranges and had a motto: Keep Your Navel Queen), the Missouri Ozark Raspberry Queens (picture giant Carmen Miranda-type head-dresses), the Peach Pit Queens, the Ghouly Girls, the Cabbage Queens, the Princesses, the No-Regrets Majorettes, the Honeybee Queens, the Brazen Strumpets, the Menopause Mafia—to name just a few. I know whoever I left out will be pissed off big time, and I apologize right here and now and will find a way to make it up to you next parade, I promise. Sonny Gilmore at Crosshaven Books in Birmingham, Alabama, chartered a bus and brought fifty-three Wannabe Wannabes to march. He said he had such a waiting list, he's already reserved three buses for next year. I call that one brave man. One group from Lakeland, Florida, had T-shirts made that read: "To hang with us—you gotta be a hip-hopping, gum-popping, forever-shopping, margarita-drinking, fun-loving, chocolate-craving, out-a-pocket, road-tripping, promise-making royal pain in the patootie!"

Well, now, that reflects our sentiments eggzackly. Those women who came, and the four jillion e-mails, cards, and letters we've gotten, indicate to us that we have struck a deep, harmonic, universal chord—that, in fact, it isn't just us and there are literally millions of people out there who either are just like us or certainly aspire to be just like us, and they are desperately seeking opportunities and, more important, leadership. This is where I come in. Because, as you know, I am not just *a* Sweet Potato Queen—I am *the* Sweet Potato Queen, Boss of all the Sweet Potato Queens, and as such I have, in my opinion, done very well by my charges: provided excellent leadership and elevated them to an exalted position of power and status, which is, of course, their rightful position in this life, and I do believe with virtually no more effort on my part, I can do the same for all of you. There's nothing to this Queen business really—just do like I tell you and you'll be fine. I promise.

A Fabulous Journey

To a great extent this book presupposes that you have read *The Sweet Potato Queens' Book of Love*. It is not an absolute necessity, but it would help, so go do that now if you haven't already. I am not going to retell all that stuff just to save you twelve bucks.

When we embarked on our careers as Sweet Potato Queens way

back in 1982, we had no idea how far we would take it—or it would take us. As always, we just wanted to have fun, and we used what we had on hand to make it, which, quite often, was just what we happened to have between our ears.

We were all such Cute Girls back then. Cute Girls: redundant. Girls are like puppies—they're all cute. It takes years of hard work, dedication, and skill, however, to become Fabulous Women. And make no mistake about it, we have worked long and hard and damn near constantly, too, to become the Sweet Potato Queens, arguably the most Fabulous Women currently living. *We* would certainly argue that point. My big old dictionary defines *fabulous* this way: "of or like a fable, legendary, hard to believe, incredible, astounding, very good and/or wonderful." Well, that certainly describes us perfectly. We are all that and then some.

My goal will be to show you the Sweet Potato Queens as we have progressed from mere Cute Girl status to our current and ongoing Fabulous Women state so that if you are yourself currently a Cute Girl, you might be spared some time-consuming steps in your own process. If, on the other hand, you are past that stage but don't feel that you are making any real headway in pursuit of Fabulous Womanhood, then this might be just the nudge you've been needing. My sister Judy thinks that some people are too far gone to hope to achieve Fabulous in this life but this just might elevate them to Adequate. A strong believer in redemption, I could not bring myself to agree with her. Suffice it to say that in all of us, there is room for improvement. We offer this book toward that end.

We feel that we can offer lots of advice regarding misspent youth. Having devoted ourselves so utterly to misspending our own personal youths, who is better qualified to teach you how to misspend yours? And fear not, if your youth has already passed without any misspending on your part, we can also teach you to misspend your middle age. That part is even fresher in our minds, since it is what we are doing currently. We like to think of the process as Building an Inventory of Good Stories to Tell in the Nursing Home. With just what we now have on hand, we are assured of being the most popular girls in the home. (Of course, being Southern, we will refer to ourselves as "girls" throughout eternity—we know what we mean.)

Today, whenever we are faced with choosing whether to do something outrageous or something predictable and boring—well, we don't even have to stop and think about it very often anymore. Unless

there is the threat of being sent to the penitentiary and/or losing custody of our children, we pretty much just wade on in up to our necks
in whatever the foolishness du jour happens to be. We think that's
good advice for you as well. Occasionally there may be some other
consequence that is slightly inconvenient or even mildly unpleasant,
but if they're not taking away our kids and putting us in the Big
House, we think it's worth the risk just to avoid being boring, not only
right this minute, but also in the nursing home. You've got to consider
your future. You don't have to do diddly-squat to get older—matter
of fact, you can't even avoid that; but getting smarter—now, that can
be a bitch if you try to go it alone.

One of the Queens, Tammy, used to spend summers at her
beloved aunt Mary's house. Aunt Mary, it seems, had a live parrot in
a cage, and Tammy was mesmerized by this bit of exotica in the Mississippi Delta. She would stand endlessly in front of the bird's cage
until finally, unable to resist the temptation any longer, she would
stick her finger through the wires of the cage, whereupon the bird,
each and every time, would bite her finger, and Tammy would stand
there, each and every time, with her finger in the bird's beak, shrieking, "Aunt Mary! Your bird's biting me again!" To this very day, Tammy
is wont to repeat ill-advised behaviors multiple times, with the same
undesirable results. We have been through this drill with her so often
that now, instead of going into lengthy discussions about what she did
again, and what happened after that *again*, we have a shorthand for
it that saves us all a lot of time. We simply say, "Hmmm. Aunt Mary's
bird is biting you again, I see."

Barbara Williams wrote to me to say that she herself was "older"
and had suffered a broken back somewhere in her travels, but now she
only wears her brace when she wants to sucker people into giving her
extra help with stuff. For instance, it got her bumped up in the line at
the bookstore when she was buying multiple copies of *SPQBOL* to
send to friends (bless her heart), and the salesgirl (emphasis on *girl*:
really young) looked at the title and made some light comment that
she hadn't read it yet but she'd always liked sweet potatoes. Well, our
Barbara just snorted and told the little whatsit to read the book and
find out what a blow job can really do for you, and with that she tot-
tered on out of the store in her back brace, leaving stunned young persons in her wake. I am so proud.

We don't want to be those pitiful old ladies who sit in the corner
nibbling on small bits of paper, never joining in any activities, never

receiving visitors, never sleeping with the male residents. Nosirree, not us, we plan to be exactly like we are right now—only a whole lot older. People will be fighting to get into our nursing home, wanting to come before they're even old enough to be there.

Back when we were mere Cute Girls, we thought a man was the answer to everything. We thought we had to have one, *the* one, Mr. Right, before we could even begin to live. We had to have a date, then we had to have a boyfriend, then we had to have a husband. Nothing would do till we got Mr. Right. Then, for some of us—too many—there came a time of being not so much disillusioned as just really pissed off big time. During this time, we still thought a man was the answer to everything. Only now everything that was *wrong* was because of a man. We thought he was the bringer of all things bad in our lives, and we were so mad about it that perhaps for a time we believed all men were the bringers of *all* things bad.

Now that we are within easy spittin' distance of fifty—or as our friend Ray Lee says, "somewhere between forty and death"—we can see that there's nothing wrong with men in general—even specifically. Most of them are just fine. Really. And while we don't want them to be the sole reason for living (nor us for them), we don't want to run them all off with a stick either. We hope we have learned a few things about choice-making. We'll share some of our hard-learned lessons with you as well as some of our cunning solutions to relationship problems.

Life is in a constant state of flux, that's for sure. One day you're a Cute Girl shyly shopping for your first real plug-in vibrator, and before you know it, your kids are nearly grown, your mother lives with you, and you walk through the kitchen one day and there she sits with your vibrator, working on the crick in her neck.

Life isn't over. Really. You're just gonna have to make a few adjustments. And your criteria for making decisions will change, we hope. For instance, we have in our circle of acquaintance this absolutely precious Cute Girl. Mary Alice is probably all of twenty-three years old and she'd been married a little over a year when we met her. In describing her like-new husband, she used these words: "He is *so fine*." Well, we all just about fell on the floor howling: "He's so fine"? This is a reason to go to the sock-hop with a guy. If he's "so fine," all the other girls will be wild with jealousy. If he's not also so *bad*, even your mother will be tickled because he is "so fine."

I didn't even know people still said "so fine." Back when I was in junior high school, shortly after the earth cooled, we even rhymed it; he would have been "fine as wine." Not that any of us had ever had any wine, fine or otherwise, in order to make such an analogy. If we had, we would have known how terribly many variations and gradations of quality that term would imply. When I was in high school, people were "so fine," no rhyme.

Being "so fine," however, is no reason at all to haul off and marry somebody. Even if it happened to be *us* who were "so fine." Naturally, we *are*, but unless you can see and appreciate some of our other many fine qualities, trust me, you won't be very happy married to us for very long. "So fine" just isn't enough to sustain a relationship through anything past the first date.

We rolled around for about an hour, shrieking about Mary Alice's like-new husband being "so fine." We got off on tangents about our own ex-husbands and ex-boyfriends, about whom all of us might have used the words "so fine" at some early point. "Yeah, he came home last night singing 'Rebel Rebel' at the top of his lungs—again, with some stranger's panties on his head—again, drunker'n even he's ever been—again. Couldn't even get the door open, I heard him scratching around with his key, sounded like a cat trying to cover crap on a marble floor, but I went on down there, and of course I let him in—again—because he's 'so fine'!" "I'm working three jobs now, on account of he's not even working one, but I don't mind, because he's 'so fine'!"

"So fine" just doesn't carry the weight it once did with us, I guess. We can tell the difference between Mr. Right and Mr. Right Now. And this is my point. We think we've learned a thing or two in our sojourn. As usual, we're just gonna lay it all out there and let you be the judge. Are we pushing the edge of the envelope? Wheeee! We hope so; but we know, by God, we are at least getting to the sticky part! It will eventually come down, as it usually does, to the age-old plea of "Lord, help us all!" and, yes, of course,

God Save the Queens!

Aftershocks

Since we did offer *The Sweet Potato Queens' Book of Love* not only as a personal testimony and mission statement about living the Queenly life, but also as a guidebook for our fellow Queens everywhere, we have been absolutely delighted with the quantity and the enthusiasm of your responses. I'd say readers' responses are split evenly among the following subjects: the Redheaded Man, the tiaras, the obituaries, child rearing, and the Promise.

And that brings to mind our discussion of bizarre sexual adventures from *SPQBOL*, notably the one involving the Redheaded Man Who Would Not Move. That story struck a chord with quite a few women across the country. I was in New Orleans at a book signing, and right in the middle of everything, this darling woman came up to me and just blurted out, "Was that guy named James?" I begged her pardon: What guy? "That redheaded guy—the one that wouldn't move!" Before I could tell her that I didn't know his name—that much, at least, had been held in confidence by the Queen who related the tale—she went on, "I swear I bet it's the same guy! I fell for it, too! He still doesn't move!" Now, I have no idea if it's the same guy or not—on the one hand, it seems like an impossible coincidence; on the other hand, if it's not the same guy, it could indicate a trend, which would be disastrous for us all.

In the same vein, I heard from a woman in California whose own personal "Redheaded" experience was with a blond German guy with a real German name like Ludger or Adolf or something. On their third date, he did the thing about "How many partners have you had before me?" and she, without guile, responded, "Oh, a couple dozen, give or take," and nearly died when he said that if a prostitute counted, she herself was number two. She married him anyway and things deteriorated from there. Apparently he was uneducable, and she just got bored blind. "Wham bam danke ma'am" was how she described it. He was stunned, literally stunned, when he discovered her copy of the *Kama Sutra*, asking her, accusingly (as if she had written it herself), "Do you mean there are more than three positions?"

My good friend Bill Fitzhugh, a book writer his ownself, sent me a newspaper clipping from somewhere in Africa where a bunch of pissed-off women had stormed a police station demanding that the cops either make love to them themselves or get up off their butts and shut down the illegal drinking establishments that were rendering their menfolk impotent. The paper said this gang of women literally shut down business in the town for a whole day with their protests against excessive drinking by their husbands and fiancés. The women said the population of the district was falling as a result of the poor sexual performance of the men, and they demanded that the police either have it off with them personally, find them new husbands, or shut down the illegal pubs. It was not reported how the police chose to respond; would that come under community service?

Many of you have experienced the thrill of wearing your tiaras in public. Nothing quite compares in my estimation—it just gives you a lift. A delightfully wise woman in my church, Miss Bettye, was a much-beloved schoolteacher for many years at an inner-city school. One Sunday she told us this story: Once upon a time, Miss Bettye had thick, thick red hair (it's still red but not so thick) and she wore it in a style that was called a "double bubble," and she had a bow pinned in between the two bubble sections. While she was going about her business at school one day, a little girl stopped her and asked, very solemnly, "Miz Bettye, do you know that you have a bow in your hair?"

Yes, of course she knew that. "Well, you sure don't *act* like it," the child replied, still deeply earnest. How, then, *should* one act if one has a bow in one's hair? she was forced to ask. "Oh! You stand a little straighter and hold your head just so, and every now and then you reach back and give it a little pat, because it's *special*. And if somebody put a bow in your hair, it means YOU'RE SPECIAL." Of course, we were all bawling because none of us had had a bow put in our hair in so very long, but, you see, that's the point: putting the bow in our *own* hair and knowing how special we are. A tiara works the same way: You know you're special, and everybody else acknowledges you're special, too, when you wear one. Even carrying a tiara in your take-on bag to the airport gives the security bag inspectors a little thrill. After all, how many tiaras are they even likely to inspect?

Katherine Gilmore, precious girl, scarcely more than a Tater Tot really, wrote that she and three of her buddies had smuggled their tiaras into their college graduation. The other girls got busted pre-ceremony by a woman so un-fun-loving, it is entirely possible she had made a pact with the devil to Cease All Fun on Earth. She didn't even allow them to wear cute shoes under their gowns. I call that harsh. But our intrepid Katherine smuggled her own tiara in under her gown—along with a roll of tape tucked in her panties (which were, of course, pretty)—and as soon as she got her diploma and got back to her seat, she whipped out the tiara and taped it to the top of her mortarboard. All the faculty members, with the notable exception of the party poopette, wanted their picture taken with her after the ceremony. I couldn't be prouder if I'd raised her my ownself.

As happy as it makes me to hear such stories from like-minded women, it is positively thrilling to hear from like-minded men. It tells me there is yet hope for the planet, and I am all for keeping hope alive. I offer this touching story—yet another from the annals of the Only Man We Ever Really Loved:

He has a daughter named Anna and he is a very good (read: doting) daddy to her. He (with significant help from her mother) raised her right—in all regards, but especially where the subject of pageants is concerned. Meaning that, while it is demeaning to have our beauty judged by strangers, as Southern women it is our birthright to be the queen of some food group as long as we don't have to walk down a runway in a swimsuit to get the crown. And so it came to be that Anna was far away in a New England boarding school and found herself in a funk and did what all girls should be able to do: She called her daddy. And he did what all good daddies should do: He fixed it. Fixed it right on up by picking up the phone and calling his buddy the Agriculture Commissioner, Jim Buck Ross. At that time in Mississippi, this act was the same as calling up God, but Jim Buck was known for much more of a hands-on, definite yes-or-no response than we have come to expect from God. Baby Anna was in a state and needed cheering up of the most immediate kind, and our hero—okay, I'll tell you this much, his name is Jim—decides that what Anna needs is to be named the Queen of Something, and Jim Buck was nothing if not a queen-maker. Overnight, Jim Buck decided he would make Anna the queen of the largest event sponsored by the Agriculture Department, the barbecue cooking contest; the crown was hers if she would agree to wear the whole entire title. And that is how Anna became the first ever Miss Hog Wild in July. That very story was the tipping point that put her into Princeton and, of course, made us even wilder about Jim—hog wild, as it were.

I was happy that so many of you shared your stories about what I like to think of as "the lighter side of death." A young man told me that his grandmother had lived with his family for many years during his childhood and the woman was just mean as a snake. She bore down especially hard on his own mother, never allowing herself to be pleased by any of his mother's near-constant efforts to make her happy. One time in particular stood out in his mind, when his mother had shopped and shopped, in the formidable Mississippi heat no less, for this particularly pretty pink pantsuit for the old biddy. To show her gratitude for the effort and the gift, the old biddy cast it aside, declaring in that gravelly old biddy-voice of hers that she "wasn't about to wear *that!*" To which his mother said, through clenched teeth, under her breath, as she walked away, "Oh, you'll WEAR it all right." And so guess what the old biddy was buried in? Tee-hee. She wore it that day, and we can dig her up a hundred years from now and she'll STILL be wearing it.

Our most favorite, most important Wannabe, George, told me he was at a gathering recently and asked about one of the guy's moms, who had been ailing of late. The friend then explained that he had gone by the nursing home to visit her, as was his habit, and she seemed fine. When he arrived home a little later, however, there was a message on his voice mail from someone at the home: "Your mama took a turn for the worse, so we called her doctor—and the coroner." Fortunately, this event had taken place long enough before that the friend was not disturbed when George and everybody else with a mouthful of liquid at that moment spewed Pepsi all over the room. It reminded me of my favorite joke of all time, so far. Sister goes on vacation, leaving brother to care for her cat, which promptly dies on his watch. Sister calls to check on cat, is told bluntly that cat is dead. Sister berates brother that this is not the way to break such catastrophic news, that he should have led with something like "The cat's on the roof and won't come down," and over a period of days, he could deliver updates such as the cat fell off and got hurt, and the cat was at the vet's and the cat was not doing too well, and then, after a suitable period of time allowing her to be prepared for the worst, he could then break the news that the cat was, in fact, dead as a boot. Brother was irritated but grudgingly agreed to be more considerate in the future. By and by, sister goes out of town again. Calls home to check in with brother, who says, "Mom's on the roof."

Knowing how I do love a good obituary, Sue Olson of Alameda, California, wrote to tell me that she and her sister had decided to go ahead and write one for each other. The following is what Sue has planned for her sister, René, should René make her departure ahead of Sue. This alone should be enough to make René live forever.

CORPUS CHRISTI, TEXAS—René (Wanna) B. Castillo passed away at a local Big K. She was trampled in a massive crowd that was rushing the store for half-price Christmas items. It was one day before her fortieth birthday.

René was a huge fan of Whataburger, so she will be buried in the company colors, orange and brown. The family is trying to get one of those paper hats for her to wear for the viewing.

René was also a lifelong member of Weight Watchers. Alas, she never reached the lifetime-member status, but she went to the meetings all the time. (Usually right before going to the drive-through at Whataburger.)

Her darling younger sister, Sue (who looked like she just spent a week at one of those California spas), said the family was devastated, but life goes on. "I'm sure René would want us to be happy, so that's why I'm taking her new graphite-blue Lincoln Town Car," Sue said.

The funeral will be held at the local Elks Club. Burial will follow at

Seaside Memorial Park. The family tried to get a plot close to slain Te-jano singer Selena's grave, but after discovering the prices, thought a view of the groundskeeper's shed would be much more fitting for René.

René leaves behind two kids, a husband, her mother, and her sweet, younger sister, Sue B. Olson. Sue, a stay-at-home mother, lives in Alameda, California, with her handsome husband, Todd, and their adorable 1½-year-old son, Nicholas. Sue is very involved with MOPS (Mothers of Preschoolers), where she serves as co-coordinator. She spends her time taking yoga classes, walking along the bay, and, of course, taking care of Nicholas. Nicholas likes his tumbling class, his play group, and living in Alameda (only an hour away from his favorite aunt, Lisa). Sue and her husband just bought a new house three blocks from the bay.

"I wish René could have seen our house," Sue said. "It's such a nice house and so well-decorated. I was hoping René could be inspired and take some of the ideas back and redecorate their mobile home."

In lieu of wasting your hard-earned money on flowers, the family is accepting cash or check (with proper ID) donations.

To date, for some inexplicable reason, I have not heard from René. If I knew my sister, Judy, had already written something like this in anticipation of my untimely death, I'd make damn sure I had one to hold over her head as well. A good friend of Tammy's, Alex, said she doesn't care at all what they say about her when she's gone, she just wants to be buried in cheese. She envisions a huge coffin-shaped hunk of cheese with a hollowed-out space in the middle for her. She didn't specify a preference for the type of cheese, having never met one she didn't want to spend eternity with.

Helen Harloe of Charleston, South Carolina, wrote to me after reading my tips on child rearing in *SPQBOL* to share with me her shining moment in Motherhood. Helen has since become a good friend and a major contender for Queendom. It seems that Helen's children—ages fifteen, eleven, and eleven, who I'm sure are usually paragons of adolescent virtue—were inexplicably acting awful at the Wal-Mart. No one knows why these things happen, but they do and it's best to have a plan. Helen had not arrived with a plan, but it took her all of about two seconds to come up with this one, and it's a ring-tailed-tooter if I ever heard one: "At the top of my lungs, I launched into 'Jeremiah Was a Bullfrog'!" And she would not stop. I picture her dancing about and using lots of gestures and facial expressions—really emoting with the song—plus, as she said, she was singing real loud and it went on for some time. People were looking around for the cameras. Surely this woman must be in a movie—what else could explain this? And her children? "One of them burst into tears, the other hit the floor, and the third crashed into a display as he was running backward." Has Helen had any further behavioral deviations from these chirren in public places? Oh no, oh my no.

Helen hoped that this would qualify her as being incredibly witty and cute and resourceful enough to be considered for at least a Wannabe slot. Man, she's a shoo-in! As a matter of fact, I am hereby officially declaring Helen Harloe Sweet Potato Queen Mother of the Year—possibly the decade.

3

Promises, Promises

Just in case you haven't yet read *The Sweet Potato Queens' Book of Love*, let me tell you that the hottest topic for discussion to come out of that book has been the Promise.

The Promise refers to the True Magic Words, guaranteed to get any man to do your bidding. All you have to do is tell a guy that if he'll just do whatever it is you're asking, a blow job is in the offing; delivering on the Promise, I hasten to explain, is not part of the deal. We describe it in detail in *SPQBOL*, which you really need to read for a full understanding—a necessity before you go out and try to employ the technique on your own. Performed correctly, it is 100 percent guaranteed, and we also guarantee that the Promise is pretty much all you will have to perform.

Readers of *SPQBOL* report nearly total success with the Promise. Kay, who gave me a very fine sock monkey she made with her own two hands, told me she has used the Promise on her husband with felicitous results: She gets her yard work done and she gets lucky—talk about your win/win! She said if she'd known about this sooner, she'd have had the Taj Mahal by now. Another woman, Nina, who sent me wonderful deviled-egg recipes, but I wish she would just come here and make them for me, said she went to a business conference and signed up for the golf tournament instead of the usual "wives' activities" and found herself in the happy situation of being the only woman playing. A highly competitive individual, Nina really wanted to win, so to inspire her teammates to give it the good ole 110 percent, she made them all the Promise. Big trophy and cash. Good work, Nina. A book club wrote me to say that they used the Promise to get a new sign for their kids' school. Not to name any names, but I did sign a Promise certificate (see our Web site, www.sweetpotato-queens.com) made out to the mayor of a very large Canadian city where some Wannabes were seeking to influence a decision on some land development. I am so proud to see that you are using the Promise for the good of your communities: The Queens are very civic-minded.

One Cute Girl wrote, however, that she was being pestered slap to death by some guy wanting her to deliver on the Promise, and she wanted to know how she could "avoid this boring part." Keep right on smiling and Promising, I told her. If he is not whining about that, it will just be something else, and you might as well keep it on familiar ground.

While we may offer the Promise, far and wide, willy-nilly, to any and all men from whom we may need or desire goods or services, we admit to a severely low tolerance for the Promise being made to—and especially accepted by—men whom we consider to be *ours*. This may appear to be a confusing set of standards to the uninitiated and also to guys, but we don't care. Our standards are our standards and we expect everyone else to live up to them fully, whether they understand them or not.

Take, for example, this most interesting case related to me by one of the Queens, Tammy, I believe it was. Tammy's dear friend Leora was constantly having trouble with her ne'er-do-well husband, Jimmy Lee (pronounced "Jimmalee" in these parts). Jimmalee, it seems, had a job that involved door-to-door walking for one of the utility companies and taking readings from the company's meter on each of the houses. As we all know, the meter reading has a profound impact on one's bill for the month, and so if anything causes that reading to be lower, well, it makes for a lower utility bill. There are many ways to accomplish a lower reading, and many of them are publicized by the utility companies themselves—caulking and weatherstripping and turning off appliances and such.

Another, probably more effective but certainly not advertised method of lowering one's utility bill involves direct negotiations with the man who reads the meter—in this case, Jimmalee. Leora related it to Tammy like this: "Jimmalee goes out on the job, and those women are just waitin' for him at the door, saying, 'Jimmalee, why don't you come on inside for some i-i-i-iced te-e-ea and a little sump'n *special.*" And way too many times, according to the highly incensed Leora, Jimmalee was indeed availing himself of the house specialties. As he would leave, Leora said, Jimmalee's hostesses would stand at the door and call after him, "Now, Jimmalee honey, won't you re-e-e-ead my meet-ah low?"

Granted, we are only hearing Leora's side of this story, but that is the only side in which we have any interest. Our job is to support Leora, and that is what we are doing. Jimmalee can get his own friends. At any rate, Leora finally had enough of Jimmalee's discount meter-reading service and decided to dissolve their marital bonds. We applaud her decision to spare his life.

It's a Scientific Fact

Some people have taken issue with our judgment that guys are obsessed with sex, particularly blow jobs, even more particularly the getting of blow jobs for themselves. Well, I say *some* people, not a lot of people—okay, maybe one person, or maybe we just talked about how nobody would dare take issue with it since it is so obviously, completely, universally true and everybody knows it. At any rate, if there is a doubter out there, the following story should terminate the issue.

I actually read, in an actual magazine from the newsstand, that some actual guys (biologists, the story said, but I'd bet money they were all guys) did an actual study and they discovered that a male zebra finch readily submits to the indignity of having a white feather glued to his head because female zebra finches find the ornament irresistible. The biologists concluded from this study that the "predilection for crests may be hardwired into the avian central nervous system." Who do they think they are fooling with that crap—their mothers? The predilection for crests? How about the endless quest for pussy? I suggest that what they proved is this: that guy birds, indeed guys of any and all species, will do absolutely anything to get it. I further suggest that they stumbled onto this crest idea in a search-and-discover mission whose sole purpose was How Can We Get More Pussy?

We all know that many beneficial products and life-enhancing procedures have come from research that was initially conducted on animals, however unpopular and politically incorrect the fact may be. I am convinced that these guys were studying the mating habits of birds with the thought that if they could figure out ways to enhance the birds' sex lives, they could extrapolate some usable data for human-type guys. I mean, I just have a hard time believing that anybody really gives a rat's ass about how birds feel about hats. That would be a tough one to get funded. If, however, you plan to do a study that provides concrete measures that male birds will take to absolutely, 100 percent guarantee that they will be chick magnets, and if you can imply pretty heavily that you are fairly sure you can come up with some human equivalencies for this study, the National Science Foundation would probably bring cash over in wheelbarrows. This would be so much more valuable than a better mousetrap.

It is only a matter of time before we start seeing guys walking around with white feathers glued to their foreheads. Here's what I think we ought to do about it: The first one you see, rush right up to him and all but devour him on the spot, admiring and fondling his feather all the while. Within seventy-two hours, every guy on the planet will have a white feather glued to his forehead. Tee-hee. You know, I bet the genesis for the whole thing was Lyle Lovett—ever look at his hair? I mean, really, it's like, pretty noticeable, to say the least. I bet those biologist guys were hanging out, wolfing brews and talking about women, of course—about actually getting women—and the subject of Lyle Lovett came up, as it so often does in these situations. Specifically, Lyle Lovett and Julia Roberts and how in this world did he ever get her—even temporarily. And maybe, in their stupefied state, they figured it must have something to do with his hair—in particular that topknot thing he wears—and they stumbled back to the lab to try to replicate this felicitous result with animals they had on hand, which just happened to be zebra finches.

They probably experimented with a variety of interesting articles on those poor bastards' heads, in attempts to attract the girls, with many failures at first. They knew it had to be very puffy and very big in relation to the bird's head and body but lightweight enough that the bird could still stand and prance about in studly bird-fashion. Wonder what all they tried? A paper clip perhaps—too business-Bob-looking; a cotton ball—too swishy; a golf ball—way too heavy; a gum-drop—too sticky and it attracts bugs, which is not altogether a bad thing for a bird, but at the moment the bird is horny, not hungry; a Q-tip—too stiff, but the shape was more appealing in a drum major or military way. And then they tried a feather, which turned out to be the equivalent of a date-rape drug for birds. The girl birds were just lying around spread-eagled (spread-finched?) all over the lab, begging for more of that hot bird-y love. The guy birds were insufferable pricks, strutting around, screwing every chick in sight. Outside the lab, it was pandemonium: Every male finch in North America was hurling himself against the lab windows, desperately trying to get a white feather glued to his head and trying to get insurance to pay for it.

The biologists will probably get, and they certainly deserve, a huge bonus not only for this huge discovery, which will be a boon to birds and men everywhere, but for solving, they believe, the biggest mystery of the millennium—namely the Lyle Lovett/Julia Roberts thing. Science knows no bounds apparently.

Of course, if they had bothered to ask a woman, she could have told them promptly and free of charge: Julia (and all the rest of us) love Lyle in spite of his hair, not because of it. We can listen to him sing "I loved you yesterday" one time and be ready to bear his children and wash his socks for the rest of our lives. Do you ever wonder why they never ask us what *we* like—just foolishly try to figure it out amongst themselves? It must be related to never asking for directions.

Magic Words ~ For Men Only

Many men have also written me about the Promise. Men have thanked me for this enormous contribution to their education, and some have expressed their delight at the dramatic increase in the number of times they have personally actually succeeded in collect-ing on the Promise. But there are, to be sure, the whiners, who com-plain that they never can collect and they are pissed off big time at how often they have been suckered in by mere words alone. Well, you are all on your own as far as the Collection Process goes. But now it is time to let the guys in on a little-known tip that will greatly en-hance your Collection Potential. Yes, there are more magic words out there—and these work on us. (Don't panic, girls: if they pay any attention at all to me, nearly all benefits will be yours. Men are, after all, easily satisfied, are they not?)

There is one sentence that all of us long from the depths of our souls to hear a man say. Six little words—the most powerful, the most seductive words we can imagine. The words are more powerful than all the flowery declarations of love, loyalty, and lifelong fidelity you can compose. I would have to say that they cause nearly the same effect on women that the Promise does on men. They make our knees weak, our eyes dilate, and our breathing heavy. We have been known to sigh deeply and flush visibly at the sound of these words. Any woman alive can tell you immediately, without hesitation, and in vivid detail the last time she heard these magical words. And she can count on one hand the times she has heard them from some man other than her own personal daddy.

The Six Words a Woman Most Loves to Hear from a Man—I'd say they are the modern equivalent of riding up on a white stallion and plucking her from a burning tower. Okay, guys, imagine this: The woman you desire is there before you, engaged in some activity. For the sake of conversation, let's say she's simultaneously trying to arrange to have her car repaired, cook dinner, unclog the sink, do the laundry, make plane reservations for an upcoming trip, cut the grass, and clean out the garage—just a typical woman's typical workload after her typical eight-hour workday, of course. Suddenly, magically almost, you appear. You stride up to her purposefully, you take her gently in your arms, look deeply into her eyes, and you say, very softly but firmly, the Six Words.

You say the Six Words to her—and say them pretty quick because until she hears them, she's liable to think that you are here in the midst of the mountain of her work feeling frisky, and if you don't swiftly disabuse her of that misconception, you could be maimed on the spot. So there she is, overwhelmed, and there you are, purposefully striding, embracing, looking deeply, and saying softly but firmly . . . the Six Words:

Oh no, let me handle this.

Gasp! Girls, can you imagine it? I swear, it gives me a tingle in my nether regions just to write the words!

Once the words are spoken, and your deliriously happy lady has finished her swoon, say them again for maximum impact. Then listen very carefully, maybe even take notes, as she gives you the necessary instructions for the task you will handle. *Caution:* If the woman is Southern, her immediate response to the Six Words will be a soft, "Oh no, that's okay, you don't have to do that." We were brought up that way, but let me assure you—WE DON'T MEAN IT! You must at this point *insist* on doing it and commence doing it immediately or all will be lost.

While *we* can hand out Promises thither and yon with nary a thought to delivery—woe, woe, woe be unto them (and any innocent bystanders) if they utter the Six Words to us and don't make good on the deal. We're not talking about your sexual favors here; we're talking about bona fide errands, goods, and/or services. We'll be more than happy to consider sexual favors after the successful completion of errands and delivery of said goods and/or services. But until such time, believe me, we will not be in the mood.

Addressing a Socratic Conundrum

One day not long ago I was out and ran into Coyt Bailey, son of my daughter BoPeep's godparents, Joanie and Buster Bailey (so he's her what—godbrother?). Anyway, Coyt and I were visiting amiably over alcohol, and the conversation moved in about three disjointed steps to the Promise. (We have all noticed this conversational trend frequently since the publication of *SPQBOL.*) What, Coyt wanted to know, would we do if the Promise did not, in fact, persuade the man to do our bidding? Now that we have put the Promise out there, what's the plan if it fails? Well, I told him, I had no idea since, to date, that has never happened anywhere on the planet to my knowledge, certainly not in my own personal experience. But, he persisted, what if . . . then what?

So I thought and I thought. Of course, this kind of abstract thinking about unlikely situations amounts to asking, "What if Jesus was a mongoose?" I do think this is the all-time stumper of illogical questions, and I whip it out whenever I'm hounded by someone for an answer to a question to which there can be no logical answer because it's a stupid question to begin with, and after I present it, the questioner will generally wander on off in a puzzled state. This question was first posed in a discussion with a small child after his first reading of "Rikki-Tikki-Tavi." Being very impressed with the speed of the mongoose in that story and also fresh from Sunday-school class, he inquired whether or not Jesus was faster than a mongoose—an excellent question, I'm sure, and I struggled to satisfy the kid. Then the discussion deteriorated, as theological conversations often do, into what if Jesus *was* a mongoose, and that is just too convoluted an issue to unravel.

I felt much the same in reaction to Coyt's question, what if we gave the Promise and it didn't work? I could, however, tell from the way he sort of hoisted up on his elbows and leaned in, his eyes all squinted up and steady, that Coyt was not about to be satisfied with "What if Jesus was a mongoose?" I could no more escape answering this question than I could the child's query. So I sat there pondering, looking into my Absolut Fredo, when revelation broke through and presented the perfect solution. There's really only one thing left for us to do at this point: Show up naked. Bring beer.

No argument from Coyt.

4

My Hors Are Moning

It may be true—and we certainly believe that it is—that everything in the world happens or does not happen as a result of blow jobs, given or withheld. But there is something else at work here, too, at the very core of it all—an unseen but nonetheless irresistible force of nature that controls virtually everything, at least on this planet, and thanks to NASA, somewhat beyond. I am speaking of hormones. Hormones—specifically *ours*—are the boss of everything. Somebody somewhere gets pissed off and launches something that incinerates somebody else somewhere else, but why is he being such a butthead? Because he didn't get the blow job he felt entitled to, or worse, because somebody else got the blow job he felt he was entitled to. But why did he not get his rightful blow job? My bet is on hormones.

We all like to think that all our actions and reactions are totally rational and appropriate to each and every situation. In fact, we bear hot resentment toward any male-type who presumes to diagnose our slight hormonal trough or surge. And if we do happen to be in a hormone-induced state, nothing makes us madder than to have a man suggest it. We can say that about ourselves if we feel like it, but woe be unto the man who tries to blame our reaction to his bad behavior on a little estrogen, plus or minus. The words "towering rage" were first used to describe just such a situation, I believe. My daddy's favorite Biblical threat toward one's enemies was "Let us cut off his head and make of his house a dunghill." Sounds good to me, and after all, it is in the Bible.

Witness these hormonal events: A woman, who shall remain nameless, calls her sister and makes the report that, not only does she not love her husband, she no longer even likes him. "Yesterday I was looking out the window and he was walking across the yard, when all of a sudden—he fell in a hole! One second he was there, the next he just dropped out of sight! I started laughing and I could not stop!" She laughed so hard, she fell down and just lay there, in a heap, cackling and whooping till the tears ran down her face and she had big black puddles of melted mascara all over her cheeks. Presently she heaved herself up by the window ledge and peered out. By this time, he was dragging himself out of the hole and she realized he had hurt himself in some manner. "I started laughing all over again! I never laughed so hard in all my life. I thought to myself, 'Just stay in that hole, you old fart!' and I laughed some more!" Eventually she calmed herself down, and he managed to haul his carcass in from the yard. She glanced up as he entered, and he said to her, "You will never believe what just happened to me." She, with a completely straight face, replied, "Oh? What was that?" Read on.

Wannabe Gayle Christopher and her former husband (not John, who is perfect—that other one she ran off) were tussling around, play-fighting, and he accidentally hurt her. She advised him of this and he had the nerve to laugh at her and tease her, calling her a "whiney baby." Gayle looked at him through eyelids squinted in menacing rage and spoke through clenched teeth (never a good omen), saying, "I will get you back, you sumbitch." And he actually laughed at her again! Talk about asking for it. "So," she tells me in only slightly suppressed glee, "I waited till he went to sleep and I got one of his mother's big old heavy silver spoons, and you know how you would pull a spoon back to flip something off of it? I pulled that sucker back as hard as I could and I popped him with it right between the eyes! He thought he'd been shot!" Miss Gayle was on the floor by the bed, laughing, fit to kill.

These were local events. From the wire services, we see a national trend. A seventy-year-old man was beaten to death with a shoe—by a woman—as he lay on the sofa. I called one of the Queens, Tammy, and inquired whether or not she was a suspect in the "Fatal Shoe Beating," since I knew she'd been enjoying very little domestic bliss lately. We agreed that you'd have to be pretty pissed off at somebody to beat them to death with a shoe. The wire service did not give us nearly all the details we craved: like what kind of shoe was it and how many times did she whack him with it? We figured it must have occurred in some strict-gun-control state. Poor woman couldn't get a handgun and had to use footwear to finish him off. Just points to the never-failing resourcefulness of women, though, not to mention their long-suffering natures. I mean, how many times do you reckon she had told him to get up off that couch? I'm quite certain she was just pushed beyond human limitations of tolerance and had no choice. That will no doubt be her defense. The hormone defense probably doesn't stand up in court. And you know she hated to ruin that shoe, too, bless her heart.

"Bless her/his heart" is a remarkable Southern device that enables us to say the very worst things possible about another human being while, at the same time, distancing ourselves from the meanness and leaving the hearer with a final note of our own sweetness. Another example: He is just a worthless, deadbeat, lying, cheating sack'o'shit, and he's going bald, too, bless his heart. Heart-blessing has another very useful function, according to exhaustive, not to mention exhausting, research conducted by our buddy Jeanne Adams. Jeanne swears it can be used as a universal response to anything a guy is whining about in which you are totally disinterested—if you are, in fact, even listening to him whine about it. Whenever he pauses for your sympathetic response, just lean in toward him, pat his arm a little bit, sort of frown in a concerned way, and say, "Bless your heart," and like magic, it's all better. Jeanne claims a 100 percent success rate with this technique, and we recommend it to you without question.

Men are not the only species to be endangered by our hormones; sometimes the tricky buggers can make us turn on our own kind. Two women were in line at the express checkout register at the grocery store. The second-in-line noticed that the first-in-line had more than fifteen items! And so she did the only thing she could do, what we've all been dying to do but were either just too chickenshit or our hormones were in balance that day. After getting her own fewer-than-fifteen items checked out, she followed the cheater out into the parking lot—and cut off her nose!

Ah, hormones. We think these brief histories—which, by the way, are surely portents of things to come as the Boomers reach menopause en masse—provide some pretty compelling evidence supporting the theory that our hormones rule world events. But it doesn't stop with the events alone. The underlying implications are far more ominous. If you are a man reading this, you are probably standing there, perhaps scratching some body part, looking perplexed. If, on the other hand, you are a woman reading this, and laughing so hard you have to sit down, then every other woman in the place is demanding to know just what is so damned funny. See, it's not only that women are doing these unbelievable things in the first place—although that is strange enough—but our reactions to this, this carnage, have all been the same—uncontrollable laughing. Guffawing. Moosing. Snorting. Shrieking. Hee-hawing. At the pain and misfortune of others.

Committing these atrocities is not ladylike. Laughing at these atrocities is unconscionable for women. Ladies, I hate to tell you this, but here's what happens when our hormones get out of whack: We turn into guys. Our actions and reactions are no longer those of the kindler, gentler sex. I can see what's coming now—it will be all over the news—multiple deaths on college campuses from *sorority* hazings, and the pinning ceremonies will reveal the Big Sisters jamming the actual pins into the actual breasts of the young pledges, laughing drunkenly as the blood and tears flow freely.

Ronnie Bagwell is a compounding pharmacist in Jackson who doesn't just fill prescriptions; he actually makes magic potions—custom-blended hormones—for practically every woman I know. He has devoted so much of his young life to our hormones that we (or more precisely, I) have dubbed him the Hormone King. Half the people who go to him now don't even remember his real name—he has become the Hormone King. He knows everything there is to know, so far, about our hormones, and we love him for this because, otherwise, I am quite sure that a whole bunch of us would be in the penitentiary by now, and countless newspaper headlines would begin with the words, "Among the injured were . . ."

Ronnie's got some great hormone war stories, too. One woman came to him after her hysterectomy and told him she was going to try his hormone concoction, and it was her second-to-last choice. He naturally wanted to know what the last choice was. Her answer: a divorce attorney. At least it wasn't the gun show. Ronnie says a bunch of his patients come in with their husbands. Can you even imagine such a thing? Ronnie says this is always fun because the woman will say that her symptoms are under control, while the husband says everything is as bad as it can possibly be. Luckily, Ronnie is also well-trained in first aid.

I despise chain letters, and the advent of e-mail has greatly increased the number of them circulating, I am sorry to say. However, I did get one I found highly entertaining. It instructed the recipient to send the letter to five other women and then to sack up your husband and send him to the woman whose name was at the top of the list and add your name to the bottom. By the time your name moved up to the top, you would have received 15,625 men, and one of them was bound to be better than the one you already have. It said that one woman (supposedly known to the sender) had already received 184 men, four of whom were worth keeping. Another success story cited: "An unmarried Jewish woman living with her widowed mother was able to choose between an orthodontist and a successful gynecologist—you can be lucky, too!" The admonition about dire consequences to chain-breakers was not the usual death-and-poverty prediction; the threat was that you might get your own husband back again.

I am telling you for true, if the estrogen supply ever dries up, it's going to be a tight fight with a short stick. Armageddon? HA! We'll see your Armageddon and raise you twenty!

5

A Pot to Priss In

There may be a certain degree of prissiness associated with being a Queen. I heard from a cutie pie in Tampa who said at the first sign of a chill in the air, she had worn her full-length mink coat to a Buccaneers game and everybody acted as if she was "Miss Priss Pot." I loved that. I hadn't heard "Miss Priss Pot" in probably forty years. It had been a favorite childhood taunt, before anybody learned to say "Miss Bitchcuntwhorefromhell," which definitely has a ring to it, but we are not as likely to wax nostalgic over it down the road. We certainly don't see this prissiness as a character flaw, at least as it applies to us. Our brand of prissy bespeaks a healthy sense of self-indulgence and is always accompanied by a sense of humor and a sense of compassion for those who, through no fault of their own, are not us. Lord knows, they would be if they could (just as we all know that every woman in that Tampa Bay stadium would have been wearing a full-length mink coat if she had one), and that alone is enough to melt our hearts toward them.

But anyway, about this prissy business—we just think that, as with most everything, there is a way to do it and also a way to completely screw it up. For instance, a former Queen, Tammy, moved far away and commenced having babies. At first she would make the trip back here for parade day, but it became unmanageable, so she abdicated. We didn't mind too much, because she was so much better looking than the rest of us. It was kind of a relief, took the pressure off somewhat, if you know what I mean. Before moving away, she had worked and slaved and generally endured hardships and deprivation—even having to do her own nails sometimes—while her husband was in medical school. However, once he got out and launched himself into doctoring full time for full money, she sat down and hasn't gotten up since except to do her makeup and such. Which is, of course, as it should be. Even we had to laugh, though, when she moved into her new house, which is on an island in a river and has a pool and every possible amenity befitting a Queen. We were teasing her about the magnificence of her new digs. Her response, by way of just putting it all in perspective for us lesser mortals and trying to make us feel better about our own comparatively sorry lots in life, was this: "Oh, no, y'all just don't know. When I'm lying out by the pool and those planes fly over, shoot, I can't sleep!"

One time, one of the regular good-looking Tammys and I went to a party where there were a whole pack of models. We took one look at them and immediately gravitated toward each other and into the next room, where there were only regular good-looking women like ourselves. The truth is that, up close and in person, they weren't any better looking than we were. They had some very odd makeup techniques going, and we needed to discuss them and suppress our resulting guffaws. Some had those brown stripes painted down either side of their noses—you know, how the magazine articles always tell you to do, to camouflage your big nose? Well, it may look fine in a photo, but somebody needs to tell these women not to go out on the street wearing that stuff on their noses: They look like badgers.

What really set us off, though, was their lipstick. How many of you out there still think it goes on your mouth? No wonder you ain't in the movies. Yeah, us too. Anyway, we were just mesmerized by their mouths. See, we were from the old school, like you, where you put lipstick on your mouth the same way you color in a coloring book: You make every effort to stay inside the lines. Imagine our chagrin to learn that in model world anything on your face from underneath your nose to your chin is considered to be mouth and is eligible to have lipstick applied to it. Liberally. If your lips are on the thin side—

hey! no problem—just take a lip pencil and draw on some new lips, any shape and size that suits your fancy, and paint them in with gobs of lipstick. It looks hilarious when they talk because only the genuine lip parts actually move: The dummy lips just sit there, gleaming but not moving. We could hardly take our eyes off of them, but then we had to leave the room so we could laugh. And redo our own lipstick, naturally. Then we were really laughing, but at least we looked like we fit in, and did we not!

Sometimes prissy goes bad on you. Overheard at a restaurant, albeit not a fine one: Middle-sized child had been talking, and overbearing grandmother had been interrupting regularly, with manners instructions and other things not at all pertinent to the child's subject of conversation. Granny clearly wasn't listening to him at all, so focused on her own nagging she was, until two words left his mouth upon which she pounced—if a fat old lady with a dour disposition can be said to pounce or even envisioned pouncing—like a swift duck on a dawdling June bug. "Willie Steve"—we do love double names down here—"how many times do I have to tell you, there ain't no such words as *maters* and *taters!* It is toe-maters and poe-taters! You just sound like such a ignerint hick sometimes, I swannee." Yes, doesn't he, though? For those of you who are not blessed with Southern birth, there is a faction of folk down here who are so adamant against any word that might possibly be construed as cursing that they won't even say "I swear." This is, after all, the much-touted Bible Belt. But, as we all know, occasions arise all day every day that make it not only highly desirable to cuss but indeed next to impossible not to, and so they have come up with substitutes, fake cussin's, like this one, "I swannee." We have also heard "shoot a monkey," "goldang it," "fudge," and, of course, "heckfire." Somehow, I think, if God does really have an opinion on all this (and if He does, I think He's just not got His priorities straight), He would care more about the spirit behind the words than the actual words themselves, and I just bet He knows the difference. But I have heard some of these folks so riled up that—shoot a monkey!—if they had the power to consign me to eternal heckfire, goldang it, they would, I swannee.

Our mainmost Spud Stud, Malcolm White, founder of Mal's St. Paddy's Parade, has been struck down once again with a genius idea. You will kick yourself when you hear it—how could none of us have thought of it before? Well, he's thought of it, and you can take advantage of it. You can buy, thanks to Malcolm, an actual Bible Belt suitable for wearing to church or honky-tonks or anywhere else! Go to www.biblebelts.net and goon these things. You've just *got* to have one, I swannee.

One of the Queens, Tammy, said she knew a sour old prissy woman once who loved to preach table manners to everybody else in the world. One of her favorite maxims was "Mah grandmutha on my mutha's si-i-i-ide always to-o-o-old me-e-e that wun shud nevah eet anything in its enti-i-i-irety." How silly is that? What is the point of deliberately leaving something on your plate—even if you are starving slap to death and want to eat the painted flowers off the dish—to be polite? If you are not hungry, fine. If the food is rotten and you simply can't choke down another bite of it, fine. But for appearance's sake? Tammy had been to a hoity-toity fashion show where this woman had been the commentator. The remark that sent Tammy flying from the room was uttered to describe what we used to call a "housedress," which we all thought had mercifully evolved out of existence: "This is just the thing to pop on when your yard man comes to the door." But to get the full effect, you should hear it said like this: "Thiiis is juuuuust th' thiiiing to pawp ah-own whin yoah yaaaaaahd ma-un cuuums to th' do-ah."

This same woman was known for planting cookies behind doors to see if the maids were on their toes. When I heard this initially, I took it to mean she was hiding the cookies to keep the maids from eating them—a greedy, stingy sort of act. But no, she was hiding just a single cookie to see if the maids were doing their job properly, checking every nook and cranny for possible dirt. Of course, what she didn't know is the maids told everybody in town she was crazy and did weird stuff with food. They were always finding cookies stashed in strange places and they didn't dare move them, thinking the woman must be going back later to hide behind the door and furtively eat cookies, careful to pick up and consume every crumb off the floor. And, of course, everybody believes the maids. Tee-hee.

I am certain I would be utterly devoted to anybody who came in and did anything around the house for me. I would want to be their best friend, and they surely would be mine. I don't have a lot of experience in the area of domestic assistance or assistants, but I have witnessed some wonderful relationships in the homes of others. A good friend of Tammy's lives in the Mississippi Delta. Tammy got Betty talking one day on the subject of child care, and Betty told the story of how she was raised by a murderess. It seems that Betty's mother, Miss Idelle, had had in her employ one Miss Eddie Lee for as long as anybody could remember. One day, in a less-than-blissful moment of domesticity in Eddie Lee's own home, well, Eddie Lee's boyfriend somehow ended up dead, and Eddie Lee ended up in Parchman Penitentiary.

This was a tragedy for Eddie Lee, of course, who was actually incarcerated, but imagine the despair, too, of Miss Idelle—that big house and all those children and no Eddie Lee to actually take care of everything. Now, Miss Idelle was no one to trifle with, and she took it just as long as she could. Then she just got in her car and drove up to Parchman, marched herself right in there, and demanded that they give her Eddie Lee. "You turn her loose right now, you hear me? Eddie Lee didn't mean to kill that man; she just wanted to give him a good whop upside the head, and Lord knows, he needed it! She never even saw that nail in the two-by-four! It was a pure acci-dent! You give her to me right now!" And they did. That was a long time ago, and she was in a family full of judges and assorted politicians, and it *was* the Mississippi Delta, where things are, they say, different. But that's how Betty ended up being raised by a murderess—and she turned out just fine, thank you very much.

Yes, compassion exists even among the prissy. One of my favorite examples of this happened for years in the little town of Canton, Mississippi, which is about twenty miles north of my home in Jackson. There was an old woman who lived out from town in a run-down house without electricity. This didn't seem to bother her; she managed to cook and to keep herself and her multitude of cats warm with the fireplace. She had access to utilities but chose not to avail herself of them, never missing them until she got a certain present. See, she was reputed to have the ability to charm warts off and perform other small, handy spells, and from time to time, the townspeople paid her visits. One time, in return for her service, somebody made her a gift of a very fine electric skillet, which she was quite taken with but could not use. It seemed like a great deal of trouble to get electricity and change the way she'd always lived just so she could use that very fine skillet. But, dang it, the thing was worthless without the juice.

She was undaunted by this little detail, however. Soon a regular occurrence in the best neighborhoods in town was this: Mrs. Jones is in her kitchen making breakfast. Mr. Jones is sitting at the table in the breakfast room, reading the paper, waiting to be fed. He smells the heavenly scent of frying pork products but doesn't see any. He does see an old woman in his garage, however, and asks Mrs. Jones who that might be. She replies without even looking up, "Oh, that's just the Cat Woman; she's cooking her bacon." Every day or so, whenever she woke up feeling like a little bacon and eggs, the Cat Woman would simply walk into town, carrying her very fine skillet and a basket of food, pop into any one of the garages on the prissiest street in town, plug in, and happily fire up that very fine skillet. It became an accepted morning ritual in the neighborhood, and folks would get their feelings hurt if she didn't get around to their house in a timely fashion. I don't know, but I think this kind of thing may not happen anywhere but small Southern towns in the homes of those "prissy" Southern women I am so proud to know.

Prissy Is as Prissy Does

Tammy is good friends with this tiny, soft-spoken, very Belle-like woman named Rosalie, and as it happens, their respective daughters also share a friendship. Tammy tells of dropping her own daughter off for a visit late one afternoon and taking time for a little visit of her own with Rosalie. They sat for a while in the sunroom, catching up on gossip and sipping iced tea. Just outside the sunroom window, living up to his familial calling, was Rosalie's yap dog, Mr. Bob. Tammy was hearing only every third word out of Rosalie's mouth and could scarcely hear herself think. All in all, it was making for a most unsatisfactory gossip session—excellent if you were behind in dog-yapping, but not much for human conversation. Every now and again, Rosalie would interrupt herself midsentence to admonish Mr. Bob to kindly shut the fuck up and go away—all in the daintiest, most ladylike terms and tone, of course, but to no avail. Mr. Bob just kept right on yipping and yapping and slobbering on the windows.

Finally, Tammy had gotten all the good there was out of the situation and started making her escape. As they were leaving, Rosalie opened the door and let the vociferous Mr. Bob into the room with them, an act that nearly rendered Tammy both deaf and insane. She bounded to her car, only to be followed by Rosalie and the still-yapping Mr. Bob, with Rosalie still sweetly asking him to please hush, which seemed only to increase his fervor and volume. Tammy leapt into her car, but Rosalie continued to talk. At least she assumed Rosalie was talking—her lips were moving—but the only sound penetrating the glass was, of course, that of the garrulous Mr. Bob. Tammy pondered for a moment the possibility that Rosalie herself had taken up the yap in concert with Mr. Bob. She rolled down her window to find out. Rosalie was uttering words, after all, but Tammy could hear only snatches of them at the odd intervals. Mr. Bob apparently had no need for oxygen, so ceaseless and seamless was the yapping. Finally, even Rosalie reached a limit for the vociferous Mr. Bob. Without so much as a warning frown or grimace—indeed her eyes never left Tammy's face—she leaned down, snatched up the hideous hair ball, and with the ever-sweet admonition to "Hush now," she hurled Mr. Bob right over the fence into the backyard, where he landed with a soft *whoosh* in a fortuitously located pile of pine straw. If he had been of slightly different shape, he would have traveled in a perfect spiral reminiscent of those expertly launched missiles of Mississippi's own Brett Favre or even our sacred Archie Manning.

The suddenness of the act seemed to shock Mr. Bob into momentary silence, during which Rosalie calmly finished her sentence with nary a trace in her demeanor to indicate that she had just fired the family dog over the fence like a rocket. We hold this up for you as a prime example of our fine upbringing in the South. Indeed, it illustrates many facets of our training and abilities that we feel necessary to the smooth running of life. Tolerance for lesser beings—she never raised her voice. Self-control—she never lost her temper, didn't even appear to own a temper. Ability to handle crises without undue fuss or muss—she did not so much as move a hair. Calm assessment of situations, quick identification of options, selection of best course of action, and speedy implementation, all accomplished in less time than it took to finish a normal-sized sentence and without a single drop of sweat. Independence and self-reliance—did she need or try to procure a man to handle this problem for her? She did not. It also clearly demonstrates that although we may appear to be deaf, dumb, and blind to your indiscretions for a time, we are most assuredly not. We are simply pretending to be, in hopes that you'll amend your ways yourself. Should it become clear to us, however, that you have no such intention, well then, we are perfectly willing and able to fling your ass over the nearest available fence and go right on our merry way, worry-free. It also indicates that down here, pretty much everybody can play football *pretty* good.

6

Wishing Is Not a Felony

There has been much discussion—indeed, nationwide—since the publication of *SPQBOL*, on the subject of Men Who May Need Killing. First you've got your group that's just all for it, literally, and for the slightest offense—a really bloodthirsty lot, this. Of course, we never meant it literally—even if a man's behavior has been universally declared hideous beyond belief, even by his own mama. We will concede that, yes, indeed, he *may* need killing and that, in fact, we might not even be real sorry if somebody did kill him, but we are 100 percent against actually setting out to do it our ownselves or even halfway suggesting that somebody else do it. The most important reason is the simple wrongness of it, of course. In addition, we would be in a whole big lot of trouble, and that would bring along a multitude of errands, which we are totally against at all times. To make the record clear, when we say a man needs killing, what we really mean is that he should be left *alive*, but alone. Southerners have a way of exaggerating. We do think it's pretty funny to ridicule shameless men, but that right there brings out the politically correct whiners who insist on taking every little ole word with a big dose of literal; and, jeez, by the time you get through explaining to them that it's just a joke (and after you explained it to them, they didn't get it anyway), it's not funny anymore. We do try to avoid any direct personal contact with this type of individual whenever possible.

I once went to school with a guy named Michael R. Warmington, and he would always introduce himself by the whole name, which I loved. He was one of the funniest people I have ever known. He used to crack me up whenever a friend of his announced he was generally pissed off at another individual: Michael R. Warmington, by way of establishing that he was completely and totally on your side, would say, with a completely straight face and a slight gasp beforehand, for emphasis, "I hate him. I hope he dies." The first time I heard him say it, I cringed in horror: You just do not say such words in a Southern Bible Belt home. After the initial shock of actually hearing the words spoken, I was utterly delighted with them and from then on have used them my ownself in exactly the same way—with, I might add, exactly the same results. Nearly everyone who hears this assessment for the first time is stunned, perhaps a tad put off, but then perfectly delighted to be supported in their rightness to such a degree.

(Another thing Michael R. Warmington used to do was to quote poetry that he claimed was his own. One of his poems was a particular favorite of mine. He would draw himself up very tall and proper and looking straight ahead, like a third grader in a spelling bee, and say, " 'Feet' by Michael R. Warmington," and proceed to recite, "You need feet to stand up straight on, you need feet to kick your friends, you need feet to hang your socks on, and keep your legs from fraying at the ends." It is one of my all-time favorite pieces of poetry, and whenever my daughter, BoPeep, has to memorize a poem for school, she always [foolishly] asks my opinion on what her selection should be; it is always the same: "Feet" by Michael R. Warmington. For some reason, she won't ever do it. I think any teacher worth *anything* would have been as impressed with it as I. Yet she refuses. Sigh. Soon after I wrote this passage, I tracked down Michael R. Warmington; he lives not far from Whitney Houston and Bruce Springsteen. Poetry paid off for you, aye, Mike? He was forced to confess that he didn't actually write that poem; it came from an old episode of *The Dick Van Dyke Show*. He thought it just sounded better when followed by his own name. I had to agree.)

But I digress. My sister, Judy, and I passed a lively afternoon once at Guido's, our very favorite restaurant and bar in Cozumel, Mexico, by listing aloud the names of all the people who needed killing. It started out on an intensely personal level, with those individuals who had wronged us grievously. As the drinks came and went, the list grew and grew to include quite a number of our fellow patrons at the bar, and then took on a universal scope to embrace low-level state employees, the occasional rude checkout woman at the grocery store, a few TV evangelists (some of the women of this ilk piss me off more than the men; you know the ones—they talk about Jesus like He was their high-school boyfriend), and assorted movie stars. One of us would throw out a name and the other would chime in with her own agreement. Then we would just laugh and laugh, as only two sisters, full of margaritas, can laugh.

Years later I found myself recounting this scenario to my boyfriend, Richard Pharr, who was entirely on board with the fun until I mentioned the name of Dale Evans. Richard is a big ole cowboy, and he was frankly stupefied at Miss Dale's inclusion in such a list. "Dale?" he queried, not a little desperately. "You want to kill Dale Evans? Whatever for? Dale?" I hastened to explain that while Dale had never done a thing to me, personally, she had somehow managed to cross the line with Judy, and I just felt it was my sisterly duty to go along with it. He was off in his own world, haunted with questions like how could he be going out with a woman who wanted to kill Dale Evans? and so he really wasn't hearing me or my explanations to the contrary—or that Judy didn't really mean it, for crying out loud: It was just a joke, Richard. In his mind all joking stopped at the mention of Dale Evans's name, she being holy and all that, to cowboys and the like. Again, as if in a trance, he repeated, "You would want to kill Dale Evans?"

My bucket of patience having run completely dry, I said, "Yeah, Richard, that's what I'm really looking for in a man: I want a man who will bring me the head of Dale Evans." Yessir, buddy, I'll believe you love me only then. And so it came to be that we have a new standard by which to judge the seriousness of a relationship. Replacing the old—Has he taken you to meet his mama yet?—is the updated scale of devotion: Will he bring you the head of Dale Evans? Isn't that what we're all really looking for? A man so utterly devoted to our happiness that, *figuratively speaking only*, he would fetch us this grisly prize, if for some totally warped reason we actually wanted it? (Okay, for the record: It's a *joke*. If you don't get it, don't laugh, but we don't want any heads sent down here. We will not love you back.)

We're still faced with this dilemma of how to emphasize to any and everyone precisely to what enormous extent some person—usually male—has transgressed against us. We hit on the idea of maiming. Instead of saying the loathsome, repulsive, insufferable dope needs killing, we could maybe just say he is a Man Who Should Be Maimed. Perhaps that would sound more palatable to the fainthearted. We've done some test-marketing on the idea, and it has been met with great approval. A vast majority of you out there are willing to embrace the maiming theory. (For you literal ones, this is a joke, too.) Still, a few holdouts couldn't even bear to hear about maiming. We suggested that they get from here and leave us be with our laughter, but then we took it (somewhat) to heart—we like a challenge anyway—and determined to explore further ways of expressing our extreme displeasure that would not offend any person on earth, with the notable exception of our intended pseudo-victim.

We consulted on this matter with one of our Bobs. This particular Bob is actually quite well-known—many of the more literate of you out there would instantly recognize his name, and he is also real smart and speaks a whole bunch of languages. We implored him to talk to us of maiming. He responded quickly, as he always does to our slightest request, and this is why he will never appear on any of our lists, except for the Promise. "Ah, yes, *maim*," Bob said, thoughtfully. "Wonderful word, that. In Spanish, of course, it is *mutilado*, but since that was used most extensively during the Inquisition, it has a sort of Old World feel to it—pincers, hot tongs, racks, et al. So you might want to use the more colloquial *mortuato en vive*, causing a deathlike feeling among the living, which was perfected by General Pinochet and now has a broader household use." Were we delighted, or what? Meeting with such success with that offering prompted Bob to come back with even more (thereby moving himself even higher on the Promise list concurrently). "Among other alternatives are *cucarachas en casa privata*, putting cockroaches in your personal home, which generally means getting under the skin in a man's very tender areas. Or perhaps even better, *blasta firmata, uno billiard, dos pelata*, one strike, hitting both the pool cue and two balls, which, for modesty's sake, I cannot explain." We figured it out our ownselves! Some might think Bob would be afraid to risk the ire of his fellow man-types by sharing such information with us, the woman-types, but when the dust settles, the truth is, Bob would a whole lot rather have us happy than a bunch of guys. Told you he was real smart.

Wishing Is Not a Felony

I had the most moving letter from a woman named Peggy, who wrote, "I am a forty-eight-year-old white woman who recently ran away from home for a weekend in an attempt to reach a meeting of the minds—via my unexpected absence and numerous credit card transactions on my husband's American Express." Right here Peggy has demonstrated a wonderful alternative to killing and even maiming: That would be the oft-overlooked method of "grudge shopping," also known as revenge spending and fuck-you-buddy charging. A blow to the wallet can be every bit as effective an attention-grabber as a whop upside the head with a good-sized stick—plus, you get some new stuff out of the deal.

But, you ask, what's to be done when *they* have been spending *our* money—is there any way for us to avoid wanting to kill them? We shouldn't have to address this, because it should never, ever happen; however, sadly, it does and with alarming frequency. Let us learn from this true-life story submitted by one of the Divas, and don't be frightened; it has a happy ending. The Diva had devoted five years of her life to grooming a guy, teaching him how to be the greatest lover ever, persisting until he even found the G-spot, for crying out loud. Her ministrations to him continued and included regular visits to him in federal prison, where he spent a year for his botched attempt at bank fraud, losing fifty-thousand-some-odd dollars of hers in the process. There's more: She furnished his house, bought his clothes, and took him on fabulous vacations—even paid for his kids' birthday parties.

I am reading her letter and trying to figure out what exactly she was getting out of this deal when I get down to the part where he started to "need space." Now, in my experience, it is pretty hard to crowd somebody when you live a few hundred miles apart, which was the case with our Diva and her scumbag. Of course, "needing space" was just a euphemism for "wanting to have sex with someone else," as is so often the case. Getting people to agree to give you your space is a good deal easier than firing them with enthusiasm for your branching out sexually. The Diva was plunged into the deepest depths of the despair pool by his defection. Here she'd spent all this time and tons of real money on this guy, wishing and hoping and somehow believing that one fine day soon, he would turn into a decent human being; everything would be perfect, and they would go away together and live in a meadow. We've seen this a million times, done it ourselves at least half a million. This is known as believing in Permanent Potential: This person would be perfect if only . . . and could be in the blink of an eye with scarcely any effort on his part. But it will never happen, even if you wait forever and he lives to be a hundred and four.

What happened in real life was that he married the other woman with whom he'd been "having space," and after a while, the Diva got to feeling better and emerged with her self-esteem unscathed and, even more important, well aware of how good-looking she is. And so it came to pass that she was out of town, minding her own business, when she rounded a corner and ran slap-dab, full-frontal, into a seedy-looking, middle-aged guy with a stringy ponytail and a holey T-shirt. Of course, it was *him*. She, on the other hand, was looking her very best, which was extremely good. It was plain to see he wouldn't have to fight for his space with anybody in the foreseeable future—everyone would certainly give him a wide berth. This was even better than having had him maimed and/or killed: She had just left him alone and he went off and got icky! Don't you just love a happy ending?

7

I'll Get You, My Pretty

As a writer, one is called upon frequently to appear on radio and television programs around the country. This helps sell books, which for a writer is just about as good as it gets. More times than one likes, however, one comes to the crushing realization that one's interviewer has not read one's book. Indeed, quite often, the interviewer has not even read the press kit or the liner notes on one's book. The interviewer is, as they like to say, winging it, or as we, the writer, likes to say, completely screwing up something as simple as a sack lunch. I mean, we know you don't have time to read every word we ever wrote, as precious as they are to us personally: You're overworked as it is and they don't give you a time slot at work for "reading." But please, it will be less painful for all of us if you can at least give the book a cursory glance before we go on the air. Or just tell us ahead of time that you haven't read it, so we can provide you with a list of questions to which we know the answers.

I personally had one such interviewer who kept asking me, regarding *SPQBOL*, to give him details about the revenge stuff. He said he understood that we talked a lot about getting revenge in the book.

Well, since there is not one single solitary word about revenge in the whole entire book—I can't recall even the word itself being used—I just blabbered about something completely unrelated that in fact had the distinct advantage of actually appearing in the book, which it is my purpose to promote. This suggested something to me, though: that there is a group out there who wants to hear about revenge. Now, the truth is that we like to keep everybody happily in line so there's no need for anything like that, but if we find that the pushing has indeed come to shoving, well, we like to think we're pretty resourceful and can acquit ourselves handsomely, if need be. So here, I got your revenge right here.

My friend Janet Mayer, who is a completely grown-up woman married to Jim Johnston, who claims to be completely grown up even though he is a man, showed up at this churchy kind of function swathed to her chin in turtlenecks and scarves, all in a stouthearted effort to conceal the fact that she was completely covered up in hickeys—passion marks, love bites, or whatever your high-school crowd called them—she had a whole big bunch of them all over her neck. She was mortified and her discomfiture was exacerbated by our hooting and howling over it. Add to that the irritating look of smugness on Jim's face—well, it just was not to be borne is all you can say. Mr. Jim was pleased with himself and his little joke for about a week, and Janet let him have his little moment and be lulled into a false sense of security by the absence of swift retribution. That's just the way she wanted him—lulled. Oh, she nailed him all right. He just lulled himself to sleep one night, the night before a big board meeting at which he had to make a major presentation, and he awoke to find himself the proud owner of a hickey the shape and nearly the size of Texas, directly beneath his left ear. Katharine Hepburn doesn't have a turtleneck high enough to hide this thing. I would score that one: Battle, Jim; War, Janet.

Not too long after Janet had married Jim, she was trying to impress him with an act of wifely Suzy Homemakerishness by sewing a button on his shirt. She had made sort of a big deal out of it, implying possibly that he was too big a simpleton to sew on a shirt button. Anyway, she got so carried away with her own wifely Suzy Homemakerishness that she didn't think about what she was doing, and when she reached for the scissors to cut her thread, she stuck the needle in the bed. Ordinarily this would have been fine except that it was a water bed. She wanted to wriggle under the thing and hide, knowing the major ribbing she would have to endure for her stupid mistake. And so she did the only thing she could do under the circumstances: nothing. She just got up (from his side of the water bed) and hung up his newly rebuttoned shirt. When no raging torrent of water appeared, she crawled into her side of the bed and went to sleep, and she let him do the same on his side of the bed, right on top of what would become, by about three A.M., Old Faithful. He woke up, soaked to the skin, thinking that he had wet the bed and was desperately trying to figure out how he was going to hide it. It is a major disappointment to me that she did not let him go to his grave believing himself to be the oldest living bed wetter. Who knows when again in this life she will be presented with such an opportunity?

But enough hearsay, you say. What about action undertaken and dished out by the actual Queens themselves? Well, there was this one time that some of us kinda sorta did a fairly mean and dastardly thing. One of the Queens, Tammy, had gotten a d-i-v-o-r-c-e, but she had not retrieved all of the stuff that was rightfully hers from one of her and her ex's several residences. Thinking that it might be a painful and traumatic experience for her to go into that house among all those memories by herself, we decided that we should help her out. It was a good thing, too. No sooner had we gotten in the front door and quickly surveyed the contents of every room than we found just what we had feared the most: evidence of other women. Oh! It just cut us like a knife and we weren't even ever married to him, so imagine the mental suffering of our poor Tammy. We just looked at one another, knowingly, and sent one of the other Tammys out for cigarettes. Oh, not for us—we don't smoke, even though we would look so grown up doing it—we needed them for his closet. The former Mr. Tammy is not a smoker either; on the contrary, he is one of the most avid nonsmokers you will ever encounter. Did I say avid? I meant rabid. So, I ask you, what else could we do but sit in his closet, smoke cigarettes, and blow smoke up the sleeves of all his fresh-from-the-cleaners shirts? We must have been in there for an hour or more, laughing fit to kill, about to puke from the smoke. I've heard it said that revenge is sweet, but it sho' do stink.

And then there was the little anniversary celebration the Queens put on for one of our friends—not a Wannabe exactly, more of a hanger-on, but a friend nonetheless. By chance, what would have been her wedding anniversary had she still been married happily coincided with a little girl-trip we were taking to the beach. We persuaded her to get in touch with an old flame of hers who lived in the area we were visiting. He met us all for a drink, and one by one we made ourselves disappear, leaving the two of them alone at the romantic beach bar at sunset. We went off carousing and generally having a delightful time, secure or at least hopeful in the knowledge that our little buddy was having one as well. By and by, we got curious about how delightful a time she might be having, and so we drove to the beach house to see if his car was outside. It was. Not only that, all the lights were out. Yippee! we thought as we drove off. We hadn't gone far before one of us remembered it was her special day and we hadn't thought to acknowledge that, so we turned the car around, killed the engine at the beginning of the street, turned off the headlights, and coasted down close to the house. We got out and crept up in the bushes beneath the window of the bedroom we thought they would most likely be occupying and commenced to sing—very loudly—"Happy anniversary to you! Happy anniversary to you!" and so on. Helpless with laughter, we made our way clumsily back to the car. As we were turning around, headlights on now, the beams caught movement at the front door. There stood our little buddy—and let me just say that naked is naked, but somehow it looks a whole lot more so in the headlights of a car—just waving and smiling. As we pulled by, we could hear her hollering, "Thank yew!" We remarked on her politeness and her nakedness, both extreme, but she did seem to be having a most delightful time, working fervently to prove the theory that living well is, indeed, the very best revenge.

And Your Little Dog, Too!

One of the Queens, Tammy, had a dog to stir up some trouble for her. YardDog, Tammy's mutt, once got into her neighbor's chickens and ate a whole mess of them all by his ownself, not even bothering to bring a single one home for Tammy to cook. The neighbor lady complained real loud to Tammy about it, too. Tammy was just starting in as to how could she be so certain it was YardDog who ate her precious chickens when who should appear grinning at her back door but Yard-Dog himself, covered in feathers. Tammy just apologized and offered to pay for the chickens. Neighbor lady said nope, Tammy had to replace the chickens. Nine o'clock in the morning on a Saturday, just what Tammy feels like doing with her day is shopping for live chickens. Forty of them. YardDog just loves chicken, and any old way you want to serve them is just fine with him. He obviously thought these were like McNuggets with legs—a little fuzzy, but tasty nonetheless.

It took Tammy a while to focus her eyes and find the telephone book, the yellow pages, and, finally, the chicken stores. YardDog had consumed a large quantity of some off-brand variety of baby chickens, you see, and the neighbor lady wanted the exact same kind in replacement—just your basic yellow puffball wouldn't do. After securing the delinquent YardDog in the house, Tammy lit out for the chicken store. She placed her order and received it—forty live chicks in little brown paper bags. They loaded them into the backseat of the air-conditioned Volvo, Tammy being afraid it would be too hot for them in the trunk, and she wanted no more dead chickens on her conscience that day. Well, Tammy is not one of your leisurely drivers even on a good day, choosing rather to sit up on the edge of her seat, cigarette hanging off her lip, white knuckles gripping the steering wheel, reenacting Talledega and striking fear into the hearts of fellow drivers—and that day the baby chickens, too, who, by their very nature were chicken-hearted to begin with, and were peeping loudly and straining at the confines of the paper bags. As Tammy careened to a stop at a red light, the bags tipped over and half the chickens made good their own escape, freeing their comrades still clawing impotently at the walls of their brown paper prisons. Soon all forty of them were hopping and peeping and pooping all over the Volvo. Tammy was thrilled to have her car's interior instantly redone in Early Chicken Coop at no extra charge, so she wheeled into the neighbor lady's yard, honking the horn. She hopped out, yanked open the rear door, shooed all the puffballs out of the backseat, and yelled, "Here's your chickens!" And Tammy roared off in a cloud of dust, cackling. That has a vengeful smack to it in my opinion.

A delightful and most resourceful reader in North Carolina wrote to describe how her erstwhile husband had made a complete drunken ass of himself at a party one night and then, when finally forced to head for home, proceeded to throw up all over himself in the backseat of our delightful and most resourceful reader's automobile. Here is where the "delightful and resourceful" parts start: She pulled over to the side of the road even though they were in the worst possible part of town and to do so was risking their very lives. He makes quite a picture: well-dressed man-about-town, on his hands and knees heaving his beets onto the already-filthy sidewalk. He finishes and is allowed back in the vehicle. They travel all of about two blocks, and he cranks up again. With somewhat less patience this time, our heroine pulls into a bank parking lot and makes him get out and take off his puke-soaked clothes, which she hurls into the bushes. He is now riding home in his underwear, and just before they get home, he barfs again—this time all over the backseat of the car itself—and being the fastidious bastard that he is, he climbs over into the very back of the station wagon and passes out. Having had just about enough of him by this time, she pulls the car into the garage, locks it, and goes on in to bed, leaving him snoring in the cargo compartment of her wagon. He wakes up at some point during the night, still so drunk he can't figure out how to get out of the locked car, but in his travails, he manages to roll around in the vomitus he's left on the backseat. He is conscious enough to know that he has done so, delicate darling that he is, and this completely discombobulates his sorry ass. By the time he sobers up enough to work the door locks, he has smeared barf from one end of the car to the other. Smelling almost as bad as he looks, he stumbles into the house to berate her for locking him in the car. To which she calmly replies that since he has ruined her perfectly good Camry, he can expect to be out buying her a new Land Cruiser by that afternoon. Don't you just love that new-car smell?

8

No, It's a Hole in the Head We Don't Need

Apparently a few readers—all men, if memory serves—somehow deduced from *SPQBOL* that we do not need them. One of them, in fact, recently asked me to compile a list of the top five or ten reasons Sweet Potato Queens don't need men. I thought and I thought about that. I must confess, I failed utterly in this task. After all, I asked myself, if there were no men, Aretha would have had no cause to sing "R-E-S-P-E-C-T," without which the world would be severely deprived. Bonnie Raitt would never have sung, "I wanna man to love me like my backbone was his own," and then where would we be? I could go on and on, but also consider this: If not men, then who would ever sing to us such memorable words as "I wanna drink your bathwater, baby"? Only a man would ever even think of such a thing. If there were no men, there would be no Johnnie Taylor to sing about the "Big Head Hundreds" and what all he wants to buy us with them. Oh, yes, sisters, we need men all right. We need them and we love them for these and many other reasons. The one and only reason I could think of that would justify our saying that we don't need men is this: We cannot borrow their shoes.

Okay, so we've gone and admitted that we need men. The problem then becomes, as related to us by many of our sisters: Where do you find them? This has just never been a problem for the Queens, as you may well imagine. Our problem is usually more along the lines of keeping the numbers manageable; therefore, we are in an excellent position to offer advice.

"They makin' 'em thangs ever'day," my daddy, who was very wise indeed, always said. Now, granted, he was referring to some manufactured product, but we can certainly give it just the slightest stretch, and it easily applies to men as well, at least in our minds, where, as you know, anything can happen and often does. The fact that they makin' 'em thangs ever'day just shows us, to our great relief, that there is no shortage. Men are in plentiful and readily available supply at all times. This is a big load off our minds, because they are so dang much trouble once you have them, that if you had to go out and hunt and scrounge around for them to begin with, well, it just might not even be cost-effective.

So, if men are everywhere, just waiting for us to pluck them off the vine, then the next question is: Which vine? Indeed, it is our experience that there are so many of them, at every turn, it is easy to get overwhelmed or even jaded and just not even bother plucking any of them. This is not a good set of circumstances. It feels awful, and we find, upon further examination, that it is often an early symptom of a hormonal imbalance; so whenever one of the Queens expresses a disinterest in men, we all immediately gang up on her and make her assess her hormones. If it's not her hormones, it may just be that she's bored with the current crop and needs a change, just like your cat will be completely enthralled with that fake bird on a bungee cord with the bells and feathers and strings hanging off of it, will play with it for hours on end and then, suddenly, it's over. The thrill, as our beloved B. B. King says so well, is gone.

When this happens, there's nothing for it but another trip to PetSmart to get a new cat toy. Sometimes you just got to have a new cat toy. But you know how it is, you go to PetSmart and there's aisle after aisle of nothing but cat toys as far as the eye can see, and they all look pretty good. I mean, it's the same basic premise with all of them—they're on some kind of springy cord attached to a stick, they all have things that jiggle and wiggle and catch your eye. Some are bigger than others, some make more noise, some are fancier while others are more no-frills and serviceable. But you can't really try them out in the store. Oh, I know, they encourage you to bring your pets in there and all that, and that may work fine with some dogs, but cats are just not really who you want to take to the mall, now are they? Even that most famous of Southern cats, Willie Morris's own Spit McGee, is not a good shopper. Cats just don't get the theory of going to the store to look at new stuff. And anyway, most of the cat toys are sealed up in wrappers, so you couldn't try them out in the store even if you could induce your cat to go shopping with you. And would you really want to buy a floor-demo cat toy for your kitty? So it is with us, sisters.

There's tons of men out there, but the only way to know if you like them is to try them out for a while. Mercy, how do you settle on one or two to try? A number of folks have shared their Rules for Dating with us. From Pensacola, Susi writes that when she and her friends were in their thirties they had the ten-year rule—you couldn't date anybody more than ten years younger or older than yourself. But Marjorie, from another Southern state, writes that, at sixty-five, she is beginning to find her fifty-year-old lover a bit old for her! Yippee! is just all I can say to that. Now that the Queens are older and, we believe, wiser, we have amended this to the new Mommer'n'em Rule, which requires that you must be younger than his mama and have never dated his daddy. The Menopause Mafia of Louisiana (they are all named Taffy because they're all teachers—and teachers get chewed on many times each day) has as its number one rule: Never date a man whose mama is not dead.

Well, the Queens have come up with a system that works for us. We find we do best in situations when we can really focus our energies and attention. For this we need a theme, and that is what we are recommending to you today: Theme Dating. It doesn't really narrow the field, just your area of focus for the moment, but for that reason makes the field more manageable for you. The theme is completely arbitrary and at your total discretion. You may select any theme, pursue it for as long as it amuses you, and then change it, with no prior warning to anyone else. It's your theme, do with it what you will. As I said, a bunch of the Queens are married and so their themes are pretty much set, for the time being anyway. For the rest of us, the theme is a constant source of entertainment. We had a long-running Jewish theme there for a while. We dated only Jewish men. At the outset, I recalled a conversation that had taken place many years before with my good friend Helen Murphey Austin, whom I actually credit with introducing me to the Joys of Jews. She was dating a man named Edward Cohen—a Jew who has grown up to be a very fine screenwriter and recent author of *The Peddler's Grandson*, which is the story of his growing up Jewish in the South. Helen and Edward got me to go out with Edward's best friend, who just so happened to be Jewish as well, named Ralph Salomon. To provide the extremely little persuasion it took to get me to go out with Ralph, truly one of the most handsome men I have ever dated, Helen assured me that "Jewish men and Southern [non-Jewish] women get along like a house afire." That may sound like, may indeed be, a cliché, but it is nonetheless true. You have only to consider the average house and then visualize it completely engulfed in flames to know you've got a fair amount of energy and excitement going on. A blazing house can be loud, but it is certainly not boring, and I can guarantee you will never forget your house burning up—or down, as you prefer. And of course, one thing you can always count on with a fire of any kind— it's damn hot, and with one of this magnitude, even when it dies down, it'll still keep you warm for a long, long time. Oh, my, yes, we do love Jewish men.

For the last good while, though, we have been on a Bob theme. This is not as limiting as you might think on first examination. Just to show you how very versatile this theme theory is: You've got your Roberts, your Robs, your Berts, your Bobbys, Robbys, Berties, in addition to your basic Bobs. And half the men on the planet are named Robert, or at least their middle name is Robert. Then there's the surname factor—Roberts, Robertsons, and the like. We are just covered up in Bobs and/or Bob derivatives. Then there's the battery-operated boyfriend (BOB) that never lets us down. Yeah, buddy, as long as them Eveready boys stay in bidness, we can rest easy. BOBs, gotta love 'em.

I was in Santa Monica not long ago with one of the Queens, Tammy, and we met a very fine young man at the Starting Line athletic shoe store. (If you are ever in Santa Monica, go there and buy your sports shoes—it is the only place I have ever been where they (a) actually give a rat's ass if your shoes fit; (b) actually know how to determine whether or not they do; and amazingly (c) won't sell you a pair of shoes that do not fit perfectly.) So me and Tammy are in the Starting Line buying shoes, as we do at least twice a year, and we find that we are quite taken with our shoe salesman. It is hard not to fall in love with a really well-trained, highly motivated, very attentive shoe salesman, is it not? I mean, he's on his knees in front of you, caressing your feet and paying attention; we can ask little else from a man. Naturally, we fell to fawning over him and praising him to the skies, which only served to increase his fervor for our feet and the shoes in which to enshrine them. Oh, it was a happy, happy circle we had going.

By and by, during this shoe purchase/courtship, Tammy asked our young man his name, to which he replied, "Adam." A momentary silence ensued. "Mind if we call you Bob?" I asked. He graciously, speedily, and without question replied, "Why no, of course not, please do." This just pushed us right over the cliff in love with him on the spot. Here was a guy happily willing to do whatever it took to please us. So fear not if there is a dearth of Bobs in your home area: A willing attitude makes up for a lot.

No Humans Harmed in This Research

Quite a few great analogous stories from the animal kingdom have been reported to me. Occasionally I will read something for myself and remember a fair number of details; more often, however, somebody else will read something interesting and tell me about it, and of that, I will remember the parts I personally find entertaining. Whether or not they are founded in fact is completely immaterial to me, as I imagine it is to you as well; otherwise, you'd be reading *Scientific American* instead of this book. No animals have told me any of the stories discussed herein. Animals don't talk to me directly, although a cat we had once willed me telepathically to name her Debbie. Otis, the brown dog who lives with my nephew, Trevor Palmer, in New Orleans and sometimes with his mother, my sister, Judy, does talk to Judy occasionally. He very softly says "Wow" when he is particularly moved about something, usually the prospect of eating a plateful of pink weenies up in the middle of Judy's bed. Otis loves them pink weenies, and he does love to eat in bed.

At any rate, I heard a story about a bird. I'm pretty sure Martha Thomas told me about it. Martha has a genius IQ, is always reading and remembering and telling me what she reads. Being the one-trick pony that I am, I make a joke out of the stuff. Anyway, I think it was the Alaskan snowy owl, but I could be wrong, so if you're a bird fanatic, don't get all in a wad. The story is what's important, and if we are attributing a characteristic to the Alaskan snowy owl that belongs to some other bird, what possible difference does it make? Don't tell them, and they won't care.

It seems that the female Alaskan snowy owl will not acknowledge the existence of the male Alaskan snowy owl until such time as he presents her with a dead mouse. Not just any ole dead mouse—it can't be one he just had lying around that maybe some other, very picky, girl owl rejected. It must be an extremely fresh dead mouse, and it must be of the appropriate size as to demonstrate clearly the degree of esteem in which he holds her, the object of his affection. He may bring dead mice for days and weeks and she will, of course, eat them right up. She will just eat and ignore him. Until the perfect mouse is presented—the, say, three-to-four-carat mouse—she will not acknowledge to her suitor that the mouse came from him. He is, by this time, wild with desire—and only for her. Doesn't he give up and write her off, taking his dead mice to a more receptive girl owl? Oh no. He becomes completely transfixed by her. He is driven to please her and only her with his mouse prowess. If he goes without getting laid for a month of Sundays, he will persist in hauling dead mice for her perusal/consumption, clinging blindly to the hope and belief that he will prevail.

Now, the story told to me did not include any suggestion that the girl Alaskan snowy owl might ever be so mindless as to just give it up for a substandard mouse, or worse, for gratis, or worst of all, just to make *him* happy. But we don't have to stretch our imaginations too far to get a picture of it, do we? I, for one, have started demanding to see some dead mice around here, and right quick, too. My current fiancé lives two hundred miles away—which makes me like him just a whole lot more—and he has to run up and down the highway all the time just to see me. He seems happy to do so. This is the appropriate attitude for a fiancé, certainly. I shared the dead mouse story with him, and he caught on to it right quick. "You want jewelry, don't you?" he asked, in a not-unpleasant tone—in fact, he actually seemed pretty jovial about it. I sighed and said, Yes, I suppose I do—just no solitaires at this point unless they are on a chain, and don't be eyeing my left hand, either, buckwheat. I've just gotten him broken in good as a fiancé, I ain't messing up this deal any time soon, thank you.

He wanted some help in picking out the right dead mouse, and I was more than willing to give it to him. He said men hate buying gifts for women because they always get the wrong thing, and even though we make a fuss over it, they can tell we hate it. So what I do, and what I advise all of you to do as well, is cultivate a relationship with a good jeweler—one who will write down what you like and keep it handy in case anybody comes in asking. Of course, your best friend should look out for you as well. When my best buddy, Allison Church, was celebrating the tenth anniversary of her marriage to the gift-igmo David, I took matters and him in hand and had the most fabulous ring in the history of the world made for her. David was overjoyed to give her something she so obviously loved. He was less than thrilled about paying for it, but hey, he got over it.

I think we should get together regularly with our girlfriends and talk about what kinds of dead mice we'd like and everybody pick somebody else's boyfriend, fiancé, or husband—maybe draw names—and advise them. Call it a Dead Mouse Party and make all your favorite Sweet Potato Queens party foods and beverages. This is as good an occasion for a party as I personally have ever heard.

About the same time I was doing all that heavy thinking about snowy owls and mice, I was also reading that "Mars and Venus" stuff about men and women. I hate to say it, but that John Gray guy makes sense. He includes at least twenty-five conversations that I personally have had with assorted men over the years—I'm talking word for word practically. Anyway, John Gray says that many problems in relationships are caused by women doing too much for guys. When they like us and we like them, we naturally want to do more and more stuff for them and be sweet to them. What could be wrong with that? Well, it just doesn't work—that is all. They hate it when we do that. This totally supports the theory advanced in *SPQBOL: Treat 'em Like Shit and Never Give 'em Any and They'll Follow You Around Like Dogs.* And I think John Gray was saying exactly that, too, only with more genteel language. And then this snowy owl business comes up. In that particular study, there was no mention of a girl snowy owl ever bringing a dead mouse to a boy snowy owl—not once, not ever in the history of snowy owls. Those snowy owl bitches have figured out the deal and they are sticking with what works.

Now, it would seem that creatures with penises are highly likely to be hardwired with a need to please creatures without penises. And since they only value what they have to work hard to get, we should cease and desist doing anything nice to attract them. It goes against their nature. Instead, we should allow them to bring us presents, but we should not be entirely satisfied with any of them, so that they can work harder at pleasing us in the future. To make them completely happy, we must reject a certain number of their offerings to provide them with even more opportunities for pleasing us.

I think I'm getting the hang of the scientific method.

9

Dating for the Advanced or Advancing

So you're dating again—or dating still—whatever the case. Let's examine the possibilities and potential problems. For instance, what if he is like this really strict vegetarian—one of those vegetarians who look like they died a month or so ago and always smells funny. You can walk in any health-food store in America blindfolded and know immediately where you are by that smell. It's not a bad smell, just distinctive. Anyway, he's one of those who looks sick and makes a big-ass deal about what all he won't eat, and he whines a lot to waiters in restaurants about what is and isn't acceptable in his food. Can this relationship be saved? Well, that all depends. If you are *also* one of those vegetarians who looks half-dead, smells funny, and whines in restaurants, then yes, by all means. Not only can it be saved, it will live long and prosper. It was custom-made in heaven for you.

If, on the other hand, you are, say, me, the big mystery would be how you ever even had the first conversation with him, let alone developed a relationship. If I am going to have to sneak around to eat my favorite foods, chances are excellent that I'd rather be hanging out with the folks I'm sneaking around with. Yeah, yeah, yeah, we all want to eat healthy and live forever and all that, but gimme a break. I'm just saying there is something bad wrong with a guy who claims he never even *wants* a cheeseburger. He's a liar—and a fool to boot—if he thinks anybody believes him. I, personally, am not destined to live my life with this man.

I heard, in this vein, from a delightful woman in Savannah who wrote to say that if she had known women like us years ago, her life would have been dramatically different (not to mention *better*). It seems she was married to a doctor for ten years ("The money was great") who only wanted a "showpiece." He required that she fulfill his definition of a "lady" at all times. The guy had such rules as "Ladies do not drink beer in public" and "They never, ever drink from the can or bottle!" It was, in her words, "a most stifling atmosphere." Well, long story short, she did not give in to her nearly irresistible urges to run over him with her Lexus (which he paid for, thank you very much) but instead merely moved on to more entertaining pastures. And now, several happy, fun-filled years later, she is happy to report that her "current fiancé" says that "she could suck-start a Harley." What a touching story, and we've got a million of 'em.

What if he is just a hideous dresser? He wears those nylon socks that won't even stay up. He wears bow ties, even when he's not dressed up in his clown costume. He parts his hair down the middle. He wears cheap shirts and, even worse, cheap shoes. One of the Queens, Tammy, has based make-or-break decisions on many relationships in her life solely (ha-ha) on the guy's shoes. Tammy simply cannot tolerate bad shoes on a man. I would have to say that if there is enough there to attract you—in spite of this outfit—he bears exploring. If he's suitable for taking out, we can deal with dressing him up. And do remember, if he's spending too much time thinking about his own appearance, he's not paying nearly enough attention to yours. I'd say buff him up a little and keep him if you like him.

What if he's fat? If I like him, I don't care—I'm a hell of a lot fatter than I used to be my ownself and therefore cannot cast a whole lot of stones. Besides, if you go out to dinner with a fat man, you know you're going to be fed well.

What if he's a tightwad? A cheapskate? A miser? A skinflint? Cheap is pretty deadly, but let me point out that so is Spendthrift. My feeling on the cheap guy would be this: If I have to pay for my own dinner, I'd rather be doing it with my girlfriends, where at least we could all talk about how cheap he is. And let me assure you, from personal experience, the Spendthrift will do all his spending on himself, with all his thrift being reserved for you. Money problems are too huge—don't fool with either one of these guys.

What if he smokes and you don't? We think this could be a plus, if he chain-smokes unfiltered cigarettes, and if he's really old, really frail, really rich, and you are his sole beneficiary. I'd say buy him a fancy table lighter and fire it up for him whenever he seems inclined to puff another one. Zippity-do-o-o-o-dah!

The Queens agree that we just couldn't survive a relationship with a humorless man. He could be guilty of several felonies that I could get over easier than this one. Life is too short and way too long to spend it laughless. I'd sooner date a gourd.

One of our funniest men friends is the Only Man We Ever Really Loved—the one from *SPQBOL* who put the butter pats on his head for us. We were recently at a party where he was also a guest. The invitation had instructed us to come attired in "casual chic." He came in a snappy navy blue bathrobe, matching turban, and sunglasses (casual sheik, get it?). He was, of course, the cutest guy there, so we spent all our time hogging his attention away from everybody else. We were his harem and happy about it. When asked what kind of women he preferred in his harem, he said, without hesitation, "Women who lie. That is to say, women who lie down and then lie about it." Perfect answer from the perfect man. No, we won't tell you his name. It's bad enough he always goes home with his wife. We're not letting anybody else horn in.

Yes, for me, a sense of humor is just about the most important thing. He doesn't necessarily have to be funny his ownself, although it's a plus, but he should at the very least be able to tell that I am funny and laugh in all the right places. And he cannot have an overly goofy laugh. We were out of town once and we met this really handsome, charming man at a party and we were all quite taken with him and we were just about to knock ourselves out flirting with him. We excused ourselves for a moment—ostensibly to powder our noses but actually to have a catfight and decide who could actually have him. I don't even remember who won, because as we started back across the crowded room to where we'd left him, waiting hopefully for our return, we heard this sound. When I say it froze us in our tracks, I am talking paralyzed us from the neck down—a thunderous emission that was sort of a cross between a hyuk-hyuk-hyuk and hoo-ee. It was stupefying. We stood there stupefied. Steeped in stupefaction. It was one of the top five worst laughs I have ever heard, and it was coming from the cute guy who, when we left the room, had five or six potential dates, but who, when we returned to that sound, suddenly had none. He was totally up for grabs again at that point.

Acting goofy is tolerated more readily, and you have only to look at the cover of this book to see why. I once dated a guy—even brought him home to meet Mama. At one point she left the dinner table momentarily and was enthralled by the sight that greeted her return. There he sat at the table, calm as you please, acting as if nothing out of the ordinary was going on, and nothing much was—except that he had two enormous wads of chewed-up roast beef stuck behind the lenses of his glasses, completely covering his eyeballs. Don't ask me what would possess a man to do such a thing, but I will tell you that we all absolutely adored him. He definitely picked the right house to do that in.

The Queens do enjoy group dating from time to time. This is not to be confused with group sex, which we are way too selfish for. Sharing the spotlight at a cocktail party is one thing; sharing candlelight is quite another—no, thank you very much. But it is big fun to have one guy take a bunch of us out—and is he ever the envy of every guy in the place. The Menopause Mafia wrote to say that they had a group date with a man who took them all to dinner. While he was in the men's room, they told the maître d' and the waiter that he was their daddy, and they were all half sisters who had just met for the first time when they arrived at the restaurant. This added a certain air to the evening for all of them.

A well-intentioned guy friend was trying to interest one of the Queens—Tammy, I believe it was—in going out with his former roommate from college. "I lived with this guy, Tammy, and I'm telling you he's hung like Paw Paw's bull!" was how he put it precisely. Coming from another guy, that's pretty high praise, I reckon.

Meeting new people through mutual friends is one way of expanding your dating pool. Intra-office dating is another. If you are me or a close personal friend of mine, I am totally against it because when you're doing it—not as in "doing it," but as in dating within the office—you think you're *invisible* and the whole thing is just your little secret. Ha! You couldn't be more conspicuous if you set yourselves on fire. Not only does everybody else know—I'm talking the people who come in at night to rake out the place? They know, and not only do they know, but they're talking to everybody in town. You ninnies!

People passing you on the interstate know—we all know what you're doing. And it is highly entertaining to watch you guys slip around, acting like you're so sly.

See, igmos, what you look like is when a cartoon character falls in love—you know, with the big heart pumping out of your chest, hearts in your eyes and floating all around your head, and your feet flapping like wings so you're hovering about a foot off the floor with this incredibly goofy look on your face. Drive by any junior high school and look at the couples—that's exactly what you look like. And that's on a good day, of course, when there are no bumps in the road of your big romance. The bad days are every bit as entertaining as the good ones—to all of us observing, anyway. And trust me, we all know when you're, as my now twelve-year-old daughter says, "in a fight," and we're taking bets on the outcome. Not only that, we're sneaking around trying to actually witness some of it firsthand to share with the others at break time.

Oh, I know, it seems so great to be able to see this person every waking minute when you're in the blush of first infatuation with him, but try to think ahead for five minutes here and imagine how much you will like spending every waking minute with him if/when the passion cools. I suggest a more practical idea would be to host office mixers. Invite all the single people from different offices to get together for meeting and pairing-off opportunities. Bill it as an opportunity for the guys to meet some potential ex-wives.

Wisdom of the Aged

We are continually delighted by letters and e-mails we receive from readers who say that *SPQBOL* has become the handbook, the manual, the catechism for them and their friends and that they have taken to memorizing passages and quoting them, chapter and verse, when the occasion calls for an immediate dose of wisdom. This warms our hearts because we do feel that we are missionaries, and the zeal of the Baptists' Lottie Moon is no match for our own in our quest to heal the lives and save the psyches of the lost, the downtrodden, and the bored.

We were in L.A., Tammy and I, on what turned out to be a Mission Trip. Actually we were in Santa Monica at the Pritikin Longevity Institute—we go there once a year now. The first time we went, Tammy's daddy semi-made us go. We were looking for a spa vacation, and he indicated that he would make a substantial financial contribution to the deal if we would go to Pritikin. Our perception of Pritikin was that we would go and learn to eat grass and dirt clods and be utterly wretched for a week, but we were persuaded to do it by two things: (1) We thought it would be a good place to meet the kind of men we really want (old, rich, bad hearts, thick cataracts) and (2) Tammy's daddy was buying. Well, we just fell in love with the place. The food is absolutely fabulous and—even better—they insist that you eat practically all day every day, which, of course, perfectly coincides with our personal preference. They have everything a spa has, but everybody on staff is an M.D. or a Ph.D., and so not only will you not be exposed to any idiotic crackpot exercise/diet fads, but you will actually come away with a pretty decent education in how to save your own life. Plus, it's in the Loew's Hotel—gorgeous—smack on Santa Monica Beach, and you can walk or bike or Rollerblade down to Venice every day to goon the weirdos and the bodybuilders. So we love the place and now we go every year at Labor Day.

This particular trip turned out—as so many of our excursions do—to be a Mission Trip. We made two new friends for life—Katie Dezember, a mere child from Bakersfield, and Charlie McGreevy from NYC. Although he didn't appear to have cataracts, he did meet our other criteria, which we shared with him. He was so happy with himself. It never occurred to him before he came to Pritikin that being slightly older and having a somewhat weakened heart would be such a boon to his social life. He was well aware that being rich was a definite asset. Having perked up Charlie considerably just by picking him as our boyfriend for the week, the three of us, Tammy, Charlie, and I, undertook the education of young Katie. Tammy and I explained to her the many reasons why she should be looking for a man just like Charlie, although we advised her that we had spoken for Charlie himself, and she dare not cross that line. We saw right off what a quick study she was going to be by how fast she grasped that concept. Charlie was deliriously happy to find himself the center of attention and the sole object of desire for not one, not two, but three young and luscious women—although one was admittedly much younger, their luscious quotients were fairly equal.

He was most eager to contribute to young Katie's education, particularly on the topic of the desirability of older men, and he spoke most earnestly to her about it. "Well, it even says so in the Bible!" he assured her. Since he couldn't quote the chapter and verse, I consulted our utmost authority on all matters, especially spiritual and sexual, Professor Larry L. King. (One of the best things that has happened to me as a result of the publication of *SPQBOL* is that I have gotten to meet some other writers—real writers, I like to call them. Larry L. King, who wrote *The Best Little Whorehouse in Texas* and a whole bunch of other equally fine stuff, has become a regular mentor to me. Of course, I know he only pays attention to me because I bandy the Promise about so freely, but hey, that's what it's for, after all. And his cute wife, the lawyer Blaine, does her best to keep us in separate states.) And Larry L., of course, knew right off the top of his head the precise passage that Charlie was referring to: "And Ashael sayeth to a maiden of tender years, Seekest thou a Man of Age; and though his eyes may weep plumgum and his hoary head be of white, fear not when he is yet full of moisture, seed, and heart. Take him to lie with, for surely he will comfort thee beyond all others and make thee exceedingly glad." Hezekiah 14:9. (This is found only in the newly revised Bible for Lechers and Other Fun-Loving Folks, most of which was personally written by 'Fessor King his ownself.)

The age factor continues to be a major point of discussion in the dating dilemma. Some folks are adamantly opposed to dating persons younger than themselves, while others don't care if their dates only recently grew their complete set of molars. I would have to say that there are more women who prefer older men than there are men holding out for older women, but it does happen. Happens to us all the time, of course, because men of all ages are clamoring for the Queens.

I, personally, had two stellar age-related events last year. The first one occurred at a swimming pool where I often take BoPeep and her buddies to loll about in the sun. Besides being the Boss of all the Sweet Potato Queens, I also happen to be the once and future queen of the cannonball, which is what I was doing when this event occurred—I was conducting, and winning, a cannonball contest with all the kids and the only other adult who will play with us, T. P. Walker. I also had my friend Bill's son and his buddies with me that day, so I was in the midst of a veritable covey of children. Bill came by to check on us and we were having the cannonball contest. I guess we had made a fair amount of racket because some of the older residents around the pool came out to see what was cooking. T.P. swam over to me in hysterics. He said that one of the women (now, she's probably a hundred and has cataracts like Coke bottles, but I don't care and neither would you) asked him who all the kids were and he said, "That's my friend Jill, and that's her daughter and her friends," and so on. That wasn't enough for her—she pointed out each child and wanted to know who he/she was and T.P. dutifully named them all. Finally she said, "But who's the one in the black swimsuit?" and he said that's the mama—that's Jill—to which she replied, "Why, she can't be anybody's mama! She can't be more than thirteen!" Let me just tell you, there are few things in life better than being forty-six and having somebody—anybody—guess that you are thirteen. As a matter of fact, I don't think there is anything better than that. I called Bill over immediately and made T.P. tell it all again. Oh, it was the high point of my life, all right; I figure it had to be all downhill from that point. Or so I thought.

Just a few short months after that I was helping a sick friend (who shall remain nameless, but for the sake of discussion, let's just call him something, say, John Doe or even Michael Rubenstein) to check into the hospital with a really brutal stomach bug, and the woman filling out his admission papers looked past him to where I was sitting and said, "And is this your daughter?" Now, I can tell you, sick as he was, he didn't look that bad, and I sure as hell didn't look that good, but hey, "gift horse," I say. I might have pushed it over the top when I spoke up and said, "Yes, ma'am, and I'm the baby—I have lots of older sisters at home." If that didn't kill him, he's bulletproof.

My friend Skip, or Skippy when he's being darlin', which is most all the time, has a pesky habit of going out with women younger than himself. Women of all ages love Skippy because, as I said, he's darlin', but the Queens don't like him paying attention to anybody other than us and especially not to anybody younger than we are. In an attempt to rid him of this predilection for pre-forties women, I explained it to him. I got right in his face and asked him what he could see, to which he replied, "Not a damn thing." Of course, I knew that because I couldn't see him, either. After forty you just can't see stuff that's real close up. This is a good thing. It's nature's way of compensating for what's happening to our faces and bodies. If we can't see it, it's not really happening—like closing your eyes and thinking you're invisible.

This explains a lot when you think about it. Like when you see a woman our age still wearing her hair real long and dressing like a teenager: It's because she can't see well enough to tell how ridiculous she looks, and she still thinks she's cute. And if she sticks to guys her age and older, they'll fall for it, too, because they can't see either. However, I told Skippy, still in his face—she can see *you!* This close, and she can still see everything! He gasped in horror. Then I walked about thirty feet away and said, What do you see now? He said that wasn't real clear either, and again I assured him, she can still see you. For two mutually old people, up close, everything gets soft and blurry around the edges, kind of like being photographed through a cheese-cloth filter—it's actually very flattering. Distance achieves the same effect. The only place we can see well without our glasses is an arm's length away, and if you light a few candles that looks pretty good, too. So the only way we would consider dating someone significantly younger than ourselves would be if he is legally blind—because we still *feel* terrific.

Everyone is tempted by the allure of youth from time to time, I suppose. A very good friend of ours found herself employing the very cutest little young thing. She guessed he was about thirty-four, which would have been young enough to disqualify him, but it turned out he was only twenty-five. I could see where she was headed from a long way off, and I tried mightily to verbally slap some sense into her before she ended up in court. She would just look me straight in the eye with a face of cherubic innocence and deny, deny, deny. My better instincts, however, told me she was just trying to get me to shut up and quit spoiling her mood, which was nearly euphoric. Then it came to pass that the two of them were off in a foreign land on business, and I could feel the sexual tension building from five thousand miles away. I was firing off e-mails on an hourly basis, desperately trying to save her and her career from certain doom. And then it came to me— sweet inspiration. I received an on-screen instant message from her. The two of them were sitting in the spring sunshine at an outdoor café in Paris, checking their e-mail on their respective laptops. So I sent her a little instant message right back: "So, how is Opie?" She read it, glanced over her screen at her very young companion, and fired back: "YOU BITCH!" And thus was she saved from her own lascivi-ousness, and just in the nick, too. Since then, the dense hormonal fog has lifted, and she has thanked me often and profusely for giving her the old slap-in-the-face-with-a-wet-squirrel that was necessary to jerk her back from the precipice.

Alas, even I am not immune to the charms of boyhood. Not long ago, as I came racing belatedly to my place on a plane, I discovered that I was seated next to a man who caused me to wonder to myself, "Hmm—just who is this sack of diamonds?" Trenton, age thirty-three and my own personal Opie—he's just the kind of guy for whom exceptions to the rules should be made. As soon as he gets all his molars, I think it will be okay to start breaking rules with him, unless, of course, he goes blind before then.

10

Marriage~ If You Must

One of the Queens, Tammy, and I were discussing the seemingly endless problems in relationships—relationships with guys, of course, since we all get along perfectly well with one another. As a matter of fact, the happiest couples we know are either gay men or lesbians. This is discouraging to us since we don't appear to be about to fall in love with each other. I mean, we think it would have struck us by now if it was going to. It is our apparent misfortune that we like sex with men, and only men, and we like it a whole lot, which means it will be necessary for us to be involved with them, and therein lies the problem. Lately, they all want to marry us.

We spent a substantial portion of our precious youth desiring, achieving, and dissolving marriages. Now we are old and have acquired good sense. After years of trying to have deep, meaningful relationships with men, we find that now we are constantly seeking shallow ones. We used to think of relationships as being some kind of rock, permanent, solid, immutable. And often we were right—except upon close examination, we found that we had somehow become lodged under the rock and it was pretty dark under there. And if you happened to roll that rock over, you discovered that all manner of crawly stuff you didn't really want to see was living up under there with you.

Nowadays, we are looking for something more along the lines of Formica. You can get it in a variety of colors and patterns, there's a never-ending supply of it, and it comes in a big roll: You just lop off the amount you need. It's inexpensive, easy to install, wipes clean, and is very easily replaced. Now that we are seeking shallowness, however, everybody wants to marry us. We chalk this up to the perversity of men, and it's apparently just further proof of the Treat 'em Like Shit and Never Give 'em Any theory. (It is fast moving from theory to law.) The more you try to get away from them, the more hotly they will pursue you. And if you want to get rid of a guy, you have only to act like you are really crazy about him. This means that when you are young, and possibly interested in marriage, you can never sleep with a man you really like. As soon as you do, he's headed for the door. You can sleep only with men you never want to see again. Once you and your men get old, you can sleep with them, but you must refuse all offers of marriage if you want the relationship to flourish.

The Queens are not unanimous when it comes to marriage. Some of the Tammys are, in fact, married, and to men they actually like. And while we are ecstatically happy for them in their good fortune, the rest of us have been so blissed out by the wedded state that we just don't think it would be fair to partake of any more of it. Not wanting to appear greedy, we will let somebody else have a turn at it. Some of us would go so far as to opine that marriage should be avoided if at all possible. The only way I can envision myself getting back into it would be if it was an old-fashioned shotgun wedding, and even then I might be tempted to size up the marksmanship of whoever was holding the gun—and maybe make a run for it.

Every year or so, somebody does a survey, and each and every time the results are the same: The happiest people on the planet are married men and single women. Now, why do you reckon that is? One report that I read said that virtually every divorced woman interviewed—even ones who had lost custody of their children—testified to "feelings of euphoria" after the proceedings were over, whereas among divorced men, the suicide rate is through the roof. We detect a pattern here.

I personally think the problem lies in too much proximity. Shared space is just death to most relationships. That old guy who got beaten to death with a shoe would probably be alive today—and perhaps even happily married—if the couple had just had the good sense to live in a duplex. Think about it: If you never had to pick up after him; never had to struggle to get up out of an icy toilet bowl in the middle of the night; if you never had to wear an overcoat in your own home in the middle of summer; if you could watch *White Palace* without someone farting and laughing during the tender moments; if you could sleep without earplugs to drown the foghorn snoring; and also if right next door lived the sweetest, funniest, most considerate man in the world, who came over on a regular basis (when invited) for dinner (followed by breakfast on many occasions), helped with the dishes, took out the garbage, brought you soup when you were sick—all the stuff he used to do before you married him—now tell me you wouldn't jump at the chance. That is my idea of true wedded bliss: close enough to be of use but not constantly underfoot. Find and marry the Right Guy (on the list of Five Men You Must Have in Your Life at All Times—see the glossary), make sure he can pay for things, and make sure the wedding is as simple and quick as possible, go on a fabulous honeymoon, come home, and move into a duplex. I guarantee you'll be happy forever.

My friend Don Yaeger said that he and his wife, Denise, had both been married before to other people, in the traditional $800,000 wedding ceremonies; after dating each other a good long while, they upped and ran off to Las Vegas and got married by an Elvis impersonator. They have the tape of their vows, which included promises to "always be a hunkahunka burnin' love" and to "never take each other to Heartbreak Hotel." Although they don't live in a duplex, he does travel in excess of two hundred days a year, and that, in my opinion, is just as effective an arrangement for achieving endless love.

A good friend of mine, longtime-divorced, recently passed what would have been her thirty-year wedding anniversary had she remained married. I could not tell how she was feeling about it. I said I knew twenty-five was silver, but what was thirty? Completely deadpan, and with no hesitation, she replied, "It's either steel wool or handguns, I forget."

For Those Who Can't Resist

When you're young, you can't wait to get married. Notice I said "get" married—no mention of "being" married. That's because you can look at gorgeous magazines and try on amazing dresses, attend other people's weddings and see close-up and personal what it is like to *get* married. Nothing on this earth can prepare you for the reality of being married. You won't listen to anybody who's done it. Don't feel bad: None of us would listen, either. However, once you have been married, if you ever do decide to get married again, it will be a whole different deal. You will know that all that money can be better spent on just about anything—a lifetime supply of chewing gum or a house or something—than a wedding. A wedding is the—well, maybe not *the*— but certainly one of the stupidest financial decisions a woman ever makes in her life. (There are many more to choose from and some of us have chosen them all, but we'll get to that after the wedding.) I don't know of even one single woman—certainly not one who is single again—who is glad she spent a bazillion dollars on her wedding. Everybody now wishes she had even half that money for plastic surgery or something else that might bring long-lasting pleasure.

Occasionally, one of the Queens will up and get married. I say "up and" because we have learned that that is the best way to do it. One day you're not married, the next day you are. Just do it, if you're so determined; don't be pussyfooting around at this stage of life. If you're contemplating marriage for the first time, you might as well skip this section. Those dresses are some powerful juju, and once you try one on, you're a goner. Of course, you could get married in whatever and then spend five thousand dollars on a few things you could actually wear in real life; and one day you will wish you had, but you don't believe that now, so go on. Just remember: I told you so.

When one of the Queens, Tammy, recently pulled the "up and get married" deal, we made notes for her, which we will now share with you. As soon as you get the proposal and acceptance part out of the way, your first concern should be: "How can I manage to pull this off without running any errands?" Impossible, you say? Well, you're right, there are inescapable errands involved in getting married, which are built in to keep people from getting a wild hair to enter into a completely binding, insoluble contract (my God, it's till you die!) and then wishing they'd just gone to the mall instead. No, they have it fixed where you cannot "accidentally" get married. You have to do it on purpose and you have to hassle.

You can manage to beat the marriage racket out of a significant number of errands, though, if you will just eliminate excessive prep time. Just call your friends and ask them to be bridesmaids—all of them, guys included. This precludes any thought time whatsoever. Just issue a blanket invitation: Tell everybody to wear a wedding dress, a bridesmaid's dress, or a Hawaiian shirt. Give these people five days' notice, at the most. If they get too much advance notice, they will have better outfits than you. Give the preacher three days' notice. This way you can avoid the four mandatory two-hour prenuptial counseling sessions. He or she will still try to snag you for forty-five minutes or so, but even at that, it's quite a savings.

The most important thing is to work out your own prenup agreement and get it carved in stone and signed in blood. The main thing you need to iron out is that you and your friends may do whatever you wish forever and that he has to do whatever you say and like it a lot. Many heartaches and divorces could be avoided if only couples would work these things out prenup. Once you're nupped, it's too late.

My favorite prenup agreement is the one I entered into with one of the mainmost loves of my life, Michael Rubenstein. We took a solemn, holy vow that we would never, ever, no matter what, marry each other. I credit that covenant with the fact that we are still in love to this very day—from a very comfortable distance.

Paperwork, blood tests, his ring: *blech*—errands, all, but alas, inescapable. Trust me, if you could get out of them, I would know about it. You have to get a license and it's a pain in the butt, especially if you don't give them seven or eight months to type it. If you want to get married this year, let alone this week, you have to know somebody who can pull some strings. You have to go to the health department and get a blood test for all the curable STDs (I'm not sure what the thinking is here; no one seems to care if your gene pool is infested with tadpoles). At any rate, it is worthwhile because when you do finally complete all the papers and tests satisfactorily, they give you a Newlywed Kit with your license. It contains, I swear to God, samples of Tide, Woolite, and Massengill, plus a discount coupon for Frederick's of Hollywood. I am not joking. Go get a marriage license and see for yourself.

Re: his ring. It's round and gold. Get it and go. Spend all available time and money on your ring.

Re: the ceremony. Let the guests choose their favorite songs and have a hootenanny. The bride or a close friend of hers should sing "My Way." Keep the vows to an absolute minimum. Don't go promising a bunch of stuff you have no intention of doing—it will come back to haunt you. Or at least cut yourself some slack. Don't be booming out these "Yeses" and "I swear to God, I wills." Smile sweetly and promise to "try real hard." The groom, on the other hand, makes another set of vows entirely. He must promise to carry you around on a little satin pillow and cater to your every whim until he is, in fact, dead as a boot.

Location can really set the tone for the whole ceremony as well as for the wedded state to follow. If I ever get married again—I won't say never because every time I say that wretched word, I end up eating it—but if I ever do, I have already picked the location. I would most definitely do it on the Mississippi Gulf Coast at a place Tammy and I found. It is right on Highway 90, easy in-and-out access, right across the street from the beach, and the sign, big as the sun, says, JOE'S TEXAS BARBECUE AND SNO-KONES! GETTING MARRIED? MINISTER AVAILABLE! Now, I ask you, what could be more perfect? You've got your reception just ready-made for you right there, and two of my very favorite foods, too. I'd a lot rather have me some Texas barbecue and a big ole sno-kone than a hunk of dried-up wedding cake any day of the week—you?

Face it, there are some basic inequities in these vows. The only hope you have of pulling this thing off is finding Mr. Right. Mr. Right is that man who believes that the sun shines brightly from your every bodily orifice. This man will eat dirt, run rabbits, and howl at the moon for you. He will tell you you are gorgeous when you aren't wearing any makeup and you know perfectly well you look like whodunit. He will say that you have the most beautiful legs, when the mirror and everyone else in the world says your knees look like globs of biscuit dough. He must be heart-stoppingly handsome, smart, funny, and a snappy dresser. All your friends and family must adore him. Otherwise, when he turns out to be an ax-murderer, and so many of them do, you will be forced to stomach endless "I told you so's." Okay, you say, these guys are a dime a dozen, and right you are. So how do I pick the right one and how do I keep him down on the farm, so to speak? Well, as you know, Tammy says to treat him like shit and never give him any and he will follow you around like a dog. And it certainly does work like a charm. However, we have noticed that whenever we don't give them any, we, at the same time, are not getting any. This is a problem.

As to making that final determination on Mr. Right, here's a suggestion. Say you have four possible suitors meeting the aforementioned criteria and grovel-potential—how do you pick one? Easy. Pick the one who doesn't have a job. This will leave him endless time to run all your errands. Trust me, this is the only satisfactory reason to get married—to get your errands run. The only way marriage can succeed is for one of the partners to commit to a lifetime of fetching and toting. Really, there is documented proof, statistics and stuff. The normal divorce rate is, like, one out of three—pretty grim, huh? But when one of the parties is not gainfully employed and spends every waking hour running errands, the numbers are one out of seventeen hundred. So if you hate errands as much as I do, and I know you do, take it from me: *If you want to be happy for the rest of your life, never be a normal workingman's wife; so from my personal point of view, get the unemployed to marry you!*

A really, really good friend of ours just loves to get married. I'm not sure how much she likes being married, but getting married just tickles her no end, apparently, on account of she has done it so many times. We keep trying to tell her, "You don't have to marry them anymore, Pam!" but she just keeps right on doing it. Whenever we get word of the latest husband, we just say, "Well, you know our Pam, she just loves a spring weddin'!"

One of her former husbands was an Elvis impersonator—well, not really, but after they split up, that's what we told everybody: most gratifying. Pam is one of the smartest women we know, who is, on occasion, just dumb as a sack full of hammers. She and Elvis were looking into buying a farm. Big yard, as in lots of grass. The Realtor suggested, laughing, that they might want to get a couple of goats. Elvis laughs, too, and says, "Yeah, and a couple of bush hogs." They walk on. Pam is standing there, mouth-breathing, her thoughts in a maelstrom. "Bush hogs!" she's thinking. "My God!" She could just see them rooting around in the front yard, all hairy and nasty. "What will the neighbors think?" she's shrieking inside her head. She is in a positive frenzy. Finally she gets up her nerve. "How big *is* a bush hog?" she asks. They tell her and she starts stomping around, waving her hands and rolling her eyes. "Will they run at me and jump up on me and run my hose? Can we just get some little bitty ones?" The two guys now realize that she is thinking of a huge, living mutant pig-thing instead of a tractor. They just let her go right on, getting more and more worried, asking more and more stupid questions with every panicked breath. Only when she finally asked, "What do they eat besides grass and how much?" did they show her the John Deere.

Sometimes people really do take my advice, and I must say, few things in life can make me happier. My friend Fran just did everything I said regarding her wedding to That Guy. (He had a name, John, which soon was lengthened to Poor John, but early on none of us could remember his name and would always ask if she was still dating That Guy, and it stuck.) I told her a hit-and-run wedding was the way to go. She gave everybody about thirty minutes' notice, and we met at City Hall—"we" being Fran, That Guy, Wilson Wong, and me. Wilson's main job in life is official consort to the Sweet Potato Queens in the persona of Lance Romance, but he is also an architect, restaurateur, professional photographer, corporate trainer, and I don't know what else; pretty much whatever we need done, he can do it. We needed him to take photos at the hit-and-run wedding. As you may know, I like themes a lot, and the theme for the hit-and-run wedding was Schnozzes and Rubber Chickens; Wilson brought both. We all met up at the appointed hour in Mayor Dale Danks's office in City Hall, and Hizzoner himself performed the nupping. I gave the bride away. When we were asked the question re: objections to the nupping from outsiders, we replied that they had plenty, so we didn't invite them. I gazed fondly at the happy couple, clasping the rubber chicken to my bosom while Wilson snap, snap, snapped away with his Brownie camera. Postnup, the three of us posed in the Wedding Schnozzes, doing a three-hand grip on the rubber chicken, grinning maniacally, much to the puzzlement of Hizzoner. He willingly posed for his own photo with the rubber chicken, however, never being shy about photo ops of any kind. (In my opinion, he is still the cutest mayor we ever had in Jackson, and no one can dispute the quality of his tan.)

Anyway, then we went to see about getting the chicken baptized, but the priest, Jerry McBride (whom I have known since shortly after the earth cooled), said na-a-a-a, we couldn't do that, but we could hold the chicken between us when we took Communion, so we settled for that. After that we put on the big rubber noses again for more pictures.

The social debut of the rubber chicken was a smashing success. It went everywhere with the newly nups. The standard "make me puke" wedding photos were transformed by the addition of the chicken. The ring photo featured the hands of the bride and groom clasped tightly around the neck of the chicken, in the time-honored celebration of the ritual of choking the chicken. (If you don't understand this term, you are undoubtedly a woman who has led a sheltered, brotherless life. Ask a guy or a woman with teenaged sons.) The gorgeous array of food took on a new aura with the rubber chicken languishing amongst the shrimp and cellophane noodles. (A hit-and-run reception with excellent eats is, after all, just a phone call away. A good caterer will do anything you say for the right price.)

Captured forever on Kodachrome is That Guy gazing adoringly at Fran, as she looks mysterious yet fairly well pleased about the whole thing. Further examination of the photo reveals the chicken's feet dangling from underneath the otherwise demure wedding gown. Instead of that ridiculous garter, picture That Guy rakishly removing a rubber chicken from Fran's silk-clad thigh and tossing it over his shoulder to the clamoring crowds.

The camera captured bride and groom offering the wedding cake, not to each other, but to the chicken. Soon everyone was snapping souvenir photos of the chicken and the happy couple and trying to wedge themselves into the photos as well. A blinding moment of flashbulbing occurred when the chicken posed between two slices of white bread just about to enter Fran's mouth—sure to be a poster one day. Someone wondered how the chicken was going to hold up under all this activity. Bets were made on the condition of the chicken post-honeymoon. Now, if only Fran had listened to the part about living in a duplex . . . The chicken fared better than the actual marriage.

Where's His Mother When You Need Her?

I really would like to take issue with the guy—and don't you just know it was one, too—who wrote those marriage vows that everybody so blithely takes all the time—specifically, the part about "in sickness and in health." Apparently there is different fine print in the vows the men take from the ones we take. Theirs says something like, "I can just get a little out of sorts and take to my bed and whine and moan and you have to wait on me and fetch and tote and I get to loll about and make your life hell." In ours, well, there apparently is no provision for getting sick. It is business as usual for us girls, deathbed notwithstanding—get over it. Shake it off, and by the way, what would be for supper? It is not just that nobody cares if Mom is sick; it's really more that nobody even notices. You are expected to carry out your duties regardless of any unpleasant or unsightly physical symptoms you are manifesting.

I once spoke to a women's group, and my opening line was "My life is over: My husband has the flu." A universal empathetic groan went up from the audience. Come earthquakes, come floods, come plagues and pestilence. Never mind wars and rumors of wars. Forget economic disaster. Staggering debt, be it national or personal, signifieth nothing. Everything and everybody can just go up in a puff of smoke for all I care—just deee-liver me from a man with a fever.

I remember, not with any particular fondness, a time when I was still married to Moon Pie. For the sake of clarity, there are a fair number of times that I do remember with particular fondness; however, not the time about which I am going to tell you. I had been fairly miserable myself the week before, having endured the flu myself. My daughter, BoPeep, who would have been about five then, had been sick as well. She had the flu on her fifth birthday, as a matter of fact. She and I weathered the storm as well as might be expected. We pretty much just took to our beds and waited it out. We got over it, rescheduled her birthday party, and emerged unscathed from our little bout with the flu bug.

Or so we thought.

Before Tragedy struck: Moon Pie got it. And we wished we had died with it when we had the chance.

This is the man who—when he had his wisdom teeth removed—complained that I filled the ice bags wrong. Wrong? I'm no nurse, but I really thought this was within my scope of capabilities. Gee, guy, it looked to me like you just unscrewed the top, put in ice cubes and water, and screwed the top back on. He had me jackknifing all over the house trying to get the ratio of ice to water correct in his ice bags. He wasn't happy if the bag was too "smooshy." I did this for one entire day, at the end of which I put the whole ice bag—ice, water, and all—in the freezer. The next morning I presented him with his totally non-smooshy ice brick and suggested, sweetly, where all he might put it if it didn't suit him or his sore jaw. Hint for the soon-to-be-married: Make him have his wisdom teeth removed before you marry him.

When 'Peep and I came down with the flu, I insisted that 'Pie call his doctor and get a prescription for amantadine, since it can help keep you from getting it if you take it soon enough after being exposed. He complained and bitched—not about having to call the doctor, but about me telling him to do it. He stomped out of the house when I suggested that the sooner he got it, the better. He would call when he was ready and go to the store when he was ready. Imagine my surprise when, several hours later, he returned with the pills, and I, just as a matter of conversation, you understand, since I truly didn't give a rat's ass at this point, asked if he had taken any of them. I'll have you know, he forgot. Self-reliance, what a wonderful thing. He didn't need me to tell him to call the doctor, and he certainly didn't need me to tell him to go to the drugstore. Someone dropped the ball, however, when it came to telling him to take the stupid pills. Apparently, that was when I was supposed to speak up. Live and learn, I suppose.

Everybody Loves a Stun Gun

Not so very long ago, my good buddy Bill Brown decided to take unto himself a wife, and for this purpose, he selected the charming Linda. I went to the Everyday Gourmet to consult with the owner/Queen, Tammy, about an appropriate gift for Bill's latest and most excellent adventure. We knew we were looking for something appropriately manly for the intrepid Bill. Tammy and I took our time to find just the right thing.

The first part was easy: I knew he had just bought himself a very large, very manly grill, so we just found the largest, manliest set of grill tools ever assembled. Done. The next part was even easier. Tammy and I went straight to it, like moths to a flame as it were. It was, of course, the Personal Bug Zapper. You must have one of these. It looks like a very small tennis racquet—only with batteries and a wire face. All you have to do is swat in the general direction of the offending insects, and it fries them on contact. Sort of a fly-swatter/stun-gun combo. How macho can you get?

Tammy said all her employees at the Everyday Gourmet and the Everyday Gardener had hooted her big time when she came back from market bearing the Personal Bug Zapper and then announced with a completely straight face that they would be stocking it. Well, of course, they cannot keep them on the shelf. The Personal Bug Zapper people are having to work overtime just to keep the supply coming fast enough. Half a dozen people bought them when I did, just because my enthusiasm was so contagious. You could tell that some of those people had plans for zapping something else besides bugs: They had some two-legged pests in mind, I do believe.

I could tell from the immediate and extremely wicked gleam in Bill's eyes when he opened his Zapper that he envisioned himself the Ruler of the Universe now that he had the only virtual cattle prod in the house. He declared that he was getting one for the office and one for the car as well, so as to never be powerless again. Just possessing it would give him, he believed, the power to subdue errant wives, children, and/or stepdogs. He would probably never even have to use it—just the knowledge that it was there would give him the Power. I read the label to him several times: "WARNING! THIS IS NOT A TOY!" But I could see the wheels turning nonetheless.

That very evening I received a phone call. The woman, laughing uncontrollably on the other end of the phone line, eventually managed to identify herself as none other than the charming Linda and new Mrs. Bill. I could tell she was calling me from the floor, where she was rolling about, shrieking with laughter. She just wanted me to know, as soon as possible, that Bill had come right home, assembled his Personal Bug Zapper, and promptly shocked himself with it! And furthermore, it was her opinion that the thing worked like a charm. I was delighted to hear it. I was equally delighted to see that, clearly, the charming Linda will be able to hold her own, and then some, with the intrepid Bill. I do so like to see couples evenly matched, don't you? Just to be on the safe side, I think I'll get Linda her own Personal Bug Zapper—I think they need to be a Two-Zapper Family.

Two of the Tammys were at a party at a fabulous house in the mountains in North Carolina. They both agreed it was easily the most fabulous house they had ever seen and, they noted, their hostess was wearing what was easily the most fabulous diamond ring either of them had ever seen. The Tammys intuitively knew there was a story here, and they made it their business to get to it. By and by, they found themselves chatting with the hostess, and they just couldn't help but comment on her ring, which was only slightly smaller than a Volkswagen. The woman threw back her head and laughed one of those wonderful laughs of delirious glee. She was obviously quite pleased with herself and, as it turned out, for good reason. The Tammys demanded to be told the tale and the woman said, Oh, there wasn't much to it really. She had found this fabulous diamond about the same time that her husband had found this fabulous house. He informed her that she would have to choose—she couldn't have both. Which would it be, the house or the diamond? What did you say? the girls wanted to know. "Ha!" she said. "I picked the diamond. Shoot, I knew *he* wanted this house!" And so it came to pass she got them both. This may be the smartest woman ever to draw breath.

11

Sex, Fritos, and the Talking Vagina

While the Queens may render a split decision on the subject of marriage, sex is something on which we are in complete accord. We do dearly love it. We all think it is a good thing. Sex is so good, Martha Stewart could have invented it had she been on the arrangements committee when the need came up. If Martha had been in charge, however, it would probably be a lot neater, more dignified, and possibly color coordinated, but, all things considered, we are pretty happy with it the way it is. And we love talking about it nearly about as much as we like having it—in some particular instances, more, but happily that doesn't occur often.

Once we were having an informal gathering at my house—just the Queens and a few Wannabes and one or two hangers-on. Let me explain that "hangers-on" is not in any way a derogatory term that we have assigned to these, our good friends, but rather the term with which they have chosen to designate themselves. They are not quite ready to take the plunge and come out, as it were, to the world as full-fledged Wannabe Wannabes, but they desire fervently to be in our presence as much as possible and soak up as much Queenliness as they can and thereby gain the necessary courage to own up and live up to their own secret desires. So, anyway, we're all there in the kitchen, and it was just like a scene from *Little Women,* each of us having a hand in the preparations and much jovial feminine chatter filling the air. One was making Fat Mama's Knock You Naked Margaritas, another was getting out bowls for Fritos.

Have we talked enough about Fritos? Can enough ever be said about Fritos? Is there a more perfect food on the planet than Fritos? Tammy and I love to go to the movies together—and trust me, when we do, we are the only ones who are enjoying it, so deplorable is our movie behavior. I have a giant purse, which we call my movie purse. With it, we can carry in any and all manner of foodstuffs not available at the concessions stand. Like, for instance, margaritas—the movie purse will hold a two-liter bottle full of them plus some plastic cups. And if we are having margaritas, we find that we must have Fritos as well; and, of course, if we're having Fritos and margaritas, we just gotta have Armadillo Dip. Fortunately, all of the above will fit handily inside the movie purse. Let me just say, there is a reason why they don't sell Fritos at concessions stands at movies. Suffice it to say, everyone there knows when you are eating Fritos during a movie. The only way to eat a Frito quietly, we have discovered, is to just put one in your mouth and suck on it until it is soft, and trust me, if you do this, you won't want more than one, so don't do it. You're never going to see any of those people again anyway, and with any luck, they'll give up and go to another theater, and we didn't want a big crowd of people in there in any event. I actually prefer nobody else to be in the theater.

Another thing we found will fit in the movie purse is Krystal hamburgers. Do they have Krystals where you live? They are similar to White Castles, and they are one of our very favorite foods. The two best times to eat Krystals are at four o'clock in the morning—but only if you've been out all night partying, which we are too old to do now. We are much more likely to have just gotten up at four A.M.—and believe me, you don't want a Krystal then. The other good time to eat Krystals, luckily for us, is anytime you can sneak them into the movies. The pleasure of eating them in the movies is multiplied many times over by the fact that nobody else has any—they know you've got them, because nothing else smells quite like a Krystal—and they now want them so bad, they'll probably leave any minute to go get some.

Actually, there is one other time that I and one of the Queens,

Tammy, love to eat Krystals and that is New Year's Eve. I personally have never had a good time on New Year's Eve in my *entire* life, so in 1982, when I buried my daddy on that day, I said, Well, fine, let's just quit this altogether, and so I did. I have not observed New Year's Eve since 1981, and I can't remember what I did that year, only that it wasn't fun. I wish I could remember it, though—it's one of those Southern things we do, remember years by the bizarre events that were taking place at the time. Like Tammy and her sister trying to re-member what year it was they went to Memphis to see the Rolling Stones, and the way they finally figured it out was that it was the same year that "Mama drove the car off into the reservoir," and they re-membered that it was, in fact, a brand-new car and they would never forget the year the family got a brand-new Cadillac convertible, would they? And then, of course, we were all diverted from our orig-inal discussion about the Rolling Stones on to the much more in-triguing tale of how it came to pass that their mama drove the brand-new Cadillac convertible off into the reservoir—in much the same way that I started out talking about sex and somehow got branched off into Fritos and New Year's Eve.

Anyway, a few years back, Tammy let it be known that she shares my aversion to New Year's Eve. We had a long discussion about the many disastrous parties and awful dates we'd been privy to on that evening, and, of course, we moved on into what we would really like to be doing on New Year's Eve, in a perfect world, which would be to eat a giant bag of Krystals (Tammy likes extra mustard and extra onions; she doesn't even care if they put the meat on there, if they put enough mustard and onions and cheese) and then just pile up in the bed with a pan of Chocolate Stuff and some black-and-white movies and happily drift off toward morning. And we looked at each other and said, as we have said to each other so many times about so many even more outlandish things we were contemplating doing, "Why not?" So we did. We began our own, now time-honored tradition of spending the early portion of New Year's Eve at the Krystal, eating those precious little burger-tiles, and making a double batch of Chocolate Stuff so that we each have a pan to take home to our re-spective beds for the actual New Year's festivities, although after eat-ing all that, we rarely, if ever, manage to remain awake for the actual stroke of midnight. Delightful. We have never had a bad time doing this, we've never gotten a ticket, never had a fight with a presumed loved one, never awakened with a hangover or a stranger: We offer this course of action to you with our highest recommendation.

But, as I was saying way back there, we were having a girls' gathering, and someone was getting out the bowls for the Fritos, someone was putting ice in the glasses, I was making Chocolate Stuff, naturally, and someone else was making Armadillo Dip. Only one in our company had been sitting idle this entire time, holding up her end in the chatting but not doing any real work—lolling, as it were—and by and by, she asked if she couldn't do something to help. I surveyed the work at hand and suggested that she might want to chop the onions for the Armadillo Dip. She said okay, got up lazily from her perch at the kitchen table, looked sort of far-off, and then she said, to no one in particular, "I guess I should wash my hands first, I just had sex an hour ago," just as casual as you please.

Well, things in the kitchen came to what you would call one of your screeching halts—meaning nobody was doing shit anymore and everybody was screeching at her, "Whaddayou mean you just had sex an hour ago? You've been here for forty-five minutes, and you haven't said a word about just having had sex right before you walked in the door! Who were you having sex with? Where were you?" Oh, all manner of questions were hammering her, but she was just irritatingly dreamy-eyed and vague. I think possibly somebody may have whacked her with a big wooden spoon—just to break the spell, don't you know—and once we had her attention, the quizzing resumed. The "who" turned out to be a salesman who passed through her office on a semi-regular basis. Seems he'd been under consideration for quite some time, and today just turned out to be the day. The "where" was in the attic space of her office. "The attic!" was the loud refrain from the audience. "Yeah, I've got cobwebs in my panties." "Well, all I can say is they sure as hell didn't grow there!" someone said sharply; it could have been me.

Whenever Tammy and I go to Los Angeles to visit our friends Ned Walton and Peter McQuaid, we make a mandatory trip to the Pleasure Chest, an enormous emporium featuring every possible accoutrement for sex that you can imagine—and many others that you probably cannot envision in your most exuberant fantasies, even with pharmaceutical assistance. There is no such store in Mississippi, where we are from, and if there was, we couldn't be seen going into it, of course. After all, we have our reputations to think of. Since we are most widely known for wearing green sequinned mini-dresses with giant tits and even more giant butts built into them, black fishnet hose, hot-pink sequinned gloves, majorette boots, and big red wigs while dancing in a trashy manner on a moving float on a public street, that may sound like a needless precaution to you. So be it. Going to the Pleasure Chest in L.A. is one of those activities that make being "out of pocket" so beguiling.

We turn into the Clampetts when we go in there, and it is humiliating for Ned and Peter, but they buck up and go with us anyway because they love us. Everybody else in there is shopping in a dignified, adult manner for the items that appeal to them personally. Tammy and I are careening around the store, picking up things and wondering aloud: What in the world can this be? Where do you reckon you put it, and, more important, why? We don't actually say "Go-llee" like Gomer Pyle, but we think it a lot.

I can't imagine how they conjure up all these trinkets for people to have sex with. Is the inventor having sex him/herself and, all of a sudden, thinks, "Gee, I wish I had a big, electric, squishy, wiggly, prickly, furry, hard, throbbing thing to do whatever with," and then gets up and manufactures it to sell to others who may have never wanted such a thing before, but when they see it, suddenly it makes sense, and they go, "Aha! I've gotta have it!" I don't follow the thought process is what I guess I'm saying. Somebody's job is to invent new sex toys. Surely somebody else's job is to make them and test them out. Our only job is to figure out what goes where and why and buy them—or not.

The most tantalizing product was the Talking Vagina. That's what it said on the box, which was not open—indeed, it was shrink-wrapped in heavyweight plastic—and I am still sick about that. I badly wanted to see a talking vagina, had visions of Chatty Cathy. People as old as I am will remember this doll: You pulled a cord on her back and she talked. Did the Talking V. have a cord like Chatty Cathy? A button? Was it voice- or sound-activated? Clap on, clap off? My doctor-boyfriend Richard Pharr has a candy dish in his office that looks like a cow, and when you reach to get a piece of candy, it moos at you real loud. Would the Talking Vagina have a similar trigger? And what exactly would one say? I never thought about such a thing before, being the proud owner of my own vagina; I admit that in all the years I've had it, I never so much as once thought about what it might say.

So naturally, when I spied it there on the store shelf, all boxed up and inaccessible, I hollered across the store to Tammy, who was inspecting the handcuff selection, "Tammy! They got a Talking Vagina over here." She ambled right on over. We picked up the box and turned it this way and that, trying to see if it was like one of those little boxes with farm animals on the sides and you turn them over and they go "moo" or "oink" or "cockadoodledoo." There was nothing audible coming from the box. We chattered away about the possibilities of what vaginas might say, now that they've got the chance. A guy was loitering nearby, eavesdropping, so we turned on him, sudden-like, and demanded to know what he thought it might say. "Go cut the grass!" he barked, in a gravelly, whiskey-sounding bitch voice. We dropped the Talking Vagina, we were laughing so hard. Tammy said, "Mmmmm! Things not so good at home, I take it?" He blurted that answer out so fast, you know he'd heard it before and with feeling, too.

And then Tammy comes to me with an ad printed out from the Internet for a Vaginal Substitute. The ad is nothing short of fabulous. By the time we finished reading it, we even wanted one, and we've already got real ones! It said that with the Vaginal Substitute, you (the guy, we suppose) could avoid any risk to yourself and/or us from STDs, and it certainly eliminates any risk of pregnancy. In our opinion, it will not do a whole lot for our sex life—this does not strike us as an intimacy-builder for couples or a precursor to any postcoital cuddling either, but still it was developed by a "medical doctor who is a world's authority on orgasm." Says he's got a patent on an orgasm monitor, even. From what we could tell, this whole thing is pretty guy-oriented. We didn't get the feeling that this medical doctor has any interest in the female orgasm, if, indeed, in his mind, it even exists, and the Vaginal Substitute makes no claims for any sexual pleasure, real or imagined, for the woman, even though it is suggested that you might want to use the device with your partner. We assume this would relegate us to spectator status.

"There is nothing magical about a vagina." It actually says that in the ad. All I can say is, with that attitude, it's a good thing this guy invented this fake one, because I can tell you authoritatively the number of real ones he's likely to have access to. He does go on, however, to add—although somewhat as an afterthought—that there is also nothing magical about a penis. Everything's got a purpose, according to our authority here, and it's all pretty cut and dried. He's got the theory on what goes where and why, but we can't help thinking he just hasn't had much fun with it all. He points out that the penis is designed to sense pressure and friction; beyond that, its tactile abilities are somewhat limited. The penis is therefore "unable to distinguish whether it is in a vagina or a vaginal substitute." It seems that the greatest tactile organ is the tongue, followed by the fingers. These two organs, it seems to me, can pretty much always tell where they are, what they're doing, and with whom or what. If, for example, you put a screw in your mouth or hold it in your fingers, chances are excellent that you can tell without looking what you've got in either location. Put a screw on a penis, however, and it will be completely baffled—not a clue. So if the lights are off or the eyes are closed, the penis, according to this guy, will be happy just to be *somewhere*, and it won't have the foggiest idea if it's in the real thing or a fake.

In our experience, we have found that it often cannot tell if it's in its home vagina, where it belongs, or has inadvertently wandered off into a neighbor's. If your personal mate is of the wandering variety, this might be just the thing to keep him home; although why you'd want to is another, more important issue. How about a Vaginal Substitute as a nice parting gift? Best wishes for the future and all that. It always pays to be nice.

12

What to Do When the Rabbit Dies

I know a lot of y'all are young and cute, which also puts you at child-bearing age. Let me tell you, dear ones, nothing will tear asunder that young cuteness quite like pregnancy and child rearing. I kept a journal and wrote voluminous letters while I was frittering away my own young cuteness being pregnant. Somehow I knew these records would be useful in my lifelong mission to help others. (Actually, I wasn't even young and cute then—I was thirty-five.)

> FROM MY JOURNAL, JULY 1987. *Well, fine. Been married an hour and a half and I'm pregnant, thank you. Yes, it's true, and I certainly hope you're satisfied. The blessed event should be just in time to screw up any plans I had for Mardi Gras, not to mention everything else for the rest of my entire life. This is a fine mess.*
>
> *This is one of those things I had anticipated reading about but never actually doing myself, you know. It's the kind of thing that happens to other people, like an earthquake or the headline* FIEND SEIZES HATCHET, SLAYS SIX *or when your mother says, "Put that down, you'll put your eye out." Never do you actually be-*

lieve that one day you'll be wearing a patch where your eye used to be. Or airplanes. Not for a minute do I believe they fly. The thing weighs a billion pounds with all those lard-bucket people wedged up in it—here's something flying soon? No, you just pile up in there and, somehow, magically, you end up in a different place, sometimes even where you want to be.

Well, I figured babies were sort of the same principle. I was the baby in my family, and the only other one I ever knew much about was my sister Judy's son, Trevor—at thirty-something he's so old now we are forced to tell people that he is our little brother so they don't think we're old enough to have raised him. He's the only baby I've ever been around, and he just sort of turned up, or so it seemed to me, still a child myself when he was born. Who knew? Well, apparently plenty of people—but who believed them? I never thought this would happen to me.

The moment I conceived, I gained fifteen pounds—in my back. Seriously, I immediately got this back like a walrus. I am now gaining weight at the rate of eleven pounds an hour, and the doctor, witty guy—a good friend of mine actually, named Rascal Odom—is pleased to announce that the baby is the size of a golf ball, max. I am so pleased.

The mood swings are pretty entertaining, I must say. Judy warned me about these. She said at least ten times a month she would go totally berserk at something her bothersome husband, Ole Shep, did or said (such as walking in the room and saying, "Hello"), and she would then announce in no uncertain terms that she was not putting up with it anymore, whereupon she loaded up everything (we're talking everything—dishes, linens, clothes, food, the works), piled it all in her car, and drove around for an hour—only to return, haul it back up three flights of stairs, and unpack it, awaiting the next provocation. [Judy was extremely young and way too energetic for her own good at the time; just reading about it wears her out today.] Well, no way am I packing up anything. No, the whole point of a mood swing is to inflict pain, fear, and/or consternation on your mate. Packing up stuff myself would seem ineffective toward that end. I prefer to stay put and say hideous things to the unsuspecting husband, Moon Pie. Trust me, no one ever had a mood swing while alone.

What to Do When the Rabbit Dies

My favorite response to anything that takes me by surprise or in any way annoys me in my newly impregnated state is to say, in tones ranging from a piercing shriek to a pitiful whimper, complete with trembling lower lip: "I'm just going to have an abortion and run away!" I must confess that after the first five thousand times of saying it, it does seem to have lost some of its effectiveness. Now Moon Pie shrugs and says something irksomely rational like "Well, okay, but you still have to have a new transmission." It sort of robs the moment.

Fortunately, I have not been afflicted with morning sickness. Actually, luck had very little to do with it. Not for anybody am I puking on a regular basis. I advised this baby if there was any unexplained nausea around here, I would know what to do about it. We understand each other perfectly and are thus managing to coexist peacefully in my body thus far.

What the name will be is a hot topic of conversation. A number of my friends want me to use the first letters of their first names to name the baby. If I do that, we'll have JAWS Conner Browne. My diminutive friend, Cynthia Hewes, wants it to be Cynthia Hewes Conner Browne. Michael Rubenstein wants Michael Rubenstein Conner Browne. I kinda like Peabo. You don't run across a Peabo just every day, now, do you? I had suggested it to Vivian White for her daughter, but she picked Mallory instead, so it's still available.

Actually, this baby is not mine. I am only having it for some friends. The girls in my aerobics class wanted one. They're all going to take turns keeping it. They swore they would.

One has to wonder about the people who keep saying to me how interesting they found all the changes in their bodies when they were pregnant. It is interesting in the same light that it would be interesting if you suddenly started to grow a tail, green scaly skin, and webbed feet. Yes, you would get up every morning and examine your body in the mirror and think to yourself, "My, my, isn't that interesting?"

Everyone, even people you don't know, beams at you and rubs your belly.

One bright spot in all this is the remarkable development taking place in my brassiere. One of the characteristics long associated with images of me is the sad state of affairs, tit-

wise. Well, weep no more, honey chile. You sho' is got some tit-
ties now!

FROM A LETTER TO MY SISTER, JUDY, SEPTEMBER 4, 1987. *Dear*
Judy, Thanks so much for withholding all useful information re-
garding pregnancy, since I am quite certain I'd have opted out if
I'd had any idea! For one thing, I have discovered that the only
people who can dress like otherwise normal adults during preg-
nancy are girls aged eight to eleven. This seems strangely incon-
gruous to me, since it is generally frowned upon in polite society
for women of such tender age to become pregnant. Why have the
clothing manufacturers devoted so much time and energy to de-
signing and producing fashions for such a relatively small (I
would assume and certainly hope) population? I haven't seen a
pregnant eight-year-old in I don't know when, but I can tell you,
if you run across one, you can take her into any maternity store
in Jackson, Mississippi, and dress her to the nines. The very
largest-sized garments in every maternity store I've been in
wouldn't fit me if I weren't pregnant and weighed one hundred
pounds less. These are the tiniest little clothes I have ever seen.
And the undersizing isn't the only problem I'm having; the
styling is absurd. Everything has a high neck, a Peter Pan collar,
and three-quarter-length sleeves. What is the deal? If I could even
fit in the stuff, which I can't, I'd look like a giant fifth grader. For
once in my life, I have a chest worthy of note and they want me
to stuff it in a Peter Pan collar? Let's have some decolletage. Let's
be cleaving while the cleaving's good.

You remember my bosom buddy since the seventh grade,
Rhonda Abel? She was in town last week from Colorado—she's
pregnant, too, and we discussed the pressing need to start gearing
up for Momdom big time. We just don't feel comfortable that we
look the part. You have to understand, we have been planning
this for years. We still have notes we wrote each other from the
seventh grade on, complete with our own artistic renderings, on
this very subject. We decided that it was time for her to go on and
bleach her hair out, start growing a big hairy mole on her cheek
and wearing polyester double-knit pantsuits. She recalled that
our early lore required me to dye my own hair asphalt-black and
wear rhinestone cat-eye glasses with a jeweled chain to hold them
around my neck when I remove them. We decided that in order

to be ready for action when her anticipated son, Sparkplug, and my own BoPeep are school-aged, we should have Suburban Mom Practice. We're going to get up and go ride around in early-morning traffic with our hair in pink foam rollers, wearing chenille robes and fuzzy slippers. We think a cigarette flopping off the lower lip is absolutely mandatory for the look we are trying to achieve. We're going to hunch up over the steering wheel and look real pissed off, and every few minutes, we'll reach over and act like we're beating the crap out of somebody in the backseat. You being a mom with many years' experience on us, we would welcome any other pointers you might have to offer us.

Your Pregnant Baby Sister,
Jill

FROM A LETTER TO JUDY, JANUARY 26, 1988. *Dear Judy: By the time you read this (hopefully), BoPeep will have made her long-anticipated arrival. If she has not, Moon Pie will likely be found hacked into many dime-sized pieces and scattered along the interstate. Pregnant women tend to get a little testy as the Time draws nigh, don't they? I have entered the confinement state of pregnancy—that's when you lie on a bed in a dark room, propped at all angles by massive pillows, and at regular intervals stare into space, weep, and eat. This cycle is broken only when one makes a visit to the powder room to empty one's bladder, which has by now apparently shrunk to the size of an underdeveloped acorn. Swelling is accomplished with no effort whatsoever on the part of the swellee.*

I don't leave the house except to go to the grocery store or the Dairy Queen, but I am easily recognized: I look like a cross between Aunt Jemima and the Michelin Man. Unclothed, I am a fugitive from National Geographic. *My face looks like a reflection in a car fender or like it was painted originally on a small balloon that has now been inflated to its utmost capacity.*

Everyone asks, "How much weight have you gained?" I'd say it is pretty much split on where the emphasis is put—some favor "How much *weight have you gained?" while others lean more toward "How much weight have* you *gained?" with a few holdouts for "How much weight have you* gained?" *I profess no preference for any of them: They all piss me off in a really big way. I mean, like I would tell if I knew! I honestly don't know.*

I get on the scales backward at the doctor's office and refuse to look.

This started the first month when I hopped on and was told that I had already gained fifteen pounds and would be needing to get some kind of grip on the situation. I would weigh myself every time I went through the locker room at the Y, and it would fluctuate all day long, like six or seven pounds a whack. It was making me completely nuts and I decided that I would have an eating disorder after nine months of that mess. So next visit, I told the doctor that, being six feet tall, I didn't think I was in any danger of going toxemic on him—worst case is I would be really fat— and that I was not willing to spend so much time fixated on my weight. Therefore I would be getting on the scales backward every month, and nobody was to be allowed either to tell me what I weighed or comment on it in any way. The good doctor Rascal gave me as stern a look as he could muster, being handicapped as he is by an advanced case of sweetness, and said that he wasn't really very happy with that proposal. Whereupon I gave him a much sterner look (not being at all hampered with sweet-ness) and said that if I had to pick somebody to be unhappy for the next nine months—me or him—I could pretty much assure him that he was the hands-down winner.

I must say it has greatly improved my mood regarding doc-tor visits. Boy, does it make the other pregnant women mad, though. You know how they do you—they herd a bunch of you into one holding area with the scales and everybody has to get on there in front of everybody else. It's not like anybody is a size two anymore, but when one contestant is not forced to confront her own excessive poundage and then listen to the subsequent lecture regarding same, well, it's pretty fair breeding ground for revolt, let me tell you. They pounce on me every time: "How come you get to get on there backwards? How come they never fuss at you?" And I just smile and say I have a special arrangement with the management. They scowl and mutter curses at me, but I am im-pervious.

What I confess I am not impervious to, however, is the feel-ing of dread that comes over me as I hear the nurse moving the weights across the bar on the scale behind my back, trying gamely to achieve balance and thus reveal the exact extent of my manifold sins in pounds. She chink-chink-chinks *the little ones across to no avail and then slides that big honking one across the bottom—the one that measures in fifty-pound increments—and then she* chink-chink-chinks *a little more and then it's back to heaving the big one over a little more, followed by even more* chink-chink-chinking *until she finally gets the Big Number. Lord, it must be big, too, because I am the size of the sun. At least they haven't told me to weigh myself at the post office on my way in—yet. I figure I'll check into the hospital and they'll clock me at around 224 pre-baby and 240-something post-baby, if my luck continues in the same vein.*

The godmothers had a very sweet, traditional baby shower for us. The invitations had my grinning face superimposed over a large (but still undersized by actual comparison) naked person, with a slightly lewd poem. Vats of wine were consumed on my behalf. BoPeep is set, having already received all the essentials for pageant school—tiara, long white gloves, pearls, and a baton. Wilson and Lynn Wong, the ever-thoughtful Young Republicans, gave me a green-sequinned set of pasties and a G-string—perfect for entertaining at home.

People take unbelievable liberties with pregnant women. Aside from fondling our swollen bellies and asking about our weight, two other sources of unquenchable curiosity for the public seem to be "Are you going to do it natural?" and "What size bras are you wearing now?" The answer to the first is: sort of. It will be drug-free but somewhat of a new departure in that everybody in labor and delivery will be naked and we are planning a nasal delivery. Margaritas will be served in the birthing suite. Re: the bras—not sure the size we're up to at the moment, but suffice it to say the cups are too big for my head. I'm thinking of making hats out of them when this is all over.

Your big fat sister,
Jill

LETTER TO FRIENDS, 8:03 A.M., JANUARY 28, 1988. *BOPEEP DOES, IN FACT, ARRIVE AMID WILD ACCLAIM. Moon Pie performed his hand-holding detail admirably. Dr. Rascal did all the hard stuff, and me and 'Peep just cruised. We all had snappy outfits for the occasion. Moon Pie looked just like a cafe-*

teria worker. They gave him a whole paper outfit, complete with shower cap. I kept threatening to rip off his little paper pants and give the nurses something to talk about.

All in all, it was a totally satisfactory experience. I had her at the Mississippi Baptist Medical Center and, I have to tell you, they have great pie. If you are thinking of coming to Mississippi to give birth, keep it in mind—great pie, also totally acceptable fried chicken. These things are important to me, especially on occasions that I anticipate will be stressful—such as having a baby for the first time ever in my whole life. I expect you are no different in this regard. Add to these important facts that the nurses were as sweet as the pie, and they didn't even know I was the Boss of All the Sweet Potato Queens, being unable as I was to fit into the outfit (I guess I was incognito—disguised as a really fat woman).

Plus, I got this really great baby out of the deal! I could spare you all the gooshy details about how wonderful BoPeep is just by saying that she is, in a word, perfect. But I won't, since I know you are dead to hear all the gooshy details. I am sorry to inform all of you currently in possession of babies that we got the best one and so you, unfortunately, did not. This baby is the cutest thing I ever saw. The only even potential flaw was the ears, and they, too, are perfect—flat on her little punkin head, just where they ought to be, like Moon Pie's, and not wafting in the breeze like her mom's. This baby is just sweetness in a little-girl suit is all she is. She goes from wide awake to REM sleep in the space of a second. I guess she dreams about the only thing she really knows anything about at this point in her small life—titties. She lights up with a big, unconscious smile and coos in her sleep as she dreams of titties, and then her little lip quivers and she starts and shudders as she dreams of that worst of all possible worlds— no titties. Michael Rubenstein confesses that his own dreams have never progressed beyond that stage.

BoPeep's preoccupation with the titties/no titties dilemma brings up another point: major life change. In one instant, I went from being Jill Conner Browne, Boss of All the Sweet Potato Queens, tantalizing woman of passion, wit, and mystery, to Jill Conner Browne, somebody's mother and personal lactating device. 'Peep sprang from the womb and promptly (and permanently, it seems) attached herself to my more-than-ample bosom,

What to Do When the Rabbit Dies

pausing only to switch sides. I imagine it to be not unlike being intimately involved with a lamprey eel, only cuter.

JANUARY 28, 1989. BoPeep turned a whole year old. This is a milestone in everyone's life—when your baby has survived your parenting for an entire year relatively unscathed. 'Peep accomplished a lot in her year—in spite of my inept attempts at being somebody's mother: She said not one but two two-syllable words, those being "titties," naturally, and "bubbles"—as in "Tiny," very fitting for the daughter of THE Sweet Potato Queen. I bet she's in a very small demographic grouping of people twelve months old who can identify Don Ho and his song. We're very proud. My sister, Judy, called every day, several times a day, for months, just to converse with 'Peep. Admittedly, the gist of the conversation was always the same—my apparently shameless sister endlessly exhorting the child to "Say 'Hi, Judy!' " We all tried to help her, actually. Every time the phone would ring or we would pass a pay phone, we'd say to her, "Say 'Hi, Judy!' " But would she say it? She would not. But then Moon Pie had one conversation with his friend Cecil, to whom he speaks maybe once every six months, and as soon as the conversation ended with "Bye, Cecil," you guessed it—'Peep has not shut up saying "Bye, Cecil! Bye, Cecil! Bye, Cecil!" with perfect clarity. Judy did have success in one linguistic venture with 'Peep, however—the two of them can deliver a chorus of "nyaa nyaa nyaa"s with matching tones and accompanying sneers. Yet another source of pride for any young mother.

It strikes me upon reflection that it will only be twelve short years before 'Peep goes to live with her godparents—Joan and Buster Bailey. Joanie was in Hawaii the day 'Peep was born and she called me in the hospital. She wept when I told her I was naming the baby after her. [No, Joan's name is not BoPeep. 'Peep's actual name is Bailey Browne.] Buster was in the background, pointing out that Bailey was, in fact, his name; Joanie only acquired it by close association. I allowed as how the baby did look a lot more like Buster, which was purely coincidental, I assured all interested parties. They could fight amongst themselves about whom the baby was actually named for—I was naming them both godparents, but there was an addendum to the deal that they might be interested in.

This baby was getting named for them and they could be

good-time Charlies for her anytime they pleased, but come January 28, 2001—'Peep's thirteenth birthday—this baby would be coming to live with them for the ensuing eight years. My own personal teenage Karma is so horrific—I still cringe at the thought of it all—I took this precaution to insure that 'Peep and I both survive until she comes of age.

[I have reminded the Baileys of their commitment each and every January 28. They are beginning to get nervous.] *I think I have hit on a swell idea here. 'Peep will still live here in town, and go to her same school, but she won't live with me. I can't afford boarding school, but this will accomplish much the same thing in that we will eliminate that personal proximity factor that makes the teenage years so tumultuous for families. It will, of course, be tumultuous to the Baileys' family, but who cares? I think of it as sending 'Peep off to a boarding home, and if you currently find yourself pregnant or in possession of a small baby not yet named, let me encourage you to pick out some friends (think gullible, easily led, sucker-types), name the baby after them, and tack on the Thirteenth Birthday Clause. The first thirteen years are a breeze—especially compared to the following eight—and you can be off somewhere having fun again while the hapless godparents are "wrassling" with your teenager. This knowledge can only enhance your sense of wonder, and gratitude, not to mention hilarity.*

By the time you read this book, 'Peep will have been under the roof and tutelage of the Baileys for at least a month, and I will be enjoying an extended and long-overdue vacation.

13

Divorce, Dating Again, and Revirgination

In *SPQBOL*, I briefly touched on what I perceived to be the many advantages of widowhood over divorcement. A close friend of mine has experienced both and has verified the accuracy of my position. The entire world is united in its support and succor of the Little Widow. Everybody invites her to everything and is even more solicitous of her little feelings if she's not up to attending. She can even use her bereaved state to get out of attending affairs that she formerly would have been forced to attend although preferring to be set on fire, if the choice was offered, and it seldom was. On the other hand, she can be lauded as brave and strong for attending, in spite of her grief-stricken condition, all the fun stuff that she would have sooner died herself than miss. When she is not taken out for dinner, food is delivered, unsolicited, to her door. Everyone is concerned about her financial state, and it is not unusual for her to receive donations. She is patted and petted by all—indeed, so many aspects of widowhood are so appealing, it is a wonder more women don't make a studious effort to avail themselves of it. We concede that, if you happen to have loved the deceased a powerful lot and feel as if part of your heart has been ripped out of your body, which our Little Widow did and does, it can quite often put a damper on your enthusiasm. But when someone shows up, as someone most assuredly will, to provide a diversion, a distraction, or something to eat, well, don't you think that might provide a little relief?

Divorce

Consider now the plight of the hapless divorcée and see by comparison how pitiful is her lot. When your husband is removed due to death, everyone brings you food. People come to help you with your children. Your errands get divided up amongst your friends. Your laundry gets done. Your house gets cleaned. Everybody wonders if you're getting enough rest: They want you to go lie down for a little while, take a nap, take a break, get out for a spell.

When your husband is removed from the marital home while you decide whether or not to divorce him permanently, and you are totally out of your mind with grief, worry, anxiety, guilt, fear—you name it, you got it—you will more than likely find yourself by yourself with all of it. If ever there was a time when you needed all that stuff done for you, this is it. As you move beyond the separation and into the divorce phase, you may become more and more isolated. Parties are planned not so much around convivial people as they are planned around convivial couples. Even if everybody hated your husband and adored you, the couple of you were invited to every party. When the party-throwers have the chance to have you, the desired one, alone without your millstone, do they avail themselves of this opportunity? They do not. Your ex-husband will, of course, retain his position on all the guest lists: Everybody wants a spare man around. Meanwhile you will only be invited to lunch with the girls because many husbands cannot be trusted to behave well in the company of spare women. You are left alone to rebuild your life from the ground up, and more often than not, all you've got to work with is your own mother wit. Fortunately, that is usually plenty.

This ties in with our overall philosophy, which we call our Refrigerator Box Theory of Life. What we're referring to is that bygone time when the best thing that could happen to you was for somebody on your block to get a new refrigerator, because it came in a refrigerator box—the best toy imaginable. All you needed to operate it was your imagination, and that box could be almost anything—castle, boat, log cabin, jail, spaceship, schoolhouse, grocery store. A refrigerator box lasted forever—or at least all summer, which felt like the same thing back then—unless somebody forgot to drag it into the garage when it rained.

When you get divorced, you've got to first look realistically at the dark side: He's gone, and you're all alone. You've got to figure it out by yourself and make a plan for the rest of your life, or at least this next little part. Okay, to do this, let's make a very slight but crucial mental shift in your thinking. Let's move to looking at the bright side: He's gone! You're all alone! You get to figure it out by yourself and make a plan for what you want to do. You've just been handed a brand-new refrigerator box all your own and you can make it into anything you want, and you can change that plan at any time without consulting anybody else to see if that might interfere with the ball game or duck season. I charge you, therefore, if you are the one in the middle of the divorce, to get up off your ass and make something good happen for yourself.

And if you are the friends of the one who is in the middle of the divorce—get over there and help her out. Do all the things for her, and with her, you would do if she were burying her husband instead of just running him off with a stick. Sometimes the whole situation is so bleak, it's a stretch to find any flicker of hope. On those occasions only other women can help women through this. We have given a few Divorce Parties for our nearest and dearest. One party was given on the occasion of a husband leaving his wife (our friend) for the Sunday-school teacher of one of their three children. He upped and ran off with the bitch, and then the bastard filed for bankruptcy. For her party, we bought a very large, black plastic rat and suspended it from the ceiling. Small plastic bats were dispensed to all attendees, who took turns at whacking the rat—just like a piñata, except there were no treats inside; we were just whacking for whacking's sake—very satisfying. Some girls, who are quite handy at cake decorating, collaborated on a delicious project that produced a large—very large—cake in the shape of a full set of male genitalia—very festive. We made song sheets appropriate to the occasion and had a sing-along. Among the crowd favorites were "Your Cheatin' Heart," "Heartbreak Hotel," "I'm Gonna Wash That Man Right Outta My Hair," "You Broke My Heart So F**k You," and of course, what gathering would be complete without "D-I-V-O-R-C-E."

On that particular song, our good buddy and the undisputed

Queen of Rock and Roll in these parts, Suzy Elkins, doctored the lyrics just the teeniest bit; we think that if Tammy Wynette were still singing it, she would love the change. You know the line that says something about me and little J-o-e going away? Suze changed it to say "that A-S-S-H-O-L-E." It fits perfectly and gives it a nice zing, don't you think? Try it at your next Divorce Party and see if you don't get raves.

But now, lest we seem harsh and unfair, let me hasten to say that if you happen to have a male friend about whom you care deeply, and all of a sudden his wife runs off with a blackjack dealer or another woman or something, then by all means throw the Divorce Party for him. That's another thing about divorce: It forces us to choose sides, and death doesn't.

Dating Again

Your girlfriend will probably need help to ease back into dating. (Your male friend will need no assistance; women will be hurling themselves on the windshield of his car.) I have been divorced from Moon Pie for a while now—oh, not to worry, he's still close by, not in the same neighborhood or anything, but certainly close enough that I can report when he does something silly and/or annoying, which is still fairly often. He has always been such a good fodder—not to mention a pretty good sport—so I could never let him stray too far afield. But anyway, there had been somewhat of a lull in my dating career there for quite some time. Being married just puts a cramp in it, don't you know. And, too, not a whole lot of guys will ask you out if you are not only married but hugely pregnant as well. I spent the next two years as a lactating device, there again not a real big dating draw. After that came that thick sort of mental fog that full-time motherhood wraps you in, and I didn't even think about dating.

So then, all of a sudden, I was in a position to date again—and who knows how anymore? Who ever knew really, but let me tell you, it is just the weirdest feeling in the world when you take it up again after a long hiatus. When it came to pass that I had the first real date looming large on the horizon, the Queens were in a state, a dither, a tizzy as it were. At that point, most of them had been married twenty years or more, and the concept of a date was mind-boggling. The date, Brint Motheral, was coming from a long way off especially for the occasion, so it wasn't like I could chicken out the night before and weasel out of the whole thing. He was going to an inordinate amount of trouble just to take me out, so I felt obliged not only to go but even to be nice the whole time he was here. I was nervous. I mean, when was the last time you tried to be nice to one person for two or three days at a stretch? Married people, don't even try to remember.

We were going to the Symphony Ball, of all things. I figured it would be some adult prom, and this would, of course, mean major dressing up on my part. I had to search and search for just the right dress because Brint advised me that his tuxedo was twenty-some-odd years old with bell-bottoms. He keeps it, he said, as a point of pride because nobody else he knows can still fit into anything they wore twenty-some-odd years ago. (I didn't mention this to him, naturally, but I would also be one of those people who can't fit into anything I wore twenty-some-odd years ago.) I was driven to find exactly the right dress that would complement and not be upstaged by a shiny, bell-bottomed tuxedo. I was tempted to have a dress made to fit over my Sweet Potato Queen outfit.

Snags in dating can crop up where you least expect them. In this particular case, the impediment proved to be my car. Now, most of you reading this will not have had the benefit of actually seeing my car in person, but for those who have, nothing more need be said. Remember when you were growing up and your mama told everybody that you were "really tough on shoes"? Meaning by that, that you could wear a new pair of Hush Puppies (if you were "tough on shoes," that's all she would buy you) for five minutes and they made it look as if your goal in life was to wear your shoes until they rotted off your feet and you were in the final stages on achieving that goal. Well, I am "tough on cars" in that same way.

The car I had at the time—its original color being blue—looked like nothing so much as a Dumpster with four wheels and a windshield, one with many cracks. See, for me, cars are nothing more than something to *go* in. My car is neither a status symbol nor a love object. Here is my essential evaluation of cars: If it goes, it is a really good car. If it does not go, it is a really bad car and should be abandoned by the side of the road. Anything remotely connected with car care, be it cosmetic or mechanical, constitutes an errand, and you should already know by now how I feel about errands of any kind. That's right. If somebody else does not do it, it won't get done.

And so it was, at the time of this big date, that I found myself in possession of a good car, meaning it was currently going, but if you were to see it parked somewhere, you would not be taking bets on its driveability. My car looked as if it had been up on blocks in a yard somewhere and a very large family of really nasty people had been living in it with all of their dogs.

Not only had I never personally washed that car, or caused it to be washed, it also had a whole lot of extraneous material inside it. Now, occasionally, I would do what I call a "big sweep" through the interior. This would entail moving about the car with a giant lawn-and-leaf bag, raking huge piles of debris, some part of which I will remember as soon as the garbage man hauls it away, like the critical piece of someone's iron lung. Every time I manage to throw something away, it turns out I desperately need it five minutes later. Having seen this pattern repeated so often in my life, I've learned to leave the stuff where it is until I need it again. Makes sense to me, but man, is it messy. And off-putting to certain people. Joe Fendley, my favorite person ever in the history of the entire world, living or dead—who decided when we were seventeen that we were meant for each other because we looked like the number ten when we stood side by side—used to pick up his feet in my car and say he didn't want to tread on the larvae of the common houseflies routinely found in filth and decaying matter, a.k.a. maggots. He intended to hurt my feelings sufficiently to spur me to clean out my car, but I am impervious to the slings and arrows of all car lovers and neat freaks alike, and also the health department—speaking of which, can a car be condemned if it still goes?

Since this guy was coming all this way—going to all this trouble on my account—just to take me to the Symphony Ball in his bell-bottomed tux, there were those who felt it an undue imposition to necessitate his obtaining special inoculations before riding in my car. My erstwhile friends were nagging me nonstop to clean up my car before I picked him up at the airport in it. Now, I ask you, if they were any kind of friends, wouldn't they know how I feel about this sort of thing, and if they really loved me, wouldn't they just do it for me while I was sleeping? Some friends. Add that to the list of things you should do for a girlfriend going through a divorce: Take her car to the car wash for her once in a while.

Revirgination

Those of you who have lived in the country or spent any time at all hiking in the woods will know that a road or a trail with regular traffic, be it vehicular or pedestrian, will remain clear and open. But let it fall into disuse, and very soon the weeds and vines will crowd in until, in scarcely any time at all, the pathway is completely obscured as if it never even existed. What we need is an intrepid new blazer of trails.

And so it is with us when our personal trails have gone unblazed for a time: We revert to our former state. And you know, of course, what an unexplored wood is called, don't you? Yes, it is a virgin forest. If we spend too much time without a regular man, we may go into a state of revirgination. This is a positive occurrence, given the high premium placed by men on virginity in both woods and women. They just do purely love to be the first one in someplace.

For revirgination to occur in a woman, it requires some changes in demeanor and comportment. It is not enough to be a virgin—or revirgin, as it were—one must also act like one. A certain degree of shyness, timidity, and wide-eyed naïveté is required. Certain props, such as hair bows, may help facilitate your transformation process (see Chapter 14 for details). You can also get good tips from romance novels: Everybody's a virgin in them.

The time it takes for revirgination to occur varies from woman to woman. Some might revirginate in a matter of weeks, while for others it might take months. Still others have honed their skills to such a level that they're able to simply spontaneously revirginate within mere moments as often as the situation demands.

Revirgination works according to our previously discussed theory "Treat 'em Like Shit and Never Give 'em Any and They'll Follow You Around Like Dogs," and it's easy to see why. If you're not just a bitch but a virgin to boot, mercy! You better like this guy a heap, because you will have to pay to have him towed away.

A reconstituted virgin is so much better than a plain ole virgin that's been sitting in storage for a hundred years. With a revirgin, all the benefits of training, experience, and the accompanying enthusiasm are retained; in addition, the equipment has been well maintained. It is not necessary or even desirable to pretend to your new trailblazer that you have never been down this road before, especially if you have one or more children who look exactly like you. No, it is enough to state, for the record, that you are a card-carrying reconstituted virgin and entitled to all manner of special considerations as such. It will then be up to him to woo and entice you to yield your most current virtue to his manly assaults upon its bastions. (He can also get some good tips from romance novels and fairy tales. I mean, who could resist a guy who rides up on a noble steed, rescues you from a dastardly villain, and gives you a kingdom or something comparable? Actually, if he could just demonstrate substantively that he is not himself a dastardly villain, he'd be pretty darned irresistible in my opinion; I'd be perfectly happy to provide my own steed and kingdom even—but that's just me.)

This revirgination thing is only useful up to a point—holding out too long is just cutting off your nose to spite your face. So do try to keep in mind how much better your face looks and feels *with* a nose.

14

How to Be a Girl

It has come to our attention since the publication of *The Sweet Potato Queens' Book of Love* that not a few men are not a little intimidated by us and the whole Queen thing. We were stunned by this revelation, since we consider ourselves to be very sweet and eminently approachable, if not dainty flowers of girlish vulnerability. Imagine our surprise when Bill Hollingsworth, allegedly speaking on behalf of men in general, advised us that we are actually, in his words, "ball-busting bitches." My, my. You just never can see yourself as others see you, can you?

This put us in quite a quandary because, as we explained to Bill, most of us are fending for ourselves out there in the big world, and although we might dearly love, above all things, to sit down in the middle of the road, heave a big sigh, and wait for the cavalry to come to our aid, experience has shown us that they just ain't coming. And furthermore, if they do show up, they want us to fix them lunch or tell them what tie to wear. Whatever needs to get done is going to have to get done by us our ownselves. Bill contends that we would have a much better shot at getting guys to run errands, pay for stuff, buy jew-

elry, furs, and flowers, as well as slobber all over us endlessly, if we
didn't act so much like guys. He actually said that we *are* guys and
that, as masculine as he himself is, he is a damn sight more feminine
than we ever thought about being.

Well! we said, in somewhat of a huff. So naturally we demanded,
not that he put his money where his mouth is (what could be more
worthless than a man with a mouthful of money), but that he buy us
dinner and give us details on how, in his opinion, we could be more
girl-like. We wanted details on how to do it, examples of when we
were not doing it, and alternative—more feminine—choices for future reference. He said he would do just that, but he insisted that we
must, to use his own words, "leave our dicks at home." He wanted to
be the only one at dinner who had one. We had to agree to be total
girls for the entire evening. We were a tad daunted at the prospect,
since we were clueless about what he would require of us.

To put ourselves into the girlish spirit of the occasion, we decided
we would try to dress the part. You know how we do love to dress up.
Thinking ruffles, pink stuff, petticoats, white stockings, little flat black-
patent shoes, we trotted off to our respective closets and returned
crestfallen and empty-handed. Who's got any of *that*? Obviously nobody we know, since we are all guys, to hear Bill talk. We did, however, fix our hair. I dredged up some old hair bows from my daughter
BoPeep's archives—great big, floppy ones. I piled my hair up on top
of my head and plunked a giant bow smack in the middle of it.
Tammy pulled her hair up on one side and secured her bow at a rak-
ish angle. Let me tell you, putting a big bow in your hair has almost
the same effect as putting on a crown! We walked different—sort of
prancy, actually—and we found ourselves tilting our heads this way
and that, even when speaking to each other. Instant Girl.

We had Bill pick us both up at Tammy's house so we could make
our bow-bedecked appearance together for maximum audience appeal. By the time he got there, we had completely metamorphosed
into giant fifth graders. Giggles and sidelong glances abounded. We
both met Bill at the door and inundated him with our girliness. We sat
up very straight and pulled our skirts down primly, hands folded in
our laps. He pronounced us "adorable." We were off to a grand start
and figured we had aced the girl thing with only a couple of simple
props. We settled in for a little light predinner conversation, just the
way girls would do.

Tammy had the first question for our mentor. She wanted to

know how to get men to buy jewelry—for us, not for themselves, for although we love the look of jewelry on ourselves, it is too icky for words on them. Bill is the perfect one to ask the jewelry question of since he personally started my own rather extensive jewelry collection for me when I was only nineteen, a mere Cute Girl. Tammy lamented that last year a man gave her a monogrammed brass cigar case—a very nice, completely lovely monogrammed brass cigar case, but there is just no way to make a pendant out of a monogrammed brass cigar case. Bill didn't even have to think a second about that one. "Well, Tammy," he said, "you shouldn't be smoking cigars, now should you? That is a guy thing, and if you want to be the girl, you shouldn't be doing it!" But he offered me one, she whined. Now, this problem is clear: She thought she was being polite by accepting the cigar; as a former president of the Junior League, Tammy can be a tad manners-obsessed. Manners are wonderful things and they serve us well, but, as with all things, there is just a time and place. According to Bill, the offer of a cigar is just the situation where we, as girls, should venture to decline a man's hospitality. He swears we can do this without giving offense, and come off looking girlier than ever. Nothing if not quick studies, we grasped his concept right away. We were just intuitively able to put that Southern spin on the whole thing, which is just about the girliest stuff on the planet. We did the little gasp thing that said to him what a big bad man he was for even *thinking* we would accept a cigar. We were positively *scandalized* at the prospect of even being offered a large, cylindrical—we can't even think it—phallic-looking—oh my!—tobacco product. The very idea! (Southern women love to say "the very idea" to emphasize how shocked they are by things.)

We put both hands on his big manly chest and shoved ever-so-slightly and said that he should just quit it! We don't even smoke, but if we did, we certainly could never smoke anything that big! Whatever was he thinking! We didn't see how *anybody* could smoke anything *that* big! We were still talking cigars, but the subliminal message was getting through, and he was positively strutting around the room; crowing should commence momentarily.

The predinner chat continued for a bit and somehow, as it so often does, the conversation turned to sex—oops! pardon my lapse—s-e-x. Anything girls want to say that is the least bit racy, they will spell out, most often in a loud whisper, which is just about the most audible tone a woman can make. Anyway, in the course of this little s-e-x discussion, we were still sitting primly on the edge of our chairs, when the subject of pleasuring oneself popped up. Tammy and I referred to it in the vernacular—"beating off." Bill was undone. According to him, we cannot say "beating off" because, as girls, we have nothing, in his definition of it all, to beat. We insisted it was just a term and could apply just as easily to us. He further insisted that yes, it was just a term, a guy term, and we could not use it, it was not feminine at all for us to use it.

What can we say then? *Masturbate* was what he came up with for us. We objected strenuously that "masturbate" sounds pretty formal for friendly discussion between friends about something you do to your own personal self; it is like talking about yourself in the third person. Besides, we tend to like earthier, folksier terms for things for private conversations. If we are speaking to a health professional, for example, we might say "breasts," whereas if we are talking to each other, we prefer the less-stilted "tits" or "boobs" (although the word *boobs* is personally offensive to me in reference to female breasts—as a product of the Sixties' South, *boob* will forever and always be a word used by Barney Fife to describe a stupid person). At any rate, Bill said we could use those words, but "beating off" was definitely off-limits. We thought only a moment before coming up with a satisfactory response. Once again, we drew upon our vast reservoir of Southern girl stuff. We looked at him, from way underneath our eyelashes, and we said, shyly, with an air of including him in a little conspiracy, "I like to touch myself . . ." (here comes the very best part: we shifted to a loud whisper and lowered our heads) *"down there!"* He fell off the couch.

After a bit, he recovered himself and seemed willing to proceed with our lesson. He said that certain references we made to men in the *Book of Love* were ill-advised when delivered in person to a guy. Specifically, Bill said that when we say that "we love men, they taste just like chicken" or when we refer to them as "cat-toys," well, it doesn't exactly, in *his* terms, make their dicks hard. We were shocked, not only at his harsh language, but at learning how thin-skinned the little SOB's are! Oops! Not a girly thing to say.

Nobody can be in Bill's presence for longer than five minutes without hearing of his undying love and devotion to me. This has been going on for, well, let's see, it started in 1971 and continues today, unabated. He nags me ceaselessly to marry him, which of course I should do, and probably would do if I wasn't so afraid of ruining the best relationship of my entire life. I would not take odds on how long the adoration would continue if I ever stupidly gave him what he thinks he wants so desperately. I'd be out a perfectly good boyfriend is all—and I do mean perfectly good. He loves me beyond reason and he lives two hundred miles away—show me the flaw in this deal. At any rate, Bill was yammering about how much he loves me and how he just had no idea if I would ever consent to even have dinner with him again and how he just had never even dared to breathe such a hope. Whereupon Tammy looked at him, tilted her little bow-laden head, twinkled for a moment, and said to him in the sweetest possible tones, "Are you just dumb as a door?" She and I both then went into convulsions of wild laughter at her blatant ball-busting, cleverly disguised with a bow and a smile. We could not stop laughing, nearly shook our bows loose. Bill looked very stern, indeed. We surmised from his look that this was a definite for the no list and so we pass along this advice to you as well: If you want to capture his heart, don't ask him, even very sweetly, if he is as dumb as a door. You probably already know the answer anyway.

My sister, Judy, said she guessed arm wrestling with them is probably out as well. Bill confirmed that. But I tell you what we did discover: You can say or do just about anything to them if you smile sweetly, look at them even more sweetly, and wear a bigass bow in your hair! We admit the bow part was news to us. We can't wait to go fully bowed to deliver our next Promise. Putty, putty, putty in our hot little hands.

15

Guys Ain't Girls

Hardly a day goes by that I don't hear about some activity that just has "guy" written all over it—no way it would ever even occur to a woman. For instance, I saw in the paper where someone was on a second-floor balcony. From that vantage point, the person was trying to show off his/her aim by throwing a watermelon from the balcony into a trash container, which was some distance away and on the ground. From the newspaper account, I gathered that he/she got so carried away with the fever of the moment that he/she did one of those things you see cartoon characters do all the time—you know, when they're bowling and they drop the ball and hurl themselves bodily down the alley toward the pins. Yes, after a hot afternoon of melon tossing, I guess the competition got the best of him/her and he/she inadvertently flung himself/herself off the balcony—to his/her untimely and totally undignified death. Now, if you had to place a sizable wager on the gender of the deceased, what would you pick? Of course it was a guy. This is a typical guy activity and it is the equivalent, but somehow more socially acceptable form, of banging their actual dicks on the table—which is, of course, the heart of pretty much all guy-type competitions.

I have a boyfriend in Montgomery, Alabama, Gary Warren, and he told me that he plays in a golf tournament *every* year that starts with what amounts to a swearing-in ceremony: They all raise their right hands and say in unison, "I am a dickhead." And then the games begin—golf, along with a fair amount of drinking ("drankin'," as we are apt to call it) and the endless telling of lies. He said there is a bar in Daytona known as "The Original Dickheads," where admission is sixty-four cents but they charge you a dollar—because they're dickheads. I admit, I like the concept.

I read with interest and alarm the missive I received from a woman named Trish, who said that a number of years ago, she had actually been arrested in Caruthersville, Missouri, for saying "dickhead." This seems harsh to me. It seems, at the time, that community had an ordinance against women using profanity. Trish didn't relate to me the circumstances that caused her to use this epithet—like, for instance, whether she directed it at a policeman who had perhaps merely stopped her for a routine traffic citation? Or did she, in fact, just use the term within the confines of a private conversation, only to be hauled off by eavesdropping jack-booted language police? If you happen to be passing through Caruthersville, Missouri, please ask them what their current policy is on "dickhead." It's information we all need. If there really is an ordinance that applies only to women using profanity, well, then, we're just gonna have to plan a road trip, now aren't we? I just want to make sure that if it's legal for *anybody* to say "dickhead," it's legal for us *all* to say "dickhead."

One of the Queens, Tammy, and I recently had dinner with these two other people. (As it happened, the other two had penises.) Now, neither of the guys had anything resembling a romantic interest in either me or Tammy—which I know is hard to believe, but it's true nonetheless. Just four buddies having dinner. Except that it was the first time the two men had met each other. What transpired was the most primitive, barbaric, and hilarious display Tammy and I had ever seen.

They did stuff early on—during drinks and what should have been pleasant before-dinner conversation among the four of *us*—that, had they been dogs, would have significantly involved trees. If there was any territory, figurative or literal, perceived by either of them, both rushed to mark it first and then, of course, last. At this point, however, Tammy and I were oblivious to the fact that we were in the middle of a full-fledged dogfight and we were just blathering away, trying to make small talk. It didn't take us too long to figure out that we were actually the only two people talking to us; the two with peni were talking only to each other. Then we realized that they appeared to have grown taller and somehow puffier. They were sitting up very straight and were looking intently at each other while pretending to have polite conversation, although not with us. If they had been actual dogs, this would have been the phase where they circled each other, maybe a little light snarling here and there. If one of them said he rode a Harley, the other one rode a bigger one—bigger and faster and louder and it was very rare; they don't even make it anymore, and they only made two of them to begin with, and the other one got sucked up in a tornado a long time ago. Oh yeah? Well, nobody actually said "Oh yeah?" but the air was rife with the implication of it. We would not have been at all surprised to hear their dialogue deteriorate to the four-year-old level of "I can fly if I want to, I just don't want to." "Huh! I don't believe you can fly. Do it." "No, I don't want to. But I can if I want to."

This went on and on until Tammy and I gave up all pretense that it wasn't happening and started talking about it, right in front of them, across the table.

"Tammy, dear, don't look now, but I think we are in the epicenter of the biggest dick contest ever in the history of the world."

"Yes, we are, aren't we? I bet we could fall over face first in our dinner and they wouldn't even pause, what do you think?"

"Well, let's just see." And then we sort of fell over on the table and lay there with our eyes bugged out and our tongues hanging out the sides of our mouths. No comment from the peni gallery whatsoever.

By and by, we sat back up. The contest continued unabated. Tammy and I wondered aloud whether shortly they would, in fact, whip out and commence table-banging. All of this "competition" somehow had to do with us, although, as I said, neither of them had any interest in either one of us. They just didn't want the other one to have us, and so battle was unavoidable. It was completely insane—and totally masculine.

Not that the female equivalent is any more sane. If two girls were out for the same guy, though, they would at least be more appealing to the guys involved, because the guys would be getting touched and rubbed on a lot by the dueling girls. This makes guys very happy! They could not care less about the source of their good fortune—they just lap it up. Which brings to mind a related guy trait that my sister, Judy, first observed and we have found to be immutable: *There is no compliment you can pay to a guy that is too outlandish for him to believe.* Make a mental note of that one; it will serve you well—we promise.

Yes, Virginia, There Really Is an Anvil Shoot

But I digress. Before I distracted myself, I was discussing weird stuff that guys are wont to do. How about this one: Ever hear of an anvil shoot? Does anybody out there have any idea what one does at an anvil shoot? Does one shoot *at* the anvil? *From* the anvil? Or is the anvil the ammo? If so, how does one propel it, and toward what target?

The man who introduced us to the fine art of anvil shooting is Gene Mulloy, sole proprietor of the Acme Anvil Company in Laurel, Mississippi, exclusive purveyor of anvils to the World Anvil Shooting Society, if you please. So I asked Gene. When are anvil shoots held? Is it a year-round sport? Indoor or out? What does one wear if one is a participant, and what does the stylish spectator wear? We especially wanted to know if any anvil-shooting clothes with sequins were available and whether hats were involved—we have a fondness for hats.

Based on the name alone, the Sweet Potato Queens decided to make anvil shooting our official sport. We were quite taken with the whole idea, even though we had no information on it. We have always thought that information is highly overrated in the decision-making process. We prefer making as many decisions as possible based solely on whatever we feel like doing at that particular moment in time, and information slows this process, in our opinion.

Naturally, we wanted to have our own personal anvils for it. We had already been thinking of getting some anvils, because you just never know when some annoying person (read: guy) is gonna tear past you in a mad dash, unaware that he is rapidly approaching a two hundred-foot cliff. And if you only had your anvil handy, you could hand it to him, à la Road Runner, and speed his descent.

We needed to get our own anvils ASAP so we could start practicing up for the Big Shoot. But first we wanted to know how the sport works. We were hoping that it involves flinging one's anvil at one's target. And, if so, do we all have to use the same target or can we each select our own? And is the target secured or does it get to run around and we have to try to hit it on the fly? If we have to use the same target, it's gonna be pretty dang hard to get a consensus—in fact, we've already had some heated discussion on the best targets. Besides the obligatory annoying guys, another top contender was any fat-armed, cig-puffing, whiskey-voiced woman yelling at her kids in the grocery store. A whole gaggle of politicos were in the running, too, of course.

So, we asked Gene, our anvil guru, are anvils one-size-fits-all? This matters much to us, since some of us are ver-r-r-ry tall and some of us are ver-r-r-ry short. We wanted our anvils customized. We were eager to schedule fittings right away, and of course, we wanted them delivered. If there was any sort of festival attached to the anvil shoot, we were volunteering to be the Queens of it. Well, actually, we were expecting to be the Queens of it—*demanding* would not be too strong a word. So Gene Mulloy, anvil aficionado, contacted me at once, begging us to come and Queen over his anvil shoot. He said that the last one they had in Laurel drew contestants "from all over." Many luminaries had participated in the event—including the mayor of Farmington, Missouri. Gene could not quite believe that the Sweet Potato Queens "really exist," but if they do, "do they come in one-size-fits-all"? I assured him that I and my Queens do, in fact, exist, although we do seem too good to be true. And as far as one-size-fits-all, it has been our experience that one Sweet Potato Queen is too much for any one mortal man. I encouraged him to recruit himself some helpers.

Oh, and he sent me a video of an actual anvil shoot. Even after watching it, I could hardly believe that grown-up people (men, of course) actually thought of this and followed through with it. I mean, if this isn't a guy thing, nothing is and nothing ever will be. Who else but a bunch of guys would go out in the middle of a field, lugging with them not one, but two, anvils weighing at least one hundred pounds apiece, a couple of pounds of gunpowder, and a fuse, with the sole purpose of watching it blow up? Seriously. They dig a hole and put one anvil down in it, put the gunpowder and fuse on top, put the other anvil on top of that, light the fuse, and run like hell. They are just wild to see how high it will go and how big a crater it will leave in the ground. I suppose they are also mildly interested in dodging the shot anvil as it crashes to the ground. I mean, really, can you picture a bunch of women pulling this kind of stunt? We would find it worth the trouble only if we could attach an annoying guy to the thing, or at the very least, his personal belongings.

It Happens Once a Year

Now here's a girl thing we find hilarious beyond words, which guys would not get at all. I know this bunch of women who have been attending the Neshoba County Fair in Philadelphia, Mississippi, every August since they were born. One of the things Neshoba County is noted for is red dirt: There is plenty of it and it is plenty red. Children are driven mad by this dirt and are compelled to roll in it, seeking to embed as much of it as possible into all their body parts and into every fiber of their clothing. The fair lasts a week, and so for real fair people—the ones who live out there in the cabins for the duration—laundry rears its ugly head about midweek. Even if you have taken every stitch of clothes your children own, water balloons and red dirt will make short work of anything resembling clean clothes. This means their mothers have to load up all the red dirt-laden clothes and haul them out to the car and drive all the way into town to the laundromat and sit there while the clothes wash and dry. This is not as exciting as it sounds.

And so it was that one group of women fell to making laundry day into their own exclusive "women only" party away from the fair and children. In keeping with the Sweet Potato Queens' closely held belief in the vital importance of the ability to make one's own fun no matter what, we heartily commend these resourceful women for this plan.

They skip out of the fair early on laundry day before that big lunch for all those people has to be prepared. They always take with them lots of wonderful salty things, like Fritos (surely the best salty food in the world), multiple pitchers of margaritas, and, of course, the laundry. Then they all pile up in the laundromat and take over. After the first round of margaritas, all the regulars give up and decide to come back later when the coast is clear of loud, potentially dangerous women.

One year after the margaritas got to flowing, it appeared to the group that one of their number had, in the group's opinion, a little too much gray hair for her own good. When they mentioned this to her, she seemed unmoved, and they felt pretty sure from her reaction that she wasn't going to do a thing about it. Well, the more they thought about it, the more unacceptable her hair became, until—well, until they just had to take matters into their own little hands. A whole bunch of them ganged up on her and subdued her—tied her up with her own dirty laundry, no less. One of them staggered over—well, maybe she wasn't staggering yet—to the drugstore, where she purchased a box of Lady Clairol in a lovely shade of brown. This was either a stroke of luck or a random act of kindness because the intended victim's natural shade, pre-gray, was a lovely shade of brown. And yes, with their good friend tied up these inebriated women dyed her hair in the middle of a Philadelphia, Mississippi, laundromat in broad daylight on a Wednesday afternoon in August.

They had not really thought this project through, though, because they hadn't allowed for the fact that her hair would need to be rinsed (or as we like to say in the South, "reenched off"), and it was going to need it pretty soon. So they all piled into a car—the victim was no longer tied up, but she did have a bunch of Lady Clairol cooking on her head—and went to a nearby neighborhood and knocked on doors until somebody answered who would let them rinse her head off. That's what I like about the South. You can go up to the doors of virtual strangers and convince them, in less time than it takes for the dye on your hair to make a sinister turn, to let you in to use their shower. It makes a pretty strong statement about the sense of community, in my opinion. To say nothing of putting the finishing touches on another great day at the laundromat.

Sizing Up Men and Women

One's perception of one's personal size, I have discovered, is heavily influenced by the style of one's private equipment. That is to say, persons with the popular Guy Style apparatus will visualize themselves one way—tall—while for persons with the equally popular Girl Style of rigging, the desirable image can fluctuate from time to time. Guys never waver—they always want to be tall and indeed will claim to be, obvious facts to the contrary. I know this because I am six feet tall and I have never personally met a man who admitted being under five-nine. I can be standing right next to him, looking smack down at the entire top of his head, and if the subject of height comes up—which it so often does in my presence—he will invariably say that he is five-nine, which would make me at least seven-two. In our midst at the time of this conversation can be another woman who is five-four, and the tops of their heads will be exactly level. The guy will stand between the two of us girls and say with a completely straight face and utter conviction in his heart that he *is* five-nine. Me and the girl will exchange glances, wordlessly communicating to each other that this guy obviously thinks that we are either dumb as a box of hair or blind or possibly both, but he's happy with his imagined stature, so we let him keep it.

I do understand this overwhelming desire to ignore the truth about one's size. I have always harbored a desire to be five-two. While I was making up impossible stuff to wish for regarding my person, I also wanted to weigh a hundred and five pounds and have long red hair, green eyes, big tits, and little feet. Oh, and I wanted to be able to sing as well. Fate was not kind. The last time I was five-two I was in the third grade, but I probably didn't weigh a hundred and five until I was much much older. I was a very tall, very skinny kid. I am still very tall. The red hair—well, I have it once a year, anyway, in the St. Paddy's Parade, but for the most part my natural color is semi-gray; it is completely natural. I didn't pay to have it dyed that way. I have not ever found it necessary to wear a minimizer bra. In fact, if I could figure out how to wear two Wonderbras, I would. And my feet. Oh, my feet. The feet I would have given myself are just the cutest little things! And my teeny little shoes would just make you cry, they're so precious. People would wonder how I could even walk on these feet, they are so very teeny-tiny. The only thing tinier on my body, if I were designing it, would be my tee-tiny little ole butt; it would be like one of them little tiny baby lima beans. I can say one good thing about the actual size of my feet: It certainly is a mercy there's that much of me folded under—otherwise, I *would* be seven-two.

A really nutty thing women do, indicating a severe distortion problem, is apparent in the clothes we buy when we have lost some weight. In our minds, before the weight loss, we were behemoths, which may or may not be founded in fact. However, once even a minimal weight loss has been achieved, we are positively elfin and we will race out and buy the clothes to prove it. We will buy clothes to put on our new bodies that, had we just recently risen to our present weight, we wouldn't dream of putting on and going out in public. Since we are on our way down the scale, we think we are Tyra Banks, and our lust for tiny spandex dresses is boundless. I have a friend—

you have one, too, I'm sure—who insists on wearing the very small-est-size clothes that she can actually squeeze herself into and zip up all the way. If that zipper closes, honey—it fits. Doesn't matter that the pleats and pockets are all stretched out, she can't move her arms, and there's fat poking out between the buttons. If she can fasten a size-four around her girth, then she's a by-God-size-four, and that's all there is to it. She would look great in a size ten, but she just lo-o-o-oves that number four. Of course, to people who don't know her, she looks like she has probably recently gained fifty pounds and can't af-ford to buy clothes to keep up with her rapidly expanding behind. All she can see in her mind's eye is that magic number four. Her mind's eye apparently can't see the woman in the mirror. We need to get her together with the guy who's five-nine. I bet they could imagine a won-derful life together.

I Prefer Clorox

I hear a lot of complaints lately about women's perfume. Actually, I have made a lot of complaints lately about women's perfume. I would much rather they have perfume-free zones in restaurants than smoke-free ones, and I am no fan of cigarette smoke. But I would say that 99 percent of all the perfumes being manufactured today actually started out as chemical warfare weapons, and as soon as the formulas were declassified, all those Calvin Klein types snapped them up and put them in fancy bottles. I have been reduced to a sneezing, snotty-nosed, teary-eyed wretch in under five minutes, simply from being in the same building with some of these "fragrances."

But let me hasten—I could fall and hurt myself, I am in such a hurry—to say that as vile as women's perfume is, men's is worse. And they have no sense whatsoever about how much to put on their per-sons at one dousing. They positively drench themselves in it. There is one guy who comes down from his shower at the gym, all buffed and shined, and smelling loud. He goes straight to the water fountain. I have made the mistake on more than one occasion of sticking my head in the water fountain right after he has been there. Big mistake. Huge. A big, ole stinky mistake. He is carrying around such a cloud of scent that a bunch of it hangs inside the water fountain and gloms onto the next poor fool who sticks his/her head in there. And there is no getting it off without a major hot shower, either. It does not wear off all day long. It sort of gets up your nose and sets up permanent residence, too. Heaven help you if one of these stinky people should go so far as to hug you. You are marred for life.

My next-door neighbors had a real mean maid when we were growing up. Mae, I think her name was. She used to yell at my friends, whose parents employed her but who were, of course, nowhere around to protect their hapless offspring. One of her favorite threats, on which she hung not even the hint of a veil, was, if they did not immediately and without any hesitation do whatever it was she wanted them to do, "I'm gone put sump'n on you Clorox won't take off!" And she always really emphasized the first syllable of *Clorox* and gave it a really long "o" sound. Cloe-rox. It was a highly effective threat and generally had the desired effect of intimidating the kids into her required state of cowed obedience. So whenever I find myself plastered with somebody else's raunchy eau de toilette (there's a fitting name), I always think of Mae, the mean maid, and her threat. Has sump'n been put on me that Cloe-rox won't take off?

It Was Only an Earthquake

Contrary to popular opinion, the chances of keeping cool in a crisis or running around screaming like a howler monkey are split pretty evenly along gender lines. There's just no predicting who will go nuts on you. I was in a crowded elevator once, going from the basement level to the ground level. That's as far as it went because it was a short building. There were mobs of people waiting for the elevator on both levels, which were only ten feet apart, max. Okay, the elevator gets stuck. I'm telling you, in less than eight seconds it was a madhouse in that elevator. One woman started yelling at another woman that it was her fault because she touched the buttons. One man started spinning in place, hyperventilating loudly. Another man literally crawled up the bodies and over the heads of everyone in front of him to get to the buttons so that he could push them himself. Being approximately three feet taller than everyone else in the elevator, I was just watching this little panorama unfold before me. Just before the shrieking started, I pointed out to them that (a) we were only maybe eight and a half feet off the ground and (b) everybody on both floors could hear that we were stuck, and help was bound to be here pronto, because those people waiting wanted to use the elevator their ownselves. Then the people with me started shrieking, and no sooner had the first blast died down than the elevator lurched up the last two feet and the doors opened, and they all walked out without even the decency to look sheepish for having behaved like pure loons in there. All that is to say, you just can't tell about people in an emergency: The male/female thing is not a good predictor.

Here's another example, told to me by our Spud Stud, Bob. Bob's buddies Claudine and Homer took a trip to San Francisco. Remember that big earthquake they had a few years back? That's when they went. Claudine is on the twenty-fifth floor of a high-rise hotel, in the shower, and here comes this giant earthquake. This, I can only imagine, is infinitely more offputting than having the doorbell ring midshower. She manages to get out of the shower and into the black hole that her hotel room has become and find a housecoat and a raincoat. Now, speaking just for myself here, I have never personally carried either a housecoat or a raincoat anywhere. But Claudine's got them both and she puts them both on and finds her way out into the pitch-dark hall and feels her way along toward the sound of a woman having a screaming fit. She finds the woman, and they both indulge themselves for a moment or two in a little well-deserved hysteria. Now, as *Bob* tells it, the two women are just sniveling mounds of housecoats and raincoats until a man, undaunted and reserved, comes by and kindly and calmly herds the two of them down the twenty-five flights of dark stairs. I doubt the veracity of this account, but they did get out into the street, where they all proceeded to go completely nuts with everybody else out there.

Meanwhile, several miles away and out in the sun, our Homer is on the golf course. According to his account, the ground just sort of rippled. They all froze momentarily and then it stopped, so they assumed it was just your regular everyday earthquake that they have out there forty times a day. Everybody behind them was playing on and everybody in front of them was playing on, so naturally, Homer and his buddies played on, too. Several hours later, as they started making their way back into town, around closed roads and missing bridges and houses bucked up and split wide all around, it began to dawn on them to be perhaps just a little afraid.

Back at the hotel, Claudine had no idea where her darling Homer was, and she was frantic with worry. Eventually, Homer appeared, and they fell on each other with relief that neither had been harmed. The joyful reunion continued until Claudine learned that while she was shivering and quaking in the streets, Homer was playing golf!

"You were on the golf course?!" And yet again, "You were on the golf course!" After steadying herself, she proceeded, "You're telling me that while I was here, not knowing if you were alive or dead, not knowing if I would live or die in this tacky housecoat with a bunch of shrieking strangers, you were playing golf." Pause. "Homer? What on earth did you do?"

To which Homer had the reckless temerity to reply, "Bogey, par, par, bogey." And somehow Homer is still alive, this very day.

16

Civil Rights, Body Hair, and Other Delicate Matters

I continue to be shocked, appalled, and dismayed at the never-ending supply of inequities in the lives of male people and female people. I'll never forget BoPeep coming home from school in the first grade on Martin Luther King Day. It was the first time she'd heard of the civil rights struggle, and she was horrified. I said, Well, do you realize that *we* could be treated just that same way in some situations? She was confused, since we happen to be white. Ah, yes, I said, but we are women, and black and white men got the vote before women did in this country. I told her that her very own grandmother was born before women in the United States of America could vote for dog catcher. She was astounded. I briefly explained that women are still considered property in many parts of the world, with no rights whatsoever. And it's not just political power that's been distributed unequally, I told her.

Consider this: I don't know if society (men) silently decreed this a thousand years ago or what, but for the life of me I can't understand how come a three-hundred-pound guy can cram himself into a

Civil Rights, Body Hair, and Other Delicate Matters

Speedo and nobody blinks. The guy can also have black, curly hair growing thickly over his entire body so that he looks not unlike a gorilla in a bikini, and nobody seems to mind. Why is this so?

Women, on the other hand, must be completely hairless. Gleaming, bald bodies are required of us. Who started this bizarre tradition of shaving our bodies, anyway? Oh, stop gagging, I do it. I'm not over here growing armpit hair while I write; I just wonder how and why it got started and how come it was never dictated that guys do it. I am of the opinion that if women's underarm hair is offensive (and I'm not totally convinced that it is), hair on a guy's back is ten times worse. Yet who among them feels the slightest obligation to do anything about its removal? Is there a woman out there who, after suffering the agony of a bikini wax, can say this is fair? I think not.

Women must also not appear to have any spare pounds in a swimsuit. As a result, there are now eighteen thousand varieties of camouflage swimwear for us to try. They are basically gaily patterned girdles, and if you want to know how well they work, squeeze a tube of pork sausage in the middle real hard. It's gotta go somewhere. It's not like we're hollow on the inside and you can just mash the fat inward and hide it.

I saw something in a catalog the other day that might just solve the world's problem of pool attire, though. (This was in a legitimate catalog. If it was a joke, they kept a straight face about it.) Called "FrogWear," it was sun-proof and covered you—totally—from neck to ankles in white fabric. I swear to you, they showed this entire family unit—Mom, Big Sister, Little Brother, Dad—frolicking merrily in the pool, wearing these ridiculous outfits just as if they had good sense. Not to mention mirrors. I mean, it looked like they were swimming in beekeeper suits. I'm sure it is the wave of the future, and not a moment too soon, either. They might consider some colors and patterns, though, in the interest of camouflage. You can still see all that back hair through the white, and if you had a spare tire, you'd look like a three-hundred-pound sack of flour floating in the pool.

And so you see, I told my precious angel who was listening raptly to my rant, we as women have special responsibilities to fight in every way we can for the rights of everyone to ensure that they are not denied to anyone, including us. She sat there blinking for a time, taking it all in. She'll be prepared all right, I'll see to that.

Men and women have vastly different habits regarding their toilettes, and their toilets as well. You won't find a whole lot of men who like to take long baths, for example. Guys like to jump in the shower and be done with it. And while we can take a quick shower when the situation calls for it, whenever time permits, we do love to get up to our necks in hot water and sit there for days.

Most men have fairly easy-care hair, while we have to fool with ours a bit more. There are the obvious exceptions, given the current popularity of head-shaving for both sexes, but by and large, men don't fuss with their hair much, and we think this is a good thing. As we discussed in *SPQBOL*, we are against men coloring, perming, or artificially replacing their hair. We are also against men having "hairdos." One of our Wannabes was married (briefly) to a man who had a hairdo, and he would fiddle with it endlessly, and if it wouldn't do right, he would pitch a fit and throw the brush at the mirror! All I can say is, if I'd witnessed that little spectacle, he'd have awakened the next morning to a bald head and a sack full of hair on the other—empty—side of the bed. There is nothing in those marriage vows about having to tolerate men having temper fits over bad-hair days. And don't even talk to me about men in hair nets!

Now, regarding the actual bathroom habits—well, you got your men and you got your women. I can't think of anything to compare this level of differentness to. Your women, for example, will use public rest rooms for number two, while your men would rather be set on fire. Men want to be on their home potty, and they want to spend the day in there. I have personally known grown men who would go through an entire workday in abject misery rather than make umps in a public rest room. They will somehow hang on until they get home to the potty where they feel free and comfy, and they will go in there with the entire Sunday *New York Times* and not come out until they have read it all, including the classifieds. There is nothing happening in that bathroom after, say, the first couple of pages of the *Times*. They are just hanging out in there—now, how weird is that?

My daddy grew up, as you may know, in Attala County, Mississippi, out from Ethel, Mississippi, to be exact, which is a suburb of Kosciusko. They didn't have any indoor plumbing back then; they also didn't have any outdoor plumbing. (Other people had plumbing of one sort or another, I am sure, but my people didn't.) In the house at night or in bad weather, they used a "slop jar" (the prissy folks called it a chamber pot), which they took outside to empty at a more convenient time. Or they just went in the woods, which were nearby and plentiful. Daddy, always the outdoorsman, made a sort of hobby, as only a guy would, out of thinking up new and interesting places outside in which to answer nature's call. His favorite was to climb a tree, select a sturdy limb with a big fork in it, drop trou', perch in the fork, and let fly. He found this highly invigorating in one of those bizarre boy ways. I personally cannot imagine any circumstances under which I could or would do this in, or rather *from*, a tree. I have not, in my informal but exhaustive survey, found any woman who can imagine such a thing, but tell this story to a guy and his little face just lights right up. Anyway, Daddy had gone to his favorite tree one hot summer day, and his dog, Rags, followed him, waiting, wagging, looking up expectantly into the leafy canopy, awaiting the descent of his boy. Daddy tried mightily to shoo him away, to no avail. Finally, nature could wait no longer, plummeting earthward and coming to rest smack on top of the dog's head. Now, Rags had no idea what was on his head, only that something had fallen out of the sky, landed on his head, and stuck there. He was completely undone by the whole thing, as any dog would be, and he took off running and hollering across the field.

Meanwhile, my granddaddy, the ineffable Harvey, was plowing behind a big ole red mule. Harvey was deaf as a post and did not know that Rags was hollering; he saw only the dog's rapidly approaching shadow coming up behind him. An affable, dog-loving kind of guy, Harvey never looked away from the row he was plowing but just reached down to pat Rags on the head as he came up alongside him and drew back a hand full of, well, freshly minted umps. *Nonplussed* I don't think would quite cover Harvey's reaction. I am at a loss to express the multiplicity of feelings that must have enveloped him. He just looped the reins over the plow handle and slowly ambled on up to the house, occasionally looking at his soiled hand and shaking his head. He drew some water from the well. As he stood scrubbing on the back porch of the old farmhouse, his wife, my grandmother Carrie, headed out to see why he had stopped plowing in the middle of the day in the middle of a row, to come wash his hands. When he saw her coming, he turned to her with soulful, searching eyes, and posed one of those haunting parental questions that will linger throughout the ages: "Maw," he asked, "what in this world could I have done to that boy to make him shit on his own dog's head and sic him on me?"

As we all know, a woman will happily use the potty at work, but if her boyfriend or new husband is in their house when the urge strikes, she will go to just about any lengths to avoid making a home deposit until she can get rid of him. In testimony of this strange truth, we offer the story of a woman we have known for many years. She is older than we are and over the years has offered us wise counsel on many subjects. I was soon to be married for the very first time, and she thought it was time to have that little talk with me—you know, the one about how will I ever have any privacy again in this life? As I said, she is older and wiser—well, she's six years older; you be the judge of "wiser." Once upon a time a newlywed herself, she had no one older and wiser to give her advice on such sensitive matters to a young girl's heart as keeping one's private matters a closely guarded secret.

She and her shiny new hubby lived in a tiny little apartment— very tiny—way too tiny for anything like sneaking into the bathroom undetected for substantial potty time. So she figured out that she could loll about in bed of a morning, waiting for him to get in the shower, during which time she would run five blocks down the street to the gas station, grab the key to the ladies' room, dash in, do the deed, return the key, and be back home before he got out of the shower. This program worked great until it rained. It was raining like a mad bastard, and though she didn't mind getting drenched anywhere nearly as much as she minded using the bathroom with him in the house, she knew there was no way to keep her little secret if she was dripping like a drowned rat when he emerged from his shower. What? Roof leak? No plausible story for even one good use, much less for the future, since she was pretty sure it would rain again one day.

As the moments ticked by, her plight became desperate. As the second hand jerked by the big numbers on her bedside clock, she was coming closer and closer to zero hour. Of course, I offered stupidly, she could have knocked on the door and told him she needed to use the bathroom for a minute, could he speed it up a little? She looked at me with flat, dead eyes that told me just how stupid that suggestion sounded to her, even now, twenty years later. He would *know*, she said, writhing, and I understood: They Must Be Kept From Knowing at any cost.

And so, she told me in hushed, hysterical tones, she did the only thing that made sense to her at the time. She scurried out of the bedroom, softly closing the door behind her, fled into the kitchen, and frantically snatched a plastic bag from the kitchen counter. The sound of the shower running told her she would be alone in the rear hallway. And yes, she did just what you are suspecting she might—and she did it in blessed privacy. As she considered her next step, however, the hall door suddenly sprang open and there she was—holding the bag— face-to-face with her still-dripping husband. Without so much as the blink of an eye, she snarled, "Are *you* responsible for *this?*"

Okay, Okay, I'm a Girl~ Just Fix the Damn Car

As a general rule car-related problems are best dealt with by human beings possessed of penises and very low estrogen levels. And here's what happens when you (a girl type: no penis, lots of estrogen) try to do something sensible for yourself about a car-related issue. Two of my nearest and dearest guy types, Allen Payne and Trey Hunt, had borrowed my car to return to Jackson from the Neshoba County Fair in the blistering heat of a Mississippi August. On their way back, something happened to the car that made the power steering stop doing that thing it does. It also made the air conditioning stop and the power windows not work. The upshot of all this is: It took both of them to steer the car. The steering wheel was just short of the melting point and, as luck would have it, they had no oven mitts, and they could not even roll the windows down. It is a wonder they didn't drown in their own sweat.

Now, I contend that movies portraying us Southerners as sweating all the time are grossly inaccurate—up to a point. They show us just going about our everyday lives, sweating like pigs at every turn— lawyers in court with big ole sweat rings under their arms, shirts unbuttoned, sticking to their backs; women working in the drugstore, rivers of sweat running down between their bosoms; kids all redfaced, hair matted to their little heads. Now, most of the time, this just doesn't happen because we invented high ceilings, ceiling fans, and sitting on your ass. The only time we really and truly sweat like they show us doing in the movies is on that odd occasion that that thing in the car that makes the power steering, the power windows, and the air conditioner work—happens to break.

So Allen and Trey rolled up at my house looking like a couple of movie rednecks. They sort of fell out on the ground when we opened the car doors. They begged us to move the sprinkler over there by them and just let them lie there for an hour or so. Feeling a certain amount of responsibility for their current slow-roasted condition, I popped the hood of the Volvo, as if I understood the first thing about any of the stuff under there. Well, butter my butt and call me a biscuit, if I didn't look down and there is this little belt-looking thing, just sort of hanging off this little wheel-looking thing, and I picked it up and said, "Hmmmm . . . I bet this is all it needs."

Thinking that car repair is not nearly so complicated as they make out, I, with broken belt-looking thing in hand, take myself to the car-parts place. It is a Saturday, midmorning, and the place is hopping. I'm talking fifty cars in the parking lot of the car-parts place. They are out there in shorts, no shirts on their hairy backs, beer guts hanging—that and no shoes. Just crawling up under the car, frying on the hot pavement, getting dirt, small bits of gravel and gum wrappers hung up in the hair on their backs, thankyouverymuch. Who are these gross individuals and where did they come from? And don't they have mamas, wives, and/or mirrors to tell them not to go to the store half-nekkid? I am gagging so bad I nearly forget why I am there, which is to buy another belt-looking thing for my car.

I go into the cool, and the car-parts guy axes can he hep me, and I hold up the broken belt-looking thing and say, "I need a new one of these." Which I thought was pretty clear in and of itself, but I went on to explain in typical Southern fashion, meaning in great detail, how some friends of mine had borrowed my car and the power steering, air conditioning, and power windows all quit working, and I bet they were plenty hot up in that car, didn't he reckon? I told him how we wondered what in this world could have caused all this mayhem, and even though none of us knew shit-diddly about cars, we were compelled to look under the hood anyway, and what did we find when we did but this little broken belt-looking thing hanging down and we just bet anything that's what was wrong and so here I was to get a new one and did he have one?

So he goes to his computer and fiddles around with it and says that, well, it could be four or five different belt-looking things, which one did I need, whereupon I held up the busted one and said I want one just like this, only not busted. So he made several trips "to the back" and he brought out a different belt-looking thing every time. I, the unskilled and unschooled, could tell from a block away that each and every one of them was twice as long and half as thick and so they were more than likely not the right ones, but he went through this painstaking process of holding them up together and comparing them closely before he determined for certain that he needed to go "to the back" and try again. He was really studying my problem hard and hmmmming and pondering a whole lot. He said, now, you don't have any idea which belt this is, do you? And I said no I didn't; all I knew was the power steering, the air conditioning, and the power windows all went out at the same time. He said, ho, that was just what he needed to know, and I said that's what I figured and that was how come I *told* him all that the *first thing*. Anyway, he finally went "to the back" and got it, but I had to take it home with me and have it put on.

I tried to get Moon Pie to meet me at the parts place in nothing but a pair of shorts and scoot around on the hot pavement under the cars with the real men. But he was too shy. It's just as well. He doesn't have what it takes to fit in with that crowd—no hair on his back.

Hey! It Works!

Truly the way to a man's heart is to ask him for help—with anything, anything at all. I promise you, it doesn't matter what it is—they love it. My friend Bruce Browning's business card is so revealing in this regard. It simply shows his name, and right underneath reads, "Perhaps I can help," and gives his phone numbers. He just lives to serve, and we do love to oblige him. Before applying this globally, we thought that this was a theory that needed road testing.

So Tammy and I went to a big barbecue shindig and hung out with the team from the Viking Range Corporation in Greenwood, Mississippi. We picked them for a number of reasons, the primary one being that since they have the best barbecue equipment, they would also have the best barbecue, and barbecue is very important to us. One thing you can count on at a barbecue contest: lots and lots of guys doing guy stuff, and this means that all but the most stouthearted women have been run off a long time ago. We dearly love a bunch of guys doing guy stuff, and we knew that the women who had not been scared off would be our kind of women as well. And it would be a great proving ground for our theory about Men Loving to Help.

We hadn't been there five minutes before Tammy announced to the team leader, Bob Gregory, that she was pretty sure that I was starving to death, so could he maybe help us find a little something to eat. ("A little something" is our favorite food because when you ask for it, you're assured of getting a big lot of something, and you know how we feel about that.) Before I could sigh deeply even once, Bob had slammed down a full slab of Viking-roasted ribs in front of me. I am happy to report that not only were they perfect, there was plenty of them, and nobody else even ate one of them. I ate the entire slab.

Then, simply by asking for their help, we got them to fetch beers, find music we liked, and dance with us. But then I put it to the ultimate test. As Tammy stared at me dumbstruck, I, with a completely straight face, told one of the guys that I could not get my beer can out of the huggy—would he help me with it? Well, you'd have thought I'd asked him to lift the rear end of the car off my mother, he was so happy to help me and so proud that he was chosen for the honor and positively bursting over his success in this endeavor. Then I pushed it—and Tammy—completely over the edge when I thanked him, blinked slowly, and asked if he would mind opening my new beer for me; it's so hard with long nails, you know. Since Tammy and I are more the type to break off the top of a stubborn beer bottle and drink the broken glass, it is beyond the realm that we would ask for help opening a pop-top. Tammy still gets hysterical whenever she thinks of it. Being a girl will just flat wear you out, I'm saying.

Occasionally there does come a situation when you've just *got* to have a guy—like when there's a spider, for instance. Your basic spider scenario creates the absolute necessity for a guy—your girlfriends are worthless to you in the event of a spider. When my friend Janet Mayer first moved to town, she and I bonded in quite a few ways, one of which was a healthy fear and loathing of spiders. Oh, yeah, yeah, I know, they are dandy little creatures that accomplish undeniable good in the world (although I personally have never observed them doing anything worthy of note). I don't care, I hate them. I wish they were all dead and gone. But Janet, *Janet* had a full-blown phobia of anything with eight legs, and when she shared with me the genesis of that phobia, well, all I can say is it would have put that Muffet chick in her grave.

Janet had just moved to a new apartment in a new town and she eagerly awaited the delivery of her new sofa. The store delivery guys brought it and put it in place. That evening, she settled in for an evening of eating crap and lolling about on the new sofa, watching TV, when her eye wandered admiringly up the back of the new sofa. There—right by her very head—was a spider the size of a dachshund just looking at her. She naturally levitated to the ceiling on the far side of the room, where she pondered what to do. New in town, she knew no one. So she called the police and told them there was someone in her apartment. They hotfooted it on over and arrived to find her sobbing and shaking outside her front door. She 'fessed up.

They yelled at her for calling 911 over a bug and turned in disgust to leave, whereupon she threw herself on their mercy and at their feet, literally, shrieking that they had to help her! Please! Since she made enough noise that people were starting to look out their windows, the cops figured they had to go inside with her. She pointed tremulously at the dreaded sofa. One cop held the flashlight, while the other one bravely yanked the cushions off. Suddenly the spider appeared and cops, flashlights, and "Whoa—shits!" were flying to all points in the room. Janet, vindicated, was yelling, "See? See? I told you! I told you! Getitgetitgetitgetitgetit!"

What with all the hubbub, Godzilla retreated to parts unknown. So then the three of them, Janet and the two policemen, were paralyzed. What to do? What to do? The cops were wishing she had called the fire department. Janet just wanted to climb out a window and abandon the whole deal, maybe move to Jersey and change her name. They had to do something. Janet suggested torching the sofa. They agreed the idea had merit, but what if there were more spiders in there and the fire just flushed them out? No, they decided it would be better to track and kill the one and then she could return the sofa as "defective," which it most certainly was.

17

Vacations: His and Hers

There is a disparity between what we (female types) think is a great vacation and what they (male types) think is a great vacation. Now, me, I think a cruise is just about your perfect vacation. One of the main selling points of a cruise is the time available for not doing Jack Shit. You can not do Jack Shit for the entire duration of a cruise. One reason is there is nothing that you can possibly need that is not on that boat. Add to that the staggering number of lackeys; as a passenger, you have at least twelve to fifteen of them assigned to you personally, and their sole reason for being is to prevent you from having to do Jack Shit. In addition, a whole covey of free-floating lackeys will come to your aid should your own personal set be out performing some other task for you when another urgent need arises—maybe a new umbrella for your drink. I do so love lackeys, and there are just hardly any at my house. Truth be told, there is only one—and she is me.

Another great thing about a cruise is the excellent food. The first qualification for food to be excellent, in my book, is that somebody else prepare it, and all I have to do is show up and eat it. And there needs to be plenty of it—especially if other people want some of it, too. On a cruise, somebody else does all the cooking and apparently they do it round the clock because there is food everywhere you look, whenever you look. You can even order every single thing on the menu at every single meal and nobody will bat an eye. I love to do this because I always want to taste everything, and plenty of times I want to eat every scrap of it. But then, I am a notorious pigwoman.

Some of my fellow Queens are also notorious pigwomen. Actually, all of us are notorious pigwomen. Our very favorite spud stud, Skippy Nessel, took two of us out to eat one night, and, notorious big spender that he is, even Skippy was staggered by the bill. Not that he complained, mind you. Our Skippy is generous and indulgent to a fault, which is, of course, why we adore him so. That and the fact that he personally purchases our fishnet stockings every year. In exchange for his purchase, he has been named the Official Seam Straightener for the Sweet Potato Queens and, as such, is responsible for making absolutely certain that each and every one of our stocking seams is straight all the way up the back of our lovely legs. It takes a real man for this job, and that would be our Skippy. No one else is allowed to call him Skippy, of course. Skippy is our pet name for him, and he is our pet and ours alone. But anyway, when he took me and Tammy out to eat, he got into a lively discussion with the waiter about the quantity of food and drink consumed and the very large bill that resulted. At some point in that dialogue, we acquired the label of pigwomen. But we are Skippy's pigwomen, and we are all happy about that.

What I'm saying is that the Queens like vacations that are luxurious and pampering in nature, ones that involve lots of lolling about in lush surroundings. Guys, on the other hand, do not.

The following is an absolute true-life example of what can happen if you give a guy a bunch of money and a travel agent. It should provide all the proof you will ever need to support this ironclad rule: Never Let a Guy Plan a Vacation.

A good friend of mine recently returned (by the skin of his teeth) from a "dream vacation" that cost a gazillion and a half dollars. My friend Bill and his friend Ron put their heads together to figure out the farthest-away place that would cost the most *possible* money and time to reach, and would offer the *worst* accommodations imaginable, where they could go to and try to kill something big. Hmmm. How about Bearplop, Alaska?

So Bill and Ron coughed up big bucks and went to an inordinate amount of trouble to go to this godforsaken place in the nether regions of Alaska in order to hunt moose and grizzly bears. See, this is what the other women and I think qualifies this trip under the stupid category. Who of sound mind would go out of his way to try to have a confrontation with a grizzly bear? A guy, that's who. And clearly, a guy with not enough fiscal responsibility weighing him down. These guys have got that old problem (I never have it myself): You know what I mean, when you get too much money in your checking account, it will start backing up on you. You have to keep it moving freely through there in order to avoid the backup problem. When the money gets backed up, you resort to absurd measures to clear it out in a hurry.

Anyway, they have to fly for a couple of days to get to the part of Alaska that has people living in it, before they can head out to their forsaken vacation spot. *Forsaken* may be a misnomer; somebody would have had to live there in order to then forsake it, and I don't think anybody ever has or ever will live where these guys went. And don't you just imagine there's a good reason for that? I mean, look at Gulf Shores and Destin—you can't sling a dead cat without hitting a condo with a thousand people in it. That's because those are desirable locations. Where Bill and Ron went, you could sling a dead cat for a couple of thousand miles and not even hit a gas station or a mobile home park. Which, in and of itself, doesn't sound all bad, but the climate isn't exactly what you'd call a big draw. Y'know?

Wheee! They are on the trek to their final destination, getting on progressively smaller airplanes at each leg of the journey, until finally, it is just Bill and Ron and the pilot in this itty-bitty plane, which the pilot informs them is still too big to fly into where *they're* going. They land on this bald knob on top of a mountain and the pilot tells them to "get out and wait right here 'cause I'll be right back." And with that, he took off, leaving Bill and Ron on top of the bald knob with no food, no water, no nothing, including no idea when the pilot was coming back. Ostensibly he was going to get yet a smaller plane, but his parting words were no comfort to our intrepid travelers: "There's a tent in that box over there. You guys can put that up for shelter, in case I don't get back." Now, I *gotta* tell you, I'd have been stroking out big time. No way would I have let that guy fly merrily off into the wild blue yonder without my person being on that plane.

So Bill and Ron were stranded on the bald knob, somewhere in Alaska, and several hours later, the pilot returned, circled the knob, and flew away. This was perplexing to our heroes, a radio being high on the list of the things they did not have, along with food, water, shelter, guns, toilet facilities and/or paper. But by and by—ten hours later—the pilot came back and landed, and took Bill away with him, with promises to Ron to "be right back." Happy Ron. "I'll be right back" is my all-time favorite line. And when *I* use it, what I really mean is: "Good-bye! If you're looking for me—I'll be the one that's gone! Just try and catch me! If I ever come back, it will be one chilly day, buckwheat!"

Eventually both made it to their vacation home, and were they ever happy then. "Home" was a Quonset hut on the side of what we in Mississippi would call a mountain or an Alp; the indigenous folk of Alaska liked to think of it as a "hill." Meals would be taken "down the hill." And down the hill it was, too—three hundred feet straight down the hill. You practically had to rappel down three times a day. Meals were then followed by the inevitable climb back up the hill. Now, our boys were both in what I would call really good shape, but nothing they had done here in the relative flatlands had prepared them for this "hill." For the first two days, they threw up whatever meal they had just eaten, getting back up the hill to the Quonset hut.

Remember, they came on this fire drill to hunt, specifically moose and grizzly bear. A fool's errand, if you ask me, but, of course, nobody did. They hired "major-league hunting guides," who sound an awful lot like garden-variety igmos to me. (But again, that is strictly my totally unsolicited opinion.) In the whole two or three weeks they were stuck off up there in the exact center of nowhere, how many moose and/or grizzly bears do you think they saw? Well, let me put it this way: I saw just as many in my very own backyard. "Hunting" with these wily woodsmen—these very expensive wily woodsmen—consisted of either (1) crashing through the brush, making enough noise to alert every bear and moose within a two-hundred-mile radius, or (2) sitting by themselves on a stump, personally selected for them by their wily woodsmen, for ten to twelve hours at a time. Sure makes me want to take up huntin'. Boy hidee, it just sounds like a bucket o' fun. I envision Bill and Ron off warming stumps, while all the bears and mooses were in the Quonset hut playing cards with the wily woodsmen.

After killing virtually nothing, not even the crazy guy who kept them up all night, every night for ten nights running, the morning of departure dawned bright and clear. Ron was the first to be extricated.

Bill was remaining until early the next morning, and this gave him time to squeeze in one more round of stump sitting. (Ron was so jealous.) Remember, they had to come and go from this Eden in a two-seater—counting the pilot—plane. So Ron bids farewell, happily, to the whole shooting match and starts the air trek back to what passes for civilization in Alaska.

Bill endures one last (he thinks) night and hops up on his last (he thinks) day in the wilds to race out to the woods and sit on a stump. Back from another exciting day of stump sitting, Bill readies himself for pickup. Sure enough, right on time—this will be the first thing to go right the whole entire trip (he thinks)—what does he hear but de plane! *De plane!* And out he runs with all his gear, looking up expectantly, only to see his transport plane circle the area and leave. There is still plenty of time to make his connections, so Bill is fairly understanding about the mountain winds and the difficulty of landing small planes. By and by, he hears the plane again, and once more he trots out expectantly with all his stuff. Again he gets the big flyover. Visualize this process repeating itself all day long—until all hope of connecting flights is dashed. Meanwhile, Ron, who got his happy hiney out the day before, is flying home, solo, with no info on Bill—like is he dead or alive, maimed, lost, did he run off with an Eskimo, or what? Nobody knows and nobody has any way of knowing because there ain't no phones or radios or any other type of communication equipment back at the Quonset hut in paradise.

This also means Bill gets to spend yet another night in the hut. Oh, it was a sad, sad night. We were feeling pretty pitiful. One little lamb lost in the woods. It was a long and lonely night for our Bill, who did confess to lying in bed and actually crying. But the night's sniveling vanished in the morning with the actual landing of the plane!

Oh, happy, happy day! This was in the top three best days of Bill's entire life. He didn't even mind (too much) his stint on the bald knob with a guy who said he was a doctor of some sort and whose conversation revealed him to be the cheapest man in the universe. Doc was living up there in the wilderness, it seems, on account of it only takes about four thousand a year. Well, I don't think we would have to resort to the wilds of Alaska to be complete and total tightwads, do you? I bet you could reside in New York City for under four thousand a year if you lived in a box with no heat or lights or running water. I mean, I think he was a little off the deep end on this frugality thing. Bill even overcame his mild bout of trepidation when he discovered that the tent in the box that could be erected for shelter, in case the pilot was unable to return that night, had been eaten by a bear.

But, as luck would have it, the pilot did, in fact, return for Bill and he did, in fact, make it to the actual airport where they have big airplanes. This brought up another issue. Out in the wilderness, it was either unnoticeable or irrelevant, but in the relative confines of the big airport, Bill could not help but notice that he smelled like a goat, although perhaps that reference is slanderous only to the goat and flattering to Bill. Bottom line: He had not had a shower in a long time and it showed—so much so that he himself could not bear it. And so, as if it made perfect sense, he goes into the men's room—handicapped stall—and strips. The man is completely naked in the men's room at the big airport, trying to de-funk himself with lavatory soap and wet paper towels. Quite a picture, no?

Several days late and somewhat scruffy, Bill did make good his return, amid great rejoicing by friends and family, who had no idea whether he would make it back alive or they would be claiming a box containing his stinky remains. All's well that ends well. Alaska is safe once more for the grizzlies and the moose.

If we were going to spend tens of thousands of dollars on a vacation, there would be things called "Sea Goddess" and "Ritz Carlton" figuring prominently. Hell, we could have plastic surgery and recuperate in a fancy hotel for that kind of money. All we can think of is how very glad we are men don't try to make us go with them and how hilarious it is that they seem to think they are pulling something over on us by slipping off on these expeditions without us. We are laughing ourselves sick all the way home from dropping them off at the airport, are we not?

Here is the Queens' ideal vacation: Delbert McClinton's Blues Cruise. Delbert, as you may recall, is one of our very most favoritest musicians in the entire world, living or dead, and he sponsors a cruise every January and books all the rest of our very most favoritest musicians in the entire world, living or dead, to go on this cruise with him. They all perform just night and day the whole time, so you can be on a cruise, getting waited on hand and foot, basking in the sun, even seeing exotic ports of call if you are so inclined. (But I warn you, the lackeys do not follow you ashore to wait on you hand and foot there.) You can have all this *plus* you get to dance with Delbert and his buddies all night every night. I cannot imagine a circumstance under which you could possibly have more fun unless you happen to own a monkey that I don't know anything about.

For all you Wannabe Wannabes out there who have been clamoring for a Sweet Potato Queen Convention, here's the deal: We're all going on Delbert's Blues Cruise! All you have to do—I'm completely serious—is call this number: 1-800-DELBERT and tell them you want to book yourself and your cohorts for a week of Sweet Potato Queens and Delbert. Don't bother paying your bills before you leave—you won't be wanting to go home, anyway.

18

More Death-Defying Recipes

From all reports, the Chocolate Stuff and Fat Mama's Knock You Naked Margaritas discussed in *SPQBOL* have done nearly everything from healing the sick to raising the dead—or at least raising the spirits of the friends of the dead. Therefore, we feel a moral obligation to offer you even more Death-Defying Recipes.

Death Chicken

Here is one we got from Tammy's friend Maggie: Death Chicken, so called because Maggie and everybody in her family has made it for funeral food so many times. When we first read the ingredients, we thought we might have to jack around with it a little bit; the spices seemed off to us. Specifically, the recipe calls for bacon, oregano, and nutmeg, among other things, and we thought that the oregano and nutmeg might possibly mess up the bacon, and we just have to say emphatically that we are 100 percent against anything that might possibly mess up bacon, which is considered holy where we come from. But we decided that we would make it just exactly like Maggie said the first time, just to see what, if anything, actually needed jacking with. Well, let me tell you—it was a pure vision, the sight of us eating Death Chicken for the very first time. It was a pure vision with a pretty hefty soundtrack to go along with it, too. Ever seen that cartoon about Precious Pup where they give him a dog biscuit and he levitates about six feet off the floor, horizontally, and he comes down real slow, clutching various parts of his body, in the throes of ecstasy, emitting loud, repetitive sounds of rapturous delight the whole time? That's kinda what we did although we all suck at levitating. It was, in a word, perfect. I wouldn't change a single thing except to make a whole big bunch more of it than we did because we 'bout took each other's arms off trying to get at the stuff.

Here's how to make Death Chicken: Start off right by lining a 9 x 13 pan with six or more slices of uncooked bacon (we recommend more, naturally; you know, some people like to say "less is more," but we are just the kind of girls who believe that more is more—and also better). This is just the perfect start to a perfect ending of just about anything, in my opinion. Next, pour a cup of uncooked rice over the bacon. I love it when you don't have to cook the rice first, don't you? On top of the rice, put some chicken pieces; happily, the skin must be left on for cooking purposes, and you may use white, dark, whatever you want. Salt and pepper the chicken a little bit and sprinkle a little paprika over it. Then whisk together 1 can of cream of chicken soup and 1 cup of water, adding a little bit of garlic salt, a pinch of nutmeg, 1 teaspoon of oregano, and 2 to 3 tablespoons of dried parsley flakes. Pour all that over the chicken and cover the whole deal with heavy foil (emphasis on heavy; it matters). Cook it at 300 degrees for two hours, with no peeking. Now, this part is most excellent because it means that you can put it in the oven and go to the funeral and come home to find your funeral food all done. And it will evermore be the hit of the funeral gathering, too, let me tell you. Make at least a double batch because, I promise you, you won't get enough of it at the funeral to suit you and you're gonna be crabby as all get out when you get home and don't have a big pan of this stuff waiting for you.

Another thing about our Death-Defying Recipes is that they all can serve a dual purpose, if need be. You can not only take it for tasty funeral food; you can use it to hasten the onset of a funeral in certain individuals, should the need arise. Say, for instance, you happen to be in possession of a very old, extremely wealthy husband who himself is possessed of a bad heart and no other heirs but you your ownself. You married him, thinking zippity-do-dah was just around the corner, but he just persists in living on, day after day after day, until you are just about ready to kill yourself over it. Well, now, a good wife would be cooking hot meals for her husband. This stuff, on a regular basis, would be just as effective as arsenic, and they can't put you in the penitentiary for it. Bacon is completely legal in all states: We checked. So you could call it Doo-dah Chicken, if you wanted to.

Connie's Death Corn Five

What was that movie—*War Games* or something with Matthew Broderick or somebody like that, where somebody was gonna blow up the world and it came in stages of DefCon 1–5? We don't remember what DefCon stood for, but we liked that part. Over the years, we have used that ranking system ourselves to illustrate the level of personal catastrophe that was occurring or about to occur: A DefCon 1 situation would be something like, oh, having a flat tire on a hot day and not being able to find your husband to make him change it and bitch him out about not replacing your tires before this kind of thing happened, while a DefCon 5 would be this same situation but when you finally do find him, he's with another woman and they have used your credit card to pay for the hotel room. So, anyway, when we got this great funeral food recipe from our friend Connie, and realized that it has exactly five ingredients—one of which is corn—well, we thought it fairly cried out to be named Death Corn 5.

You take one package of yellow rice—being Southern, we naturally prefer it be Zatarain's. You have to cook the rice ahead of time and that's a pain, but it can't be avoided. Fortunately, the rest of the recipe only involves dumping stuff in a casserole dish and stirring it up. So you cook the rice just like the box says, only you don't put any oil in it. Don't worry, there will be fat in a minute. You know whoever said "time heals all wounds" is just an idiot. Time doesn't heal shit-diddly, not by itself anyway. If something rotten happens and you just sit down and wait for it to pass, I promise you, no matter how long you sit there, if you don't eat something good, you are gonna feel every bit as bad as you did when you started—worse even because you'll be starving slap to death. No, time does not heal all wounds; fat, however, does. I can't think of a situation bad enough that fat wouldn't improve significantly.

So, anyway, you've got your Zatarain's yellow rice cooked without oil. Now dump it in your casserole (a quart size is probably big enough—but here again, why don't you just go on and make a big vat of it and freeze some of it?). Then dump in a can of Mexicorn (that canned corn with red peppers and other stuff thrown in), a can of cream of chicken soup, a stick of butter (melt it first), and a cup of shredded cheese—cheddar or hot Jack, if you like a little kick, which I do. Dump and stir, as I said, and maybe put a little more cheese on top—you can just never have too much cheese, you know—and cook it for about 20 minutes or so at 350 degrees.

Please note that all five ingredients are yellow. Can you imagine a more cheerful dish to take to the bereaved? I'm sure it will perk them up no end. Note: At a cooking demonstration I once commented that you could make this recipe with nonfat soup, nonfat or low-fat cheese, and Benecol (instead of butter) and it would be pretty low fat, but I wouldn't do it for somebody I loved: They deserve the full-fat treatment, in my opinion. Susan Trott, leader of the Cooter Throb Queans (not a typo) of Memphis, Tennessee, came up to me afterward and declared that there was nobody in the world she disliked enough to make a fat-free casserole for.

Larrupin' Good Sweet Potatoes

Lest you forget of what we are the Queens, here's the best thing involving sweet potatoes you ever put in your mouth. I first got this recipe from a guy I used to work with, Mark Magee. Well, actually, I got it from his wife, Pam, by way of Mark. He's a sweetheart and a multitalented guy, but I'm quite sure cooking ain't one of 'em. Whenever there was a covered-dish event at work—the only justification I can see for working at a real job as opposed to being self-employed—involving everybody toting massive amounts of fattening foodstuffs to work with them for public consumption, we would all just wait by the door with a spoon for Mark to arrive because Pam would pack him off to work with this incredible sweet potato stuff. We would just hover, like so many vultures with spoons, and as soon as he set it down and took the foil off, it was as good as gone. Reta Washam, the only white woman I have ever known who could keep up with me on a dance floor, told me that she got this same recipe from her mamaw

(Yankees: that's grandmother) and it was "larrupin' " good. My daddy used to say larrupin', too (it rhymes with *terrapin* but has nothing to do with turtles). I never knew the definition of *larrupin'*, but I did infer quite early on that if something was larrupin' good, I should get as much of it as possible, and I advise you to do the same.

Okay, to make this larrupin' sweet potato stuff, you first want to boil a bunch of sweet potatoes. (Don't even think about using canned sweet potatoes in any recipe I ever told you about. There are certain things that are acceptable, even desirable, to get from cans, like cream of anything soup, but canned sweet potatoes are a sacrilege.) You want to end up with about 3 cups' worth of mashed ones, so ever how many 'taters that is, use that many. I'm sure a cookbook can tell you; I can't. I just boil a big pot full of sweet potatoes; Julia Child, I ain't. Here's the deal, though: If you boil the sweet potatoes with the skins on, after they're boiled, the skins just slip right off in your hand, practically. On the other hand, trying to peel one raw sweet potato, let alone a whole pot full of them, would be enough to sour you on this recipe from the get-go.

So boil 'em, then peel 'em, then dump them in a big bowl and put in *at least* 1 cup of sugar, ⅓ cup of milk, a stick of butter, and a teaspoon of vanilla. You know when I say a teaspoon of vanilla that I mean for you to let the vanilla run over the sides of the spoon for a little bit before you stop pouring. You also need just a dash of salt in there or it will taste flat. The sugar part you have to do to taste: Start with a cup and if it needs more, then by all means, put more in. After you get done tasting and testing, then beat in two eggs. Trust me, you do not want to put the eggs in first and then go to tasting it to see if you've got enough sugar in there: The sweet potatoes are just hot enough to make the eggs poisonous but not hot enough to cook them. After all that's done, put the 'tater stuff in a greased casserole. (Once again, you can make a vat of this and freeze it.)

The topping is the kicker. You want a cup of dark brown sugar (why do they even make the light brown kind?), ⅓ cup of butter, ⅓ cup of flour, and a cup of pecan pieces. Stir it all up together and spread it over the top of the 'taters. Kay North wrote me that she also puts a cup of coconut in this same topping. I tried it and it's a killer. Sometimes I'll make it with coconut on one side and regular topping on the other: This is the height of luxury, I believe. After you put the topping on there, you bake it at 350 degrees for about a half hour. I have often thought of putting this in a pie crust, since it's better than any sweet potato pie I ever had in my life. As it is, though, it gets served as vegetable, which means, of course, that it doesn't count as dessert, and you can have that, too.

"Get Back, Granny" Sweet Potato Cobbler

There is a saying in the South—of baffling origins—that when something is tasty in the extreme, it is "good enough to make you slap your grandmaw." Why would the consumption of something yummy provoke one to an act of violence—and against a senior adult at that? I cannot fathom how this got started. Perhaps William Safire could be of assistance. At any rate, I got this recipe for sweet potato cobbler from my friend Ray Lee who told me when he brought the dish out to serve, "This stuff is so good, it'll make you slap your grandmaw." And, I must admit, if there was any truth to that maxim at all and I was a whacking sort of gal, this stuff would endanger the quality of life for grandmaws everywhere.

First thing, boil some sweet potatoes (remember the skins come off easily after they're cooked). You need about 2 cups of sweet potato chunks to make this stuff. Now melt a stick of butter in a 13 x 9 x 2 pan—anything that starts out like this is gonna be good, don't you know? Okay, then heat 2 cups of water and two cups of sugar until the sugar melts. Then make a dough out of 1½ cups self-rising flour, ½ cup shortening and ⅓ cup milk. Roll that dough out to a rectangle about ¼ inch thick and sprinkle it with 1 teaspoon of cinnamon and one of nutmeg. Put your sweet potatoes on there, roll it up, and pinch the ends together to seal them. Then slice that roll into about 15 or 20 pieces and put them in the pan of melted butter, pour the sugar syrup over them, and bake the thing at 350 for about 45 minutes.

Just to be on the safe side, don't serve this when your grandmaw's around.

Country Club Eggs

Mary Ellen, leader of the Shreveport, Louisiana, Crude Queens, sent me this recipe that she got from her mother-in-law. It sounds hideous, but you know I wouldn't suggest anything using deviled eggs that wasn't fabulous, knowing that I love deviled eggs more than life its ownself. A deviled egg is nothing to be trifled with, no indeed. Mary

Ellen says her mother-in-law, Mimi, called these Country Club Eggs, and I must admit, they are pretty high-falutin. You start with regular ole deviled eggs—you know, mayonnaise, mustard, pickles, paprika, etc.—and you put them in a casserole dish. Don't they look yummy? This is the hardest part for me—looking at those eggs just sitting there, begging me to eat them. I must have eaten a thousand deviled eggs before I ever got this recipe made the first time. Delaying gratification has always been tough for me. Anyway, you put them in there and then as quick as you can (before you eat them all), cover them with tomato soup (it could take more than one can, unless, of course, you've eaten all but, say, one of the deviled eggs, in which case it won't take much soup at all), and then you cover that with lots and lots of sliced Velveeta cheese. Velveeta is just like other cheese in that you can never have too much of it. You bake this concoction at 300 to 350 degrees until it gets bubbly around the edges. It's a good thing this is so much trouble—I'm not sure it would be prudent to eat it as often as you're gonna want to.

Dinksy's Gooey Bars

My friend Mary Rathbun, who owns the Great Acorn store in San Anselmo, California, where you can get just about anything worth having, sent me this recipe for a behind the size of the sun. This will, as they say around here, put some junk in yo' trunk, as if we needed any help in that department. We are just about to give up on looking for rich half-dead guys and focus on guys who like fat women. Wouldn't you just love to be with a man who never thought you were qui-i-i-ite plump enough? "Just eat a little sump'n, baby," would be his litany, spoken low and sweet in our happy little ear. Mary claims she got this recipe from her friend in Beaufort, South Carolina, who is four-ten and called Dinksy. She does not say how much Dinksy weighs; my guess is, though, since she is called Dinksy, she doesn't eat this stuff herself. Good. More for us.

To make Dinksy's Gooey Bars, you start with a Duncan Hines Devil's Food Cake mix—already off to a good start, I say—and mix it up with a stick of butter (not margarine, but I don't think we have to say that, do you?) and an egg. Put it in a 9 x 13 pan. Then mix up 8 ounces of softened cream cheese, a box of powdered sugar, 2 eggs, a running-over teaspoon of vanilla, and a cup of chopped pecans (not walnuts, not almonds—*pecans*). Pour all that over the cake stuff in the pan and bake it at 350 degrees for around 40 minutes. Do this all in secret while everyone else is gone; otherwise you're gonna be forced to share.

Bacon Monkey Bread

I know you've had Monkey Bread—where you take the little hunks of canned biscuits and roll them in butter and cinnamon and sugar and pecans and you put them all in a bundt pan and bake it and then you eat it by delicately plucking off little wads of yum off the pile. (We call those canned biscuits "whomp" biscuits because you used to have to whomp the can on the counter to pop the seal. Now you're just supposed to peel back the label and it pops open, but we all still whomp it on the counter because we like to.) Well, I wouldn't have thought there could be any variation of that theme that would please me as much, but Leslie Monk has come up with a new version that's every bit as yummy, and since it falls into the Salty Food Group, you could actually have both, which would pretty much make your life complete, as far as I can tell. I can't think of what else you could possibly expect life to hand you after this unless you are just too greedy to live.

Leslie calls this Bacon Monkey Bread, and so you know from that that it's got to be good. I can't think of a food containing bacon that I don't love. First you cook a big wad of bacon. Now, this is at least as big a problem for me as the deviled eggs—I am completely powerless over bacon. I rarely buy it for this reason: However much there is is what I consider to be a "serving"—be that two slices or two pounds. If it is cooked and in front of me, I'll eat it till I gag—can't help it. So, anyway, you cook enough bacon so that when you get through eating it, there's still a bunch left for the recipe—you're gonna need at least a dozen slices for the recipe, I'd say. Crumble them up (they need to be crumbled for the recipe, but this will also inhibit further pilfering on your part). Mix the bacon bits with ½ cup of Parmesan cheese and a small chopped onion. Okay, now melt a stick of butter. Take 3 10-ounce cans of whomp biscuits and cut each biscuit into quarters. Dip the biscuit hunks in the butter—but don't *just* dip them: Roll them, bathe them in the butter. Put about a third of them in a lightly greased bundt pan and sprinkle some of the bacon stuff over them. Fill up the pan with layers of buttered biscuit hunks and bacon stuff, ending with biscuit hunks. Bake it at 350 degrees for around 40 minutes, but for goodness' sake, don't burn it. Let it sit in the pan for a few minutes after it's done and then dump it out onto a platter and jump back to avoid being trampled.

Twinkie Pie

Also known affectionately as "White Trash Trifle," this is just the most embarrassing recipe we know of, and it's a tribute to our character that we can confess not only to owning such a recipe but making it often and loving it as well. You would think we would be too proud to admit all that, but we think pride of this sort is a sin, and besides, we want you to have some because it's so shamefully good. Also, we are trying to popularize being fat so that we will be on the cutting edge of fashion. If you will do your part and eat lots of this and all the other stuff in here, I think we'll have a pretty fair start on your basic groundswell movement.

You start with a crate of Hostess Twinkies—don't even mention the fat-free variety to me: They are an abomination and should be outlawed. You know you're gonna need a billion of these because you'll eat them as fast as you can open the packages. Try this—take one out of every package and eat it on the spot. Take the other one and cut in two lengthwise and put it in a 9 x 13 pan—or whatever size you want, depending on how hungry you are. Now us, we lean toward your big pans, and we think you're like that, too. Then make up some vanilla pudding—the kind in the box, whatever brand you grab first, it doesn't matter. Spread the vanilla pudding over the Twinkies. Cover all that with sliced bananas, strawberries, peaches—whatever kind of fruit you want. Now, if you are really and truly just absolute total white trash at heart, you may use fruit cocktail. We think you should try to overcome this urge, however; it really doesn't speak well of you at all. Put it in the refrigerator, and when it's cold, eat it until you either get full or sick. And don't tell anybody where you heard about this.

One of my very favorite men and writers in the whole world, living or dead, Bill Fitzhugh, sent me a recipe, and Lord knows, he meant well. I mean, it's got chicken and sausage in it, after all. But on further inspection, I saw that it specified that the chicken, although thighs, should be skinless and trimmed of fat. Well, I could tell it was gonna deteriorate from there, and I was right. At every turn, he had you draining off fat and such as that. It was called something or other "maque choux"—and I have no idea what *maque choux* means, but I'm certain that it has nothing to do with cream of mushroom soup, Velveeta, or even bacon. The sausage called for turned out to be Italian, which everybody knows is deficient in fat content.

Bill Fitzhugh is a fine man, a precious darling man, and an excellent writer—I highly recommend you read all his books—but he has apparently been living in Elle-Aye for a little bit too long and has done got way above his raising, if you ask me. I mean, I got to the end of the recipe and he wrote—in his own hand—that the *maque choux* should be accompanied by "crusty bread." Now, no Southerner has ever said such a thing in his life. Cornbread certainly, but everybody down here knows that bread crust was made only to serve during shipment as a protection for the soft white middle and should be cut off cleanly before serving.

Bless his heart, let's get him home and feed him.

19

The Time Is Now

I cannot imagine who came up with that phrase about "time march-ing on." For whom is time merely marching? And I have to wonder why it seems to be moving so slowly for them: Poor things must be bored slap to death. For us, on the other hand, time is whipping by so fast, we feel like the way dogs look when they hang out the window of a fast-moving car—hair and ears blown straight back, tongues hang-ing out, grinning and blinking in the wind. This must be because we devote so much of our lives to having fun. We love to play.

One year, for my birthday, a couple of the Tammys had a party for me at Ton-O-Fun. This is a locally owned establishment, much like the national chain Discovery Zone, only better. It's a big, indoor play-ground thing, full of things to climb on and through, things to swing on and slide down, and the best part of all—the big pit full of plastic balls to land in. They rented the whole place one night after closing time for an adults-only party. Problem was, we all had to show up be-fore closing time and be there, in our little party room, with all the tiny little chairs and tables, while they ran all the actual children out of the play area to make way for us. We got some dirty looks from some of those tots that were fairly advanced. Their parents seemed only too happy to leave, however, having been there for hours watching the kids play, never getting to join in.

The second they were all gone and the doors were safely locked behind them, we went berserk. Mothers and fathers, CEO's, Junior League presidents, pilots, TV personalities, doctors, lawyers—all that was forgotten in the mad rush to be the first one through the maze of tunnels and slides to land in the big ball pit.

Let me just tell you, the big ball pit is IT. If they would put one in the break room of every workplace in America, they could quit making Prozac. If the post office had these areas, the disgruntled postal worker would be a thing of the past. If the waiting room at the doctor's and dentist's office were big ball pits, nobody would mind waiting and nobody would ever be late for their appointment. Instead of installing a hot tub in your house, I beseech you to consider a big ball pit. We played there for hours, just laughing fit to kill the whole time—it felt like we were about six years old. Fabulous.

We got out and had the funky pizzas—you know, they're all cheese because the kids won't eat anything else—and Fat Mama's Margaritas—we brought those with us—and birthday cake. The staff sang to me and I got a T-shirt and everything—just like a real kid. Best birthday party I ever had.

We got the idea because the year before, on Tammy's son Timothy's birthday, she had rented one of those space jumps. After about an hour, the kids got tired and distracted and went off doing other stuff, and Tammy and I got in the thing and made ourselves sick jumping and laughing. We made so much racket, the kids heard us and came back; and, of course, they wanted to get in there again now that it looked like so much fun. We wouldn't let them, naturally, partly because we were afraid we would jump on one and crush him, but mostly because we are selfish. Eventually they shamed us into getting out, but we didn't forget how much fun it was, so when my birthday rolled around, well, it just seemed like the natural progression of things. That's how we think.

See, one of our secret weapons, as Sweet Potato Queens, is the power of play—the restorative, almost magical healing powers of play. Dressing up the way we do is a big part of it. When you are wearing something so completely outlandish, it imparts a certain degree of freedom to your behavior. I mean, no matter how we act (or act up, as it were), it is still difficult to live all the way up to the outfit. Those outfits set an incredibly high standard.

This year before the parade, Tammy decided we needed a bull-horn for the parade. I have no earthly idea why she thought we needed a bullhorn, but she was adamant and could not be dissuaded in her pursuit of one. She took the prescribed course of action in this pursuit, of course: She told one of our ever-dancing-in-attendance guys she needed one and set him off in search of it. She chose Michael Rubenstein for this errand, and it was an excellent choice because he located one that very day. And so the night before the parade, as we were gathered at Tammy's waiting for our limo to take us to Hal and Mal's for the big party we were flinging for the Wannabe Wannabes from all over the country, suddenly the voice of God came booming through the walls: "Sweet Potato Queens! Come out with your hands up!" We determined that, although the voice was very Godlike, the choice of words probably was not and, upon further investigation, it turned out to be not God, but Rube.

Well, that was all it took for Tammy. The borrowed bullhorn im-mediately became her favorite toy. Anything said through a bullhorn by anybody, let me just tell you, takes on surprising heft. We managed to pry it out of her hot little hands after a bit and dragged her off to the party. She forgot all about it on parade day—whatever the urgent need had been had evaporated—but the next day (that would be Sunday) she popped out of bed with nothing but bullhorn on her mind. We all loaded up in the car to go down to the Edison Walthall (the official hotel of the Wannabe Wannabes) for breakfast. Tammy has the bullhorn in the car (trust me on this, a bullhorn is too loud to be used inside an automobile) and insisted on running by a few folks' houses to give them a little shout, as it were. We pulled up to the home of the revered Southern writer Ellen Douglas—who is our friend, lucky for all of us, and her, too—and addressed her, from the street, naturally (when you've got a bullhorn, you don't need to go to the door): "Ellen Douglas! We know you're in there writing those trashy books! Come out with your hands up!" When you've got a bull-horn, it is just second nature to demand that everybody come out with their hands up.

Then we passed First Baptist Church. Now, here's a real bone of contention in Jackson, Mississippi. The Baptists wanted to build a sky-walk across North State Street so their members wouldn't have to go to the light at the intersection or jaywalk to cross the street. And they did everything but harelip the world to get that skywalk built—it was against all manner of laws, ordinances, and regulations, and promised to be a hideous eyesore, but they were persistent, as Baptists are known to be, and they got their silly skywalk, and don't you just *know* that not a one of them use it, *ever*. I personally have never seen a single Baptist up in that skywalk. It just irritates the fire out of everybody in town that they won't use it: Drivers will honk and gesture vehemently at the jaywalking Baptists, indicating with an extended digit that they should not only go up into the skywalk but also what they should do once there. Now, we are not a community against jaywalking by any means. First Presbyterian Church is right down the street, and the Presbyterians jaywalk all day long and nobody minds, because they didn't harelip the world to build an ugly skywalk and then refuse to use it. Anyway, as we were driving by the Baptist church, we spied a covey of dressed-up Baptists casually jaywalking (directly *under* the skywalk) and Tammy addressed them with the bullhorn on that issue: "Hey! You Baptists! Get up there in that skywalk! You whined for it! Now get up there and use it!" It was a cathartic experience, I tell you.

Then we went by our beloved Eudora Welty's house, and as it was her birthday, we sang to her through the bullhorn, but very softly, as we went by. Can't be hollering at Miss Eudora. It must be said that Tammy fairly hogged the bullhorn all day long. We thought we were gonna have to buy her some Depends, she was laughing so hard. Now she wants one of her own, just so she can call her cat, her cat being one who would respond better to the voice of authority; your basic "Here, kitty kitty" just doesn't move him much. I swear, we are so easily entertained—it's one of our best qualities.

I got an e-mail one day—Rachel Kahan, our beloved and devoted Wannabe on staff at our publishing house, Crown, in New York, forwarded it to me—an amazing message from Kathi Lamonski, owner of the Fig Garden Bookstore in Fresno, California. Kathi declared that *The Sweet Potato Queens' Book of Love* was her bestselling book of all time, and asked whether there was any way under heaven that the author might be persuaded to come out to Fresno for a visit. I just picked up the phone and called Ms. Lamonski at the Fig Garden Bookstore in Fresno, California, and said I would be tickled pink (with sequins on top) to come out there, if she would only send me a plane ticket. And that conversation led to the First Annual Festival of Queens in Fresno.

The Time Is Now

They sold tickets, forty dollars apiece, to a dinner—open to all Wannabes, consorts, and/or spouses (Spud Studs). The store sold out of tickets before any notice of the event ran in the newspapers, and they were forced to add more tables to accommodate the crowds. They gave every person a tiara and had great door prizes like baskets of Fat Mama's Knock You Naked Margaritas and Come Back Sauce and other of the Queens' favorite foods. There was a dress requirement for the event: You had to wear whatever made you feel Queenly. Attendees were encouraged to think fantasy—old prom dresses, majorette boots (for those lucky enough to have them), long gloves, dangly earrings. They could declare themselves the Queen of Whatever They Chose, one of the basic tenets of the Sweet Potato Queens' philosophy. Since they were all going to be dressing for the evening, I took my outfit, even though we practically had to buy the thing its own airline ticket, it's so huge.

Let's just say the attendees got it, in a big way—and then some. There were *some outfits* out there, let me tell you. (Keep in mind the attendees selected their own Queendoms.) One tiny little woman was proudly sporting a banner across her bosom that proclaimed her to be . . . Queen of the Whores. (She wore a blouse. Not a tunic, a blouse—as in nothing else but sheer hose and high heels. I went up to her and said, "Darlin', I think you must have misread me. I said, 'Never wear panties to a party'—I didn't say nothin' 'bout not wearing pants!" She just laughed and laughed with her little nekkid self. I loved her.) The Queens Most Likely to Be Eaten—Queens of Chocolate— had Hershey's Kisses stuck all over themselves.

The official emcee for the evening was the cutest man in the whole world, living or dead, and his name was Wheatie. Wheatie himself wrote me after the event and said that the party looked like a middle-aged spring break, and he thought it was a wonderful thing for all those women to give themselves permission to have that much fun, and he was so happy that he got to see it. There's a message—or two—in that for all of us.

I know this wonderful—magical, really—woman named Sandra Williams. She is a marvelous watercolorist. She will paint a picture of you and your favorite celebrity, depicted engaging in the activity of your choice. Think about that. I think I would have me and Sean Connery in a passionate embrace; he is and always will be the sexiest man in the history of the entire world, living or dead. Sandra's self-portrait shows her in a big clawfooted bathtub full of bubbles and James Garner—the two of them sipping champagne and looking re-e-e-eally happy. Maybe I would have Sean Connery carrying me in his arms. Is that the sexiest thing or what? If you have never seen a soap opera even once in your life—who are you trying to kid?—you can turn on any one of them on any given day and see somebody getting carried off to bed by somebody else. Nobody on TV ever has sex unless they get carried off—usually up some stairs—first. Now, this is one of those things that no guys in real life ever do. Why is that? Obviously, women love the idea of it or they wouldn't show it to us every single day on every single TV station from eleven A.M. until three-thirty P.M. (I can remember watching *As the World Turns* before I started school. I can remember the very first episode of *Days of Our Lives*, and people have been getting carried off to bed that whole time, every day of the world.) You would think that something that has gotten that much publicity on such a regular, long-term basis might have trickled down to a couple of guys by now. I can't figure this out. This is information we want them to have.

I believe I have told you that I am a very large woman—six feet tall, no shoes. I read where Elle MacPherson is six feet tall and weighs a hundred and thirty pounds. As I said, I am six feet tall. There will be no discussion in my book about my weight, thank you very much. Suffice it to say, I outweigh Elle by a few. A guy would need to be spending some time in the gym before he took to hoisting me up a flight of stairs. One of the Queens, Tammy, is what our precious Michael Rubenstein so sweetly refers to as a "normal-sized" woman, like myself. Tammy and I have discussed at length, on many, many occasions, how the only reason we wish sometimes we were tiny is so that men would snatch us up and prance off with us from time to time. We felt better when all the itty-bitty Queens confessed that nobody is snatching and prancing with them, either.

At any rate, normal-sized Tammy works out at the Y with me every morning, and our favorite birthday present to give and receive each and every year is getting picked up by Orange Young. Orange is this large, gorgeous law-enforcement officer who works out in the mornings when we're there. The Queens do so love law enforcement; we are under the personal protection of the Sheriff of Hinds County, Mississippi, Malcolm McMillan. But back to Orange. He's a big dog now and is usually in regular-guy-shirt-and-tie stuff. On rare occasions, he will have on his actual cop suit—with the badge, the gun, the handcuffs, the whole deal—and we just go into veritable paroxysms of delight at the sight of him. There is just something about a man in uniform. Maybe it's the handcuffs that set us off. We are effusive with our praise and panting after him. Orange just grins. One day we said, "Orange, you look so fine in that uniform—we bet you sleep in that thing!" "Just the top," he said, grinning. We were on the floor. Anyway, Orange has biceps—big, big biceps—the kind for which the term "guns" was coined. So when Tammy's birthday arrives each year, I ask Orange to just march up to Tammy in the weight room, sweep her off her feet, and stroll around with her a little bit. She has Orange do the same for me. This is the best present we ever got.

Before I got sidetracked, I started telling you about Sandra Williams. Besides painting, the other thing Sandra Williams does is that she is a federally certified Wildlife Rehabilitator. You probably didn't realize that it is illegal for you as a regular uncertified human being to fool around with wild animals, even if you are trying to save their lives. Probably not a lot of tickets are given for the offense, but just the same, you're not supposed to be doing it. Sandra, on the other hand, is supposed to be doing it. She has been so ordained by our own federal government and, I personally think, by God as well. She provides a wonderful, miraculous service.

Any mother can attest to the sinking feeling one experiences when one's child has discovered a wounded or stranded baby animal. The child looks to you—the great and powerful mother—to fix this poor creature. Alas, your skills at breast-feeding are rusty at best, and even at peak performance were pretty much restricted to baby people. The child cannot believe there is nothing you can do; the child believes you can do anything. Sandra makes it possible to do something. You can sack it up, whatever it is, and take it to her in the comfortable knowledge that she will most likely fix it. I have taken her tiny baby squirrels—so young they were still pink and hairless—that had either fallen or were for some reason pushed out of the nest. Sandra not only raises them to adulthood, she does it so the squirrels can return to the wild, completely able to take care of themselves.

Snow White is what Sandra is. Remember in the movie, how the animals and birds would hang around and sing and talk to Snow White all the time? Well, the first time I ever took BoPeep with me on a mission of mercy to Sandra's house, Sandra was standing on her front porch waiting for us to arrive, with one bluejay on her head, another on her shoulder, several on low-hanging tree limbs in front of her: They all seemed to be having a little chat. As we walked up, she turned and walked in her open front door. When she did, all the birds went in with her—into the living room. And they were in there flying around, squawking away. When she got ready to come out again, she offhandedly said, "Y'all come on out now," to the jaybirds, and they did. 'Peep just stood there, mouth slightly ajar, completely mesmerized by this woman whom the very birds of the air obeyed.

We were delivering some fallen baby chimney swifts for her care. I have no idea if these birds exist all over the country and I am not about to go look it up, but around here, if you don't have a cover over your chimney, in the spring these birds will come and build their nest in there. They are chimney *swifts*, not sweeps. Sweeps are those people who figure prominently in *Mary Poppins;* swifts are birds—federally protected birds, I might add. Did you know it is a federal offense to disturb one of their nests—with a large fine as well? Yet every exterminator under the sun advertises in the yellow pages that he will happily come out and remove all of your chimney swift nests. This makes Sandra slightly wild.

Anyway, we had this nest in our chimney—a delightful experience, let me tell you. Once the babies hatch out, if you make the slightest noise in your house—like if you sneeze or something—they start screaming. There are usually just a few of them in there, but, man alive, are they ever some loud sumbitches! Their screams echo and amplify down that chimney. It's as if several thousand people with extremely long fingernails were scraping the world's largest blackboard, and the sound was being run through some big ole Peavey speakers for your listening pleasure. And it lasts until the babies are big enough to fly out of the nest and go away. You will not have this happen to you more than once; you will cover that chimney in religious fervor every year for the rest of your life. Anyway, we had some one year, and before they could get grown and fly off, they got to roughhousing around in their nest and knocked it down. So now, instead of screaming and hollering halfway up the chimney, they were screaming and hollering right there in the den with us—at us. And they were never going to grow up and fly off because their mama couldn't feed them since grown-up chimney swifts don't land on the ground *ever*, according to Sandra. This meant we had to (a) wait for them to starve to death (there's something fun you want to do with your three-year-old); (b) feed them ourselves (which I imagined would involve catching and partially chewing up worms to spit into their tiny, uplifted, wide-open, screeching birdie beaks; or (c) scoop them up and take them to Sandra.

I picked C. 'Peep got a shoe box and put a warmed towel in it, and we dug around in the sooty fireplace until we found the little boogers. You have heard it said all your life, and so have I, that a baby anything is darling. I believed that to be true until I viewed baby chimney swifts: Let me just say that they look just about as good as they sound—not quite, though. Them's some ugly babies, plus they're nasty from living in the chimney, and even more so after wallowing around in ashes. Even BoPeep thought they were homely, and babies just love baby animals. 'Peep still wanted them saved, but even she had no desire to keep them at home, which was lucky for me. We called Sandra, and she said she would be happy to have them; she could use her bathroom for the aviary. Said she wasn't worried about them hurting anything: The raccoons had taken all the wallpaper off the walls already and there was a wood duck in the bathtub. As I said, she was communing with the bluejays when we arrived and 'Peep handed her the box of birds. She reached in, as delicately as if this was a newborn's bassinet, and lifted each tiny swiftlet out and clasped them all to her bosom to impart body heat to them as quickly as possible. She then whisked them off to check their status, feed them, and get them settled in the aviary.

Several weeks went by before we heard from Sandra. She called to tell me the most miraculous, wonderful story I have ever heard: When the chimney swifts are old enough to be released into the wild, it is a very dangerous undertaking for them. Sandra must be absolutely certain that they can fly high enough to reach a tree limb; if they cannot, they will die, because chimney swifts do not land on the ground, they live in treetops only. And remember, her bathroom was the only aviary these particular birds had ever known, so they'd never actually flown higher than nine feet. So she took one bird at a time and gave it a slight toss into the air. If it couldn't fly, she'd catch it and take it back inside for a few more days of strengthening. But, she said, the most incredible thing would happen when she released one that could fly high enough. Out of a clear sky, no other birds in sight, when this baby bird flew up to the trees for the very first time in its life, out of nowhere would come two adult birds to meet it. She said she stood on the ground and wept as she watched. The two birds would stay with the youngster, guiding it for a time. And it happened again and again. Each time another one would reach the trees, two more birds would come to help it. I just bawled when she told it to me and can scarcely repeat the story today without crying.

The first person I told the story to was my beloved Beth Jones, to whom I dedicated my first book, as she was dying of cancer. We agreed that if God can make and implement a plan for a chimney swift, as utterly unappealing a creature as you might ever find in a worldwide search for ugly beings—if God looks out for them, He must surely have a plan for us and send us help when we need it, even when we don't know what we need or how to ask for it.

Another cherished, departed friend of mine, Ronnie Wesley, a saxophone-playing fiend, used to say, "Ain't no danger—just ain't no danger." I always took this to mean that we should live life to the fullest, without fear. I tell this to BoPeep when she has the occasional clingy moment, worried about me flying in a plane or something. I'll tell her that if God wants me, He's not just waiting for me to get on an airplane to snatch me up; staying in my house, under the bed, night and day, wouldn't ensure that I would live forever. We all die, some sooner rather than later. We are all just a breath away from it, all the time.

Don't fear being near-death—but rather fear, dread, loathe, and do all you can to avoid *near-life* experiences. Nobody goes to the grave or to the nursing home wringing their hands and gnashing their teeth and just wishing they'd served on a few more committees, worked a few more hours. Too often we are waiting until we (and then later, our children) finish school, waiting until the mortgage is paid off, waiting until we lose weight, waiting until we retire. We are always, as we say in the South, just "fixing to." After this thing or that one happens, *then* we will travel, write, play, rest, visit friends, *then* we will live. And, lo and behold, before any of that stuff can happen, it is over, and we never got around to living.

No more near-life experiences, please. Whatever it is you are going to do *someday*, well, *someday* is here. Have at it. I am here to tell you, it is way better to live your dream than it is to dream it.

20

Matters of the Heart

I've written this whole entire book to avoid writing this chapter. Just writing that line has made me cry, but it must be written. I must tell you about two men.

Whenever I sign a book for a guy, I write in it, "To the only man I ever really loved." So if your husband comes home with that inscription in his book, relax; I've written it to every guy on the planet and I only meant it once. Winston Brown really is the only man I ever really loved. Oh, I have been in love, deeply so, with some others—even married some. But I never loved anybody the way I loved Winston Brown. I was only sixteen when I met him. He was eighteen and he had the blackest hair and the bluest eyes. His eyes were the color—well, in Mississippi, around October every year for about two or three days the humidity will drop and the air will get very, very clear and the sky turns this amazing shade of blue—it is deep yet bright, and it makes your heart feel funny to look at it for very long. Also about that time of year, the leaves on the sweet gum trees turn a vivid yellow, and when you look at those leaves against that sky, it makes the sky seem even bluer, and that's the exact color of Winston Brown's eyes.

When we were grown and I hadn't seen him for twenty years, every October of those twenty years I would see Winston's eyes in that sky. My love for him was different because I was so very young. It was overpowering and it was totally without guile or reservation. I had never been in love like that and so it never occurred to me not to trust it and him completely. Since I had no frame of reference for heartbreak, I had no armor. To this very day, out of my entire life—including the birth of my precious child—the very happiest moment of my existence was when Winston Brown told me he loved me. There's a hymn that says "and suddenly there were thousands and thousands of angels"—that's the way it felt. Because it was the one moment—totally free of fear—of pure, unadulterated joy. It is my treasure.

But, by and by, he did break my heart, and though I have certainly loved others, the knowledge that love can hurt so much tempers and restrains just ever so slightly.

I loved Winston then, still love Winston, will go to my grave loving Winston—he just tickles me. That's all I can say. He just tickles me slap to death—his turn of phrase, his laugh, just him. He loves to be in the woods. He was telling me one time about trying to teach his new dog to hunt and the dog was real smart and doing great for a while, but now it seems all the dog will hunt is armadillos. How in the hell did that come about, I wanted to know. Well, he guessed it was really his fault. The dog had run up on one and chased it down and he (the dog) was so happy with himself, he (Winston) shot it for him (the dog), and so now he (the dog) thinks that's what he (Winston) wants him (the dog) to do, and so each and every time they go into the woods, he (the dog) thinks they are on another armadillo hunt. So basically the dog is useless for hunting now? I asked. "Well, yeah," he said, "except one good thing about it is, if you get lost in the woods, the first thing you want to do is find an armadillo."

Well, I had never read this particular tidbit in any hunting/hiking/camping material about what to do when you get lost in the woods. I've never known anybody to advise finding an armadillo for any worthy cause. Most folks down here don't even believe there's such a thing as a live armadillo anymore; it does seem like we'd run out of 'em sooner or later, as many as we run over. So I pressed him urgently to find out why it is, when you are lost in the woods, you must find an armadillo—and by the way, how lucky he was to have a trained armadillo-hunting dog. Winston was so happy and proud to contribute to my outdoor education. "You want to find an armadillo and follow it," he said, " 'cause that sumbitch is heading straight for a road."

Anyway, Winston broke my heart, and we didn't see each other for twenty years, but what I did do as soon as I could form a thought in my head after we broke up was the only thing a girl could do, under the circumstances, I started dating his best friend, Bill Hollingsworth. I went with Bill for several years and then we broke up and then life just sort of got away from all of us until the next thing we knew, it was twenty years later. So there we were twenty years later and who did I run into but Bill and he told me Winston was lawyering in a small town in north Mississippi, where everybody in town adores him, and that he'd built a house out in the woods on a little pond and he hunts all the time.

So what did I do but pick up the phone and call his office. He answered the phone and I didn't say hello or anything, just, "Well, I thought since it's been practically twenty years to the day since you ripped my heart out and stomped the fucker flat, you might have the decency to come to town once in a while and take me to lunch." He didn't even ask who it was, just said, "How about Friday?" And I, of course, said Friday would be just fine, thank you. So he came and took me to lunch and proceeded to tell me that he had loved me his entire life and that his one regret—the one thing he would change if he could—was losing me. I said if I had written him a script and paid him to read it, he couldn't have done any better, and I felt all that, too, but that since we did find ourselves married to other people at the moment, perhaps it would be best if we didn't date. But we stayed in touch and had lunch from time to time and he would come to the house if he was in town on business and we would call Bill to come go out with us. So here we'd go—me and Moon Pie and my two old boyfriends—out on the town. Hilarious.

More time passed and Moon Pie and I came to our parting of the ways, and who handled all the divorce stuff for me? Winston. Then I wrote *SPQBOL*, and who are the first two people at my first book signing? Winston and Bill. The Queens threw a huge party at Hal and Mal's after the first book signing, and there sat Winston and Bill—the whole night. Whenever I would introduce them to anybody, they would announce that they were my two oldest boyfriends and they had both been in love with me for thirty years, and then they would argue back and forth over which one of them loved me the most and, more important, which one I loved the most. Oh, it was entirely satisfactory, let me tell you.

From then on, whenever I had a book signing within four hundred miles, they would be there, the two of them, telling their tale to whoever showed up. It was pretty gratifying. And it all felt so safe and wonderful; I'd known and loved these men for literally thirty years and here we were again, hanging out, just like high school.

Picture this: I am in Tupelo, Mississippi, signing books at this great bookstore there, Gum Tree Books, and all of a sudden, a woman strides in the front door, walks past everyone standing in line, comes up to me directly, and asks me if I am Jill Conner Browne, to which I have no choice but to respond affirmatively, whereupon she, without a word, hands me a blue folder. If you have ever in your life been sued for anything, you know what a blue folder is—it's a court summons. So I'm standing there, in front of Lord knows how many people, and I have just been served with a court summons. You have no doubt heard the expression about not knowing whether to shit or go blind: Those seemed to be about my only choices at the moment.

I opened the blue folder and started scanning the pages. The best I can tell, I (and my publishers) am being sued for $5 million by some women named Tammy Bochamp, Candy C. Wygle, Brandy D. Prichard, Georgia Pennypacker, Heather Sharp, and Deloris Thigpen—all of whom, according to this official court document, are actual former Crowned Sweet Potato Queens from Vardaman, Mississippi (the self-proclaimed Sweet Potato Capital of the World). (I noted with interest that Deloris Thigpen used an "X" to fill in the signature space.) The litigants were, it seems, incensed that this book *SPQBOL* was on display and being sold at "Thigpen's Feed and Seed on Highway 8, west of Calhoun County, Mississippi, a mere seven miles from the town of Vardaman." And that this book, it went on to say:

> dishonors the solemn position and grand stature of the award of being a Crowned Sweet Potato Queen. That since the publication and dissemination of the publication the Plaintiffs have been unable to walk the streets of their home town of Vardaman without unseemly remarks being directed at them as a direct result of contents of said publication. That the contents of the publication was published with the knowledge that it implies that the Plaintiffs would lie about the performance of certain unnatural, unspeakable, and illegal sexual

acts (crudely referred to in the publication as "Blow Jobs") in order to get members of the opposite sex to perform menial tasks. This was done with full knowledge that real Sweet Potato Queens do not and would not lie. That the contents of the publication was published with the knowledge that it belittles the Plaintiffs' participation in pageants and contests of beauty, poise, and breeding to the point that it brings into question not only the intelligence of all participants involved in pageants but also the legitimacy and importance of such activity as a self-actualizing exercise and life-learning lesson for all participants.

The suit further stated that "at no time during any competitions present or past has 'butt tape' been used to secure clothing to a contestant's body. Moreover a roll of 'butt tape' cannot even be found within Calhoun County, Mississippi." When it got around to listing specific damages suffered by the Plaintiffs, this one figured prominently: "Georgia Pennypacker would show that she suffered special damages in that her fiancé called their scheduled wedding 'off' after reading only a portion of the publication and stating to Miss Pennypacker that 'There is no way I am going to marry a woman that thinks it is OK to make a promise of something like that and not actually deliver,' and thereafter accused Miss Pennypacker of being a 'communist' and stormed out of the room. She has not seen him since." In conclusion, it stated that, if awarded, the Plaintiffs would use the five million bucks "to assist and be applied to their never ending quest for World Peace and Prosperity as each promised when Crowned."

The attorney listed on the summons was Honorable Armis ("Jabo") Thigpen, but of course, I knew his true identity. Indeed, as I looked out the window of Gum Tree Books, I saw the real author of this six-page "legal" document strolling (and grinning) down the street. It was Winston, of course, with Bill Hollingsworth right beside him. He had typed this whole thing up himself, driven to Tupelo, gone into an office and somehow convinced a woman he'd never seen before to get up from her desk, leave her office, and walk down the street and into the bookstore to deliver to me this phony lawsuit. God, don't you just love a man who knows how to play?

In May of 1999, I had a book signing scheduled at That Bookstore in Blytheville, Arkansas, which was a pretty good distance away, so I decided I would drive halfway—to Oxford, Mississippi—and spend the night, get up and drive the rest of the way to the signing, and then come back to Oxford afterward. Winston and Bill planned to meet me for drinks and dinner in Oxford both days. I got to the City Grocery (a great bar and restaurant on the Square in Oxford) first and ordered a drink. Shortly, Winston came in and ordered. We sat, drinking and visiting, waiting for Bill. Winston was sweating buckets—it was hot outside but cold in the bar, and he just wasn't cooling off. He used all the cocktail napkins on the bar mopping himself off, and I finally asked him just what the hell was wrong with him, anyway. He said he'd eaten some bad pizza a few days earlier and had just felt like shit ever since. I said, Is your stomach upset? No. Do you have fever? Didn't think so. I felt him—like ice. I've got something tightening in the pit of my stomach, and I ask him, Does anything hurt? His shoulders. "Well, that does it," I said, "let's just go get you one of them EKG's." He says no, it's not his heart—the pain doesn't go down his left arm. And I said yeah, and this ain't TV, and I don't care if it doesn't look like all the heart attacks he's seen on TV, he's having one now and we are by God going to the hospital and there's no point arguing because I am not gonna shut up about it and don't make me go call an ambulance because I will and it will cost you a fortune.

He wanted to wait for Bill and to finish his drink and his cigarette. I said this whole thing won't take ten minutes; if you're not having a heart attack, we'll be back before Bill even gets here. I finally convinced him to go, but of course, he had to drive. We get to the emergency room, and I tell them I want an EKG on him ASAP, cited three days of cold sweats and chest pains, forty-eight-year-old heavy smoker whose father dropped dead at fifty-something of a heart attack. They asked him if the pain was constant; he proudly answered that oh, no, it comes and goes—as if that was a good thing, which it isn't. About that time his blood pressure pops up on the machine—something impossible like 198/125—and they snatched him up so fast and ran him down the hall, he didn't have time to protest. They told me he was having a massive heart attack as we spoke. They told me what all they wanted to do to try to stop it, and I told them by all means to do that and then some.

I went back to speak to Winston and he was asking the doctors how long all this was going to take—how long would he be here? They told him about five days. Five days? He'd still been counting on a few more drinks and dinner, it seems. I told him that I would find Bill, and then Bill and I would call Winston's wife, Barbara, and explain to her why he was going to be five days later than anticipated getting home. They're wheeling him off down the hall and he's hollering back at me, "Well, dammit, I want a rain check!" The medical personnel had not previously had any heart attack victims quite like Winston.

Now, I go out to the phone in the ER and try to track down Bill. I get his answering service. The little girl on the phone tells me that Mr. Hollingsworth is in a meeting at the moment and cannot be disturbed. I politely informed her that I didn't care where he was or who he was with or what they were doing, this was a freaking emergency. Find him, I demanded, and tell him that Jill is on the phone and she's calling from the emergency room, and I promised her that he would want this information. I was so right. He dove into his car and called me on the fly—literally, I think he was airborne. When I told him what had happened, he immediately accused me of having induced this heart attack. "You were in bed with him, weren't you? And now you've killed him, you ho!" He's just laughing and hollering about how he knew if he was five minutes late, something like this would happen, and how he had to watch us every second and be there constantly to keep me from running off and making time with "the Brown."

Everybody in the ER is listening with rapt attention to this conversation; they only need to hear my half of it to deduce what is being said on the other end. Except they don't know it's all a long-running joke, and they are looking at me like I am, in fact, a ho, and a mean one at that. Through clenched teeth, I tell him that I can't really play right now; just get down here so we can call Barbara. He makes the forty-five-minute drive in about eleven minutes, I think, and by the time we'd called Barbara, they had stopped Winston's heart attack, and we got to go in and play with him in Intensive Care. We were all so scared and so relieved and so happy to have one another to hold on to, we carried on scandalously in the ICU. The two of them were doing their same shtick pretending to fight over me, and the nurses were wide-eyed. I told one I bet most people who came there to have heart attacks didn't have this much fun, and she allowed as how that was the pure truth. We never did explain to any of them who was who, and when Barbara arrived, they were even more confused. Bill and I went on off and had dinner and I, for one, had several drinks. I did my book signing the next day and Bill and I pretty much spent the weekend in and out of the hospital visiting Winston, who never looked better in his life. And a few days later they sent him home from the hospital. He died that very night.

The grief was—and is—staggering, stunning. I go out to the cemetery. He's buried in Jackson next to his father. There's no headstone on Winston's grave yet, just a marker with his name on it. It looks so out of place there. I'm most accustomed to seeing that name written over and over on my high-school binders, preceded usually by "I love." There is a marker flush with the ground in front of Winston's grave that bears the name "Humphrey," and I sit on Humphrey and talk to Winston. Quite often, I lie down on Humphrey and look up at the sky above Winston, which is sometimes, but not often, the color of his eyes. I am overcome by the knowledge that he's almost directly below me such a short distance. From this distance, if he were across from me, I could see his laugh lines and extend my hand to touch his face, but he's not across from me, he's beneath me and he's in a box. I saw him in that terrible box before they took him away to bring him here. I combed his hair; it was parted wrong. I kissed his face, his hands. I all but crawled in that damned box with him. And I cried from a place so deep inside my soul, I never knew it was there before. As I lie on his grave and contemplate the nearness of his body, I know that it is only that, his body. It is the body Winston lived in—the part of him that I could see and touch and feel and hear and smell and taste—and I know that the stuff that was in that body that made him Winston is not in that box, but it is gone from me, and that's the stuff I am lost without.

And then, a few months later, Willie Morris—one of the South's, the country's, most treasured writers, much-loved husband of my precious friend and editor, JoAnne, father of my friend David Rae, friend to untold numbers of people in all walks of life, mentor to me, and surrogate grandfather to my daughter, Bailey—I don't know how anybody so important to so many people could do such a thing, but he did: He upped and died on us. He was fine when he woke up that morning, got to feeling real bad all of a sudden, went to the hospital—laughing and joking with all the nurses in grand Willie style, inviting them all to the premier of the movie made of his book *My Dog Skip*, and introducing JoAnne to them all as "the best wife I ever had"—and they took him off down a hall and he just died. Well, he didn't die immediately; he was in a coma, but they said he couldn't survive, it was only a matter of hours. JoAnne called a few of us and the word spread quickly. Within minutes it was on TV that Willie Morris had suffered a massive heart attack.

And as long as I live, I'll never forget that day and the beautiful, generous, truly loving thing that JoAnne did for Willie and for all of us who loved him and her. Instead of barring all visitors and sitting alone with him, she flung open the doors and told the nurses to turn no one away. Anybody who showed up was going to be someone who loved this man and he would want them there and so did she. And we all sat around him, on the bed, on the floor, everywhere, and we held his hands and we stroked his hair and we talked to him. Willie's favorite thing in this world was to be in the midst of a bunch of friends talking. And so we talked to him and told him how much we loved him and how much he had taught us, and we thanked him, and oh, it was incredible. When we came in, his blood pressure was just barely registering, he was ice cold. As we sat, holding him and talking to him, we saw his blood pressure come up, point by point. We felt the warmth return to his hands and face, saw the color come back to his cheeks. We knew he felt the love. And then he was gone.

An old man I used to know, whenever he was asked to pray at gatherings of one kind or another, would always do pretty much the standard fare of things requested and things appreciated in his address to the Almighty, but he always ended with asking that God grant us "a peaceful moment in which to die." I had never fully understood that phrase until that day we all gathered close and helped our beloved friend to die. What a priceless gift to give someone—a peaceful moment in which to die. What a holy moment to be allowed to be present for.

And I had to tell you about these two men I loved and lost this year, Winston and Willie, because when I was writing my first book, *SPQBOL*, JoAnne Morris was my editor. She would work on it in the daytime and Willie, the night owl, would work on it at night. How lucky could a Wannabe-writer get, to have probably the two best editors in the country working on her little book? Sometimes Willie would do nothing but change one single word on a page, and it would be transformed. JoAnne and I would just look at each other and shrug—no need to ask each other why we didn't think of it, we would have if we could have, but only Willie could. He loved all the wild, silly stuff in the book, and he laughed and laughed over it, but he told me, You must bring them back to the sweetness. Sweetness, he said, is the core of this book and you must bring your readers back to that at the end.

And so I've thought and thought of how Willie would want me to end this book and I think it's this: The first time I met Willie, he told JoAnne after I left, "She's kind. And she's solid." I can't think of a finer compliment I've ever received in my entire life. That was one of Willie's many gifts—making you feel really visible. He took the time to pay attention to you and size you up, and whatever good qualities he found, he told you about them and made you want to be more of that kind of person. I think Willie's lesson for us all—by his splendid words and loving actions—is we've got to *be* good people, we've got to *know* and really show our love for good people—right now, while we can—and we've got to *raise* good people. So do your part.

How's that, Willie?
Love,
Jill

GLOSSARY OF SWEET POTATO QUEEN TERMS

Here are some commonly used words and terms in Sweet Potato Queen jargon that will be helpful to you.

Boyfriend: Any and all heterosexual male persons who buy you dinner, take you to the movies, etc.

Come Back Sauce: The Official Condiment of the Sweet Potato Queens. The recipe is in *SPQBOL*, but for hopeless slackasses, it may be ordered from Hal and Mal's at 1-601-948-0888.

Fat Mama's Knock You Naked Margarita Mix: The Official Margarita of the Sweet Potato Queens—mix available from Tammy's store, the Everyday Gourmet; call toll-free to order (1-800-898-0122).

Fiancé: Any and all heterosexual male persons with whom you are currently having sex. Fiancé status does not have any bearing, real or implied, on the ultimate future, if any, of the relationship.

Five Men You Must Have in Your Life at All Times: According to Lydy Henley Caldwell, and she ought to know, these are: one you can talk to, one who can fix things, one you can dance with, one who can pay for things, and one to have great sex with. The good news is: All but one of them can be gay.

Four Major Food Groups: According to the Sweet Potato Queens, these would be Sweet, Salty, Fried, and Au Gratin.

Lolling About: The Official Activity of the Sweet Potato Queens, sometimes referred to as Not Doing Jack Shit.

Promise, The: The True Magic Words Guaranteed to Get Any Man to Do Your Bidding, a physical act of a personal, oral nature—or rather the Promise of such an act—very popular with males.

Spud Studs: Men in the entourage of the Sweet Potato Queens who make themselves useful in various and sundry delightful ways. May include current and/or former boyfriends, fiancés, and husbands. No one is ever allowed to escape.

GLOSSARY

Tammy: The Official Name of each and every Sweet Potato Queen, used to preserve some shred of a semblance of anonymity.

Tiara: The outward physical symbol of the inward spiritual act of embracing one's own Queenliness, should be worn for some part of every day—it's important.

www.sweetpotatoqueens.com: The Official Web site for Sweet Potato Queens information and merchandise—visit it often, bring your credit card.

Zippity-Do-Dah: The Official Funeral Song of Sweet Potato Queens for late—and unlamented—husbands. This song definitely does not apply to all departed spouses. We quickly acknowledge that some—perhaps even most—are indeed greatly lamented and sorely missed.

ACKNOWLEDGMENTS

In a perfect world, there would be some stupendous act or feat that would clearly demonstrate the tremendous wave of gratitude I experience toward certain people connected with this book. In a perfect world, I would know what this act is and I would perform it daily, on a stage, perhaps, for all the world to see and know of my great debt of appreciation. But things being what they are—I'll just say thanks.

To Chip Gibson, Steve Ross, Teresa Nicholas, Brian Belfiglio, Pamela Roskin, and Rachel Kahan—all of Crown Publishing, the *only* publishing house I ever *really* loved. And to David Tran, who comes up with my book covers, which no one can resist.

To Steven Wallace of Random House, who has been my champion since before the beginning, and to his great crew, Ed Brazas, Toni Hetzel, Eileen Becker, Julie Kurland, and Bill Stich for their support.

To Marlyn Schwartz and Larry L. King for encouragement, advice, and belly laughs.

To Sambo Mockbee, famous architect and Buckethead, always a man of extraordinary vision, for giving Malcolm four hundred dollars of the money he inherited from his sweet mama to buy the flatbed trailer that became the once and future float for the Sweet Potato Queens.

To James Griffin for keeping us dancing—for *all* these years.

To Bill Croswell and G. C. O. for their generous sponsorship of the Queens.

To Larry Bouchea, Official Chaplain to the Sweet Potato Queens for Spiritual Guidance and Ejaculatory Prayers.

To Ginger Tucker, for doing the hard part on the computer.

To Liza and Rick Looser of the Cirlot Agency in Jackson, Mississippi, for creating our award-winning Web site (www.sweetpotato queens.com). To Greg Gilliland of Cirlot for his design and patience. Rick and Greg are total Spud Studs; Liza is the ultimate Wannabe.

ACKNOWLEDGMENTS

Thanks to Jay Sones for all his help so freely given to maintain our Web site—I promise we're gonna start paying you, Jay. Thanks to Sarah Babbin and Bailey Browne, without whom no merchandise would ever actually be shipped to anybody.

To The Junior Leagues of America, for their enthusiastic and un-expected support.

And finally, thank you so very much to all of you who have writ-ten to me of your own Queenliness and especially to all of you genuine Wannabe Wannabes who came all the way to Jackson, Mississippi, to march in our parade—for helping us teach the world: The Higher the Hair, the Closer to God.